Books by Alex Shoumatoff

Florida Ramble
Westchester: Portrait of a County
The Rivers Amazon
The Capital of Hope
Russian Blood

THE MOUNTAIN OF NAMES

A HISTORY OF THE HUMAN FAMILY

by Alex Shoumatoff

Simon and Schuster

Designed by Barbara Marks
Manufactured in the United States of America

Most of this work originally appeared, in slightly different form, in *The New Yorker*.

Library of Congress Cataloging in Publication Data
Shoumatoff, Alex.
The mountain of names.

Bibliography: p.
Includes index.
1. Kinship—History.   2. Family—History.   I. Title.
GN487.S56   1985   306.8'5'09   85-2053

ISBN: 0-671-49440-6

for our boys,
André Luis and Nicholas Neto,
and all their little cousins,
known and unknown

CONTENTS

PART I

A History of the Human Family

1

The Need for Kinship

HUMANS HAVE PROBABLY ALWAYS BEEN SURROUNDED BY THEIR kin—those to whom they have been related by blood or marriage. But the size, the composition, and the functions of their families and kinship groups have varied tremendously. People have lived not only in the "nuclear family," made up of just the parents and their offspring, which is standard in the West and has been found almost everywhere; they have lived in extended families and in formal clans; they have been "avunculocal"; they have been "ultro-lateral"; they have been conscious of themselves as heirs of lineages hundreds of generations deep. However constructed, the traditional kinship group has usually provided those who live in it with security, identity, and indeed with their entire scheme of activities and beliefs. The nameless billions of hunter-gatherers who have lived and died over the past several million years have been embedded in kinship groups, and when people started to farm about ten thousand years ago, their universe remained centered on kinship. Now that there was a durable form of wealth which could be hoarded—grain—some families became more powerful than others; society became stratified, and genealogy became an important means of justifying and perpetuating status.

During the past few centuries, however, in part of the world—in Europe and the countries that have been developing along European lines—a process of fragmentation has been going on. The ties and the demands of kinship have been weakening, the family has been getting smaller and, some say, less influential, as the individual, with a new sense of autonomy and with new obligations to himself (or, especially in the last decade and a half, herself), has come to the foreground. A radically different mental order—self-centered instead of kin-centered, and traceable not to any single historical development as much as to the entire flow of Western history since at least the Renaissance—has taken over. The political and economic effects of this rise in individual self-consciousness have been largely positive: civil rights are better protected and opportunities are greater in the richer, more dynamic countries of the West; but the psychological effects have been mixed, at best. Something has been lost: a warmth, a sanity, and a supportiveness that are apparent among people whose family networks are still intact. Such qualities can be found in most of the Third World and in rural pockets of the United States, but in the mainstream of postindustrial society the individual is increasingly left to himself, to find meaning, stability, and contentment however he can.

An indication of how far the disintegration of traditional kinship has advanced is that a surprising number of Americans are unable to name all four of their grandparents. Such people have usually grown up in stepfamilies, which are dramatically on the rise. So is the single-parent family—the mother-child unit, which some anthropologists contend is the real nucleus of kinship; having already contracted to the relatively impoverished nuclear family, partly as an adaptation to industrialization, kinship seems to be breaking down even further. With the divorce rate in America at about fifty per cent and the remarriage rate at about seventy-five, the traditional Judeo-Christian scheme of marriage to one person for life seems to be shading into a pattern of serial monogamy, into a sort of staggered polygamy, which some anthropologists, who believe that we aren't naturally monogamous to begin with, see as "a return to normality." Still other anthropologists explain what is happening somewhat differently: we are adopting a delayed system of marriage, they say, with the length of the marriage chopped off at both ends. But many adults aren't getting married at all; they are putting "self-fulfillment" before marriage and children and are having nothing further to do with kinship after leaving their parents' home: their "family" has become their work associates or their circle of best friends. This is the most distressing trend of all: the decline in the capacity for long-term intimate bonding.

At the same time, there is evidence of nostalgia for the continuity and the sense of belonging which traditional kinship provides: the widespread fascination with the Mafia, the recent wave of interest in "roots," the way politicians of every stripe are coming out for "the family," as if it is no longer a given in people's lives, but a beleaguered institution in need of support. Some social scientists, who believe that historical processes are cyclical, claim that the period of intensive individualization which began several centuries ago may have just peaked in what has been called the "Me Decade," and that Western society is entering, out of necessity and as part of a general trend toward conservatism, a more kinship-oriented phase. Some Americans, of course, have never lost the strong family sense. The Mormons have active cousins' clubs and immense family reunions, and are among the world's most indefatigable genealogists. Each Mormon is required by his religion to "seek after your dead" and to perform certain sacraments for them which will assure that they all meet again in the Celestial Kingdom. The sacraments are performed not only for known ancestors of living church members but for anybody whose records are obtainable. The Mormons have done enough genealogy to realize that *everybody*, in the end, is kin. In what can be seen as a joyous extension of the church's missionary program, Mormons, scattered all over the world, are microfilming records and sending them back to an indestructible repository—a literal "mountain of names"—outside Salt Lake City. So far about a billion and a half of the six to seven billion names of the dead thought to exist have been collected, and a small but significant part of the human family tree has been reconstructed; and more names are coming in every day. Several years ago, though a "gentile," I was allowed to examine in some depth the Mormons' multimillion-dollar operation, which employs some of the most sophisticated records-processing technology in existence.

Because the course our society is charting and the technology it is developing are almost completely new, it is impossible to predict with certainty what the future role of kinship will be in it. But one can study what its role has been up to now, and look for patterns. The *history* of kinship is still a largely untouched field, however; while sorting out the intricacies of traditional kinship systems has been the traditional business of anthropology, most anthropologists, as one of them recently explained, have taken a "synchronic" approach to the subject, rather than a "diachronic" one. When seen in historical perspective, some of the current developments seem less distressing. There is a precedent for practically all of them.

The unavoidable conclusion from such a study is that the prospects for kinship, on the whole, look good. With the world's resources steadily diminishing and its population steadily growing, there is bound to be increasing want and competition—and kinship thrives in these conditions. It is already thriving in many parts of the world, where Western individualism is still an unknown and alien mental order. In other places, the idea of individual self-fulfillment has recently been introduced but remains an impossible dream. Even the young single urban career person whose family has come to seem like an alma mater that keeps sending fund letters is marked for life by genetic, cultural, and psychological transmissions from his parents and other relatives. The family is still the crucible. It still provides the most intense, intimate, and permanent relationships most of us will have; and this is not likely to change. There may even be, as many scientists believe, a basic human need for kinship. Perhaps, like other animals, we are "wired for attachment." If this is true, then the history of human kinship begins even before the appearance of man.

❡

Many of the common patterns in human kinship are found in other species. Over ninety per cent of birds, for instance, are monogamous. After inseminating his mate, the father bird generally stays around and may help in various ways: by providing her with food as she broods her eggs; by brooding them himself; by finding and defending the nesting site and actually building the nest; by feeding and guarding the young. Mated Canada geese stay together until the following nesting season. Mourning doves are even more constant lovers, clinging to their mates until death. California condors mate for life and take several years to raise their young, but the nuclear families of most birds dissolve after one season. Of the species that go in for polygamy, like turkeys, with a flock of females for each gobbler, or long-billed marsh wrens, some of whom are bigamous, polygyny (one male with more than one female) is by far the more common arrangement, which is also true of human polygamists. The handful of species, like the wattled jacana, that are polyandrous (one female with more than one male) seem to have reversed sex roles. The female is larger, more aggressive, more brightly colored. She courts the males and defends their nesting territory, while the males brood the eggs and care for the young, even though they don't know which of them is the father.

The breeding systems of mammals are generally not as straightforward as those of birds. There is perhaps only one universal feature in all their families and societies, including those of humans: the mother-child unit. That is because only the female can produce milk, and her initial role in child rearing is therefore critical. Some species, like tigers and pandas, are classified as solitary, but even they, as the field biologist George Schaller has told me, run into their neighbors at scent posts from time to time and are aware of each other's movements; even they have to be social during the mating season. Other carnivores, especially members of the dog family, tend to pair off as birds do. Coyotes and foxes, golden jackals and black-backed jackals, for instance, are all committed, long-term monogamists. A wolf pack is really an extended family consisting of a dominant male, his mate, and their adult offspring, who often give up the chance to start families and packs of their own to bring their mother food so that she can keep producing big litters. Some packs contain three or four generations of uterine kin.

Lion families are essentially mother-child units, with the father playing an indirect role as teacher and provider—catching food for himself, but sharing it with his young if they fight with him for it. There is evidence that lions transmit what they have learned to younger generations—that they have a capacity for culture, in other words. Early in the century (my source again is Schaller), the lions around the Ngora Ngora Crater, in Kenya, stopped roaring because they recognized that their roars attracted hunters. This went on for several generations. But now the lions there are protected, and they have begun to roar their heads off again. That many surburban animals have changed their schedules and become nocturnal to avoid humans and their pets is another example of acquired behavior passing down in families, and cultural inheritance is also a factor in the eating habits of some Japanese monkeys: one group has taken to washing in the ocean the sweet potatoes it eats, apparently because a particularly fastidious female several generations back started doing it.

Male elephants play an even more peripheral role than lions in the lives of the children they father. The field biologist Cynthia Moss, who has spent a decade observing elephants, mostly in the Amboseli region of Kenya, has discovered their social system to be many-tiered and female-dominated, with the mother and her children as the "immediate family." The next circle of kinship is a "family unit," consisting of the mother, her daughters, and her granddaughters and immature grandsons. This unit often forms a "bond group" with another family unit; members of the same bond group move, feed, and rest together, and greet each other excitedly after periods of separation. The bond groups in turn mix with larger groups which Moss calls "clans," and the clans associate with one of the "subpopulations" that make up the entire population of the area. Males are driven from the immediate family when they reach sexual maturity, at about the age of fourteen or fifteen, and thereafter they approach the cows and calves only to mate.

Few of the nonhuman primates go in for long-term, stable pair-bonding either: only small arboreal species, like marmosets (whose males take over much of the child rearing), titis, gibbons, and tamarins (which can also be polygynous and polyandrous). The most common breeding arrangement among primates is a single, dominant male attached to a group of females, with the other males cruising in nearby groups, continuously trying to displace him. Sometimes the dominant male will admit a younger apprentice, who will eventually succeed him, and several high-ranking males will often form a coalition.

The male's reproductive strategy in this type of system—and some scientists believe that all primate males, including human males, have the same strategy—is to gain access to as many females and to produce as many offspring by them as he can, because by his doing so, his genes will have the best chance of surviving and proliferating. The female's strategy is different because the number of children she can have and perpetuate her genes with is limited—twenty children in a lifetime is a lot for any primate—she is selective, choosing to mate only with those males who look as if they will give her the greatest number of viable offspring. (Female chimpanzees in rut, however, seem to mate freely with all comers.) The nonhuman female primates also concentrate on eating well as a way of maximizing reproductive fitness, while the males devote their energies to courtship and to competing with other males for access to them. This fundamental difference in the reproductive strategies of the two sexes seems to carry over to humans. The man tries to mate with as many women as he can, while the woman withholds her favors for the mate who seems strongest (not physically, but socially and financially) and most stable, who looks as if he will be the the best provider and most likely to live up to a long-term commitment.

Gorillas are polygynous. The number of consorts an adult "silverback" male will have—seldom more than five, nine maximum, often only two—varies from group to group and from subspecies to subspecies. The main job of a dominant silverback is to protect his females from other males (even though gorillas in practice, despite the famous chest-pounding displays of the males, are among the gentlest and most low-key of the primates), and so a more puissant one will attract more females; but diet also determines the size of the group that can travel together. Western lowland gorillas, which eat fruit exclusively, have smaller families than eastern mountain gorillas, whose staple food, leaves and stems, is more abundant.

According to the social biologist Irven DeVore, the hamadryas baboons of Ethiopia are most like human tribal people: everybody lives together, but sexual access is delineated. They have three levels of organization: the clan, made up of a high-ranking male and his permanent "harem" of up to ten females; the band, consisting of several clans who go off together on foraging expeditions; and the troop, which can have as many as seven hundred and fifty individuals from different bands, who sleep together on cliffs or rocks in the arid acacia grasslands. The male "sequesters" females for his harem when they are still immature two-year-olds. He mothers them, grooms them (which is unusual for male baboons to do), and directs hostile stares at them or even gives them painful neck bites if they stray too far. The females accept the bullying passively. Once in a harem, that is their life. Dominated by the male, they have little chance to be selective or to vary their sex life, unless they manage to sneak off. The savanna baboon, however, which is so closely related to the hamadryas baboon that the two species interbreed where their populations are in contact, has a very different social system. The females are more assertive and political, with dominance hierarchies of their own. Groups of females form to defend access to certain trees whose nutritious fruit enhances their reproductive success. New males are not admitted to their band without their consent. They seem to be the matrix of the society. The primatologist Richard Wrangham has proposed the terms "male-bonded" and "female-bonded" to describe the different systems of the hamadryas and the savanna baboon, and he has told me that "with a few wrinkles" male-bondedness and female-bondedness seem to be evolutionary prototypes of patrilineality and matrilineality, the two routes of descent between which most elementary human societies have chosen. Along the Awash River, in southeastern Ethiopia, the male- and female-bondedness of the local baboons correlates neatly with the distribution of wild fruit trees.

The other primates, particularly, seem to foreshadow humans, with their comparatively stable monogamous or polygynous bonding; with the enduring groups of male or female allies which many species, including gorillas, baboons, chimpanzees, and macaques, inherit through their mother, and which seem only a step away from human descent groups. Macaque troops have even been found to recognize a "pecking order of lineages," and since 1965 evidence has been accumulating that many species have a tendency to avoid incest, which previously only humans were thought to do. This evidence has made it necessary to revise a central thesis of Sigmund Freud and Claude Lévi-Strauss, that exogamous marriage and the establishment of incest taboos—a man forswearing a sexual relationship with his sister or daughter and giving her to another man—are the first acts of the morality and culture which define our species.

In 1964 a series of important papers by the English biologist W. D. Hamilton offered a Darwinian explanation for the practice, observed in many animal species, of close kin coming to each other's defense, even at the cost of their own lives, which seems to contradict Darwin's theory that individuals are primarily concerned with their own preservation and perpetuation. Hamilton developed his theory from work done in the nineteen-thirties by the geneticists J. B. S. Haldane and Ronald A. Fisher and from his own study of wasps, which are well known for their readiness to give their lives in defense of the hive. After observing many acts of suicidal altruism by wasps, Hamilton began to see a pattern: that the individual wasp was particularly ready to give her life for other wasps to which she was closely related. Because of their peculiar mode of sex determination, closely related wasps share an unusual number of genes; three-fourths of the genes of sisters, for instance, are identical by descent. Hamilton concluded that the wasps' altruism was therefore only apparent, that their self-sacrifice was in fact a means of insuring the survival of more of their own genes, in the bodies of their threatened relatives, than they themselves incorporated. He called his theory "kin selection."

Since Hamilton's papers came out, all sorts of animal behavior has been examined in the light of the broad implications of kin selection: altruism in species ranging from spiders to wild horses; the "hurt-wing" trick that mother killdeer use to lure predators from their young; the alarm calls that individual starlings and other birds give to warn their flock of approaching predators, but which draw attention to themselves; the similar behavior of female ground squirrels; infanticide among mice; the tendency of sexually mature blue jay, jackal, and wolf offspring to be "helpers at the nest," helping their parents raise a new brood instead of going off and starting a family of their own. Other studies have confirmed that close kin tend to associate and cooperate in ways that are not self-sacrificing—that blood-related Japanese monkeys, for instance, feed together regularly, while unrelated ones rarely do; that if three hyenas come on a dead gazelle and two of them team up to prevent the third from having any of the meat, the two are probably more closely related (a type of alliance which Richard Wrangham has called "interference mutualism"); that it pays for kin to stick together, in other words, or one day they may find themselves without an ally.

Another pattern under study is the uncanny ability of many animals, like bats and various pelagic birds, which nest in huge colonies, to recognize their own kin in large groups of their own species. How is it, as the biologist Joan Graf has recently reported, that "certain sweat bees, guarding the opening to their nests, will exclude nonrelatives and admit kin even though they have never met either"; or that "some toad tadpoles prefer schooling with brothers and sisters to schooling with unrelated tadpoles and are often finicky enough to prefer to mingle with full siblings rather than with half-brothers and half-sisters"?

But humans are more complicated than wasps or tadpoles, and there is a lot of disagreement about the usefulness of kin selection as a framework for interpreting and predicting human social behavior. One of the most enthusiastic endorsers of the theory for humans is the cultural anthropologist Napoleon Chagnon. Chagnon spent four years among the Yanomamo Indians, a group of about twelve thousand hunters and simple horticulturalists who live, isolated from the outside world by rapids, in the mountainous jungle of southern Venezuela and northern Brazil. Except for the introduction of steel axes, aluminum cook pots, glass beads, and a few other trade items, the Yanomamo are considered much like people living in the Neolithic. During his stay among them, Chagnon collected and later linked by computer the genealogies and marriage histories of about three thousand Yanomamo, living and dead. He was thus able to work out the exact relationships of the participants in an ax fight he photographed in one of the villages in 1971. The results were striking. All of the seventeen people who came to the aid of a young man named Mohesiwa, one of the major figures in the fight, turned out to be related to him, often in several ways. They were eight times more closely related to Mohesiwa than to his opponent, and two times more related among each other than to the village at large. Chagnon also found that when meat was brought into a village by a hunter, the people shared it "in decaying order of relatedness" to him, and that when people broke away from a village to start a new one—an event known as "fissioning"—they too tended all to be related.

Students of Chagnon have since learned that monkey troops and Amish communities also fission along kin lines. It is not really surprising that when communities break up, blood should usually prove thicker than water. Many of the Norse sagas tell how small groups of closely related Vikings sailed from established communities in search of a new home; they are also describing "fissioning."

The villages of Senegal and the Gambia have genealogical

relationships of their own. When they get to be a certain size, frictions usually develop, and some of the people leave. If it is started by the nephew of the headman, the new village is the "nephew" of the old one, and its inhabitants are all "nephews" of the old village's inhabitants, on top of whatever blood relationships they may already have.

When the theory of kin selection is applied to humans, however, questions arise. Why, if there is a biological need for relatives to be together and to be supportive of each other, do so many of the things people do, particularly in modern society, seem to run counter to the interests of their relatives, or to demonstrate complete indifference to kinship? Why, to begin with, is homicide committed most often by a member of the victim's own family? (One reason, of course, is that there are fewer restraints or taboos on aggression or violent expression of rage within families; another is the particularly volatile and irrational nature of jealousy.) Why do mothers sometimes stop feeding their babies, and have "anger displays"? Why are there generation gaps? Why are elderly parents and their adult children having increasingly little to do with each other? Why is even the nuclear family in trouble? Why are increasing numbers of women delaying motherhood and having fewer children, or forgoing the experience altogether? How could the followers of the Reverend Jimmy Jones have killed their whole families at his community in Guyana? Why, if it is to our advantage to associate and cooperate with our kin, aren't we maximally inbred? (The genetic consequences of inbreeding will be gone into later.) Why, instead, are we becoming an increasingly outbred, "panmictic" society? Are there not very good reasons having nothing to do with reproductive success for poor people to have a lot of children?

Some of these contradictory patterns are explained by the fact that as human society has grown more complex, other factors have come into play. Chagnon, who has been charged with "biological reductionism" for his endorsement of kin selection as a predictor of human social behavior, explained to me recently that "the environment of kin selection is a hundred, a hundred and fifty people. Most of us now live in cities—a completely different social environment. Nor should all behavior be expected to be adaptive. Not everything an organism does is preserved by natural selection." The sociologist Pierre van den Berghe has explained the declining fertility rate by proposing that an organism which has become "self-conscious"—a woman who has decided that she wants to do something more with her life than just having children, for instance—can override the interests and instructions of its "constituent genes." The cultural anthropologist Thomas de Zengotita has argued in a paper about the collective suicide at Jonestown that "not just the limiting case, this socio-cultural mutant, but the great historical stream of functional social systems, from hunting and gathering bands to theocratic states to modern industrial nations—all of them [lie] at the point of origin, beyond natural explanation." To him, each of mankind's rich array of customs and rules is a product of an often arbitrarily imposed "mental order," and this very capacity for "culture"—the constant possibility of our countermanding the genetic imperative or any other kind of natural causality—is precisely what makes us human. "People can do any damn thing they get into their heads," de Zengotita told me recently, "and they're doing it all the time. The difference between having an incest taboo that includes fifty cousins, say, and another that includes no cousins at all can't possibly be attributed to anything genetic."

But the fact that human inventiveness is virtually boundless does not rule out the possibility of there also being an ancestral human need for kinship, ultimately of biological origin. The anthropologist Robin Fox, whose career has been devoted to reconstructing how human social systems may have emerged, and to working out plausible explanations for the many forms they have taken, has written, "Kinship groups are as natural as limbs and digestion. They are the outcome of adaptive responses and natural selection over millions of years; they are not peculiar to human society. They do not depend for their existence on the equally natural ability to classify and name which characterizes our species; in the absence of language and rules, they would still occur."

Most of the differences between the breeding systems of the other primates and human kinship systems, Fox maintains, can ultimately be attributed to man's "hindsight"—his "ability to look back to his ancestry . . . to calculate degrees of relationship and to utilize them for the forging of social bonds." Other species, of course, have the same spectrum of relatives, but they can't conceptualize them; they lack categories like second cousin once removed, can't remember who their sixth great-grandfather was, and don't create honorary kin (although they may have surrogate parents). According to Fox, this hindsight has been "as much a factor in [man's] successful development as the claws of a tiger or the neck of a giraffe were in the survival of those species." The trait seems, at any rate, universal in man. In villages throughout the world, there is usually somebody who knows how each person is related, who can recite as many generations of everybody's ancestry as are needed for that particular social system to work. This "remembrancer" is usually an older person with some predisposition to the role—a good memory, perhaps, or a feeling for the past—and his or her position, though valued, is seldom official. In the feudal societies of Europe and Asia, a special bardic caste was often found, whose job was to draw up, and often to make up, pedigrees and to celebrate their patrons' ancestry in verse. The deeper a man's pedigree, the greater his prestige usually was. One of the early English definitions of a nobleman, in fact, was "he who knows his pedigree." The word pedigree itself is a product of European feudalism. It comes from the old French, *pied de grue*, "crane's foot," and alludes to the form in which pedigrees were drawn up in the Middle Ages.

Although there is no society in which relatives do not recognize each other and form special relationships with each other, because humans can do anything they "get into their heads," there is much more diversity in their kinship systems, and the important questions about human kinship are still hotly debated: What is the real building block of the human family, are we naturally monogamous or polygamous, and even, what *is* human nature?

Traditional Kinship

IN 1975 THIRTEEN DIMINUTIVE HOMINIDS OF VARYING AGE AND sex, belonging to the species *Australopithecus afarensis*, were found in the Afar Triangle of Ethiopia. The absence of other remains and the way the bodies were clustered together suggested that they were some kind of family group which around two and a half million years ago had met with an accident; they were hailed, in fact, as "the First Family." Considerable evidence—from the other primates and from contemporary tribal people—suggests that humans have essentially always lived in bands of close kin—in families of some sort—which probably contained more than one adult male. But what sort of family we originally had—a nuclear unit or a gorillalike troop, whether the father stayed with his mate and children, and what sort of relationship existed *among* families: did they hunt and sleep together and share food?—is not at all clear.

Owen Lovejoy, one of the discoverers of the First Family, has argued on the basis of our anatomy that we are a monogamous species. The modification of our lower limbs for "upright bipedality"—the oldest characteristic in the paleontological record which defines humans—evolved when men had to bring food to their mates and children, Lovejoy maintains, after we had come down from trees and moved into open country. Our "feminized" canine teeth he interprets as a further indicator of monogamous tendencies. Among the other primates, only in species whose males must fight with each other for access to the females (most species, in fact) do the males have large, intimidating canines, while the canines of stably pair-bonded species like gibbons and marmosets are reduced like ours. He suggests, moreover, as the science writer Desmond Morris has argued in *The Naked Ape,* that the epigamic characteristics of women—enlarged breasts, luxuriant hair, unhairy skin, the heightened responsiveness of their lips, nipples, and genitals, the flushing of certain areas during coition—evolved as signals to men that they were permanently available, not only at the moment of ovulation, like other animals which get together only when the female is in estrus; and thus encouraged permanent pair-bonding. Finally, Lovejoy argues that humans could not have afforded to spend so many years as children and thus delay reaching sexual maturity unless there was some assurance that a high percentage of the children would survive. This would have required the men to redirect their energies from competing with each other for "consort success" to becoming more involved as parents; and that would not have happened unless the men were sure that the children were theirs—unless monogamy, with sanctions against adultery, were in practice.

The challenge of finding a mate and, especially these days, of maintaining the relationship for any length of time; the joys of having children, going through life, and growing old together, are such common human objectives that it seems almost inconceivable we could be anything but monogamous. Plato already recognized that each of us is fundamentally incomplete because we can only be of one sex. In the *Symposium* Alcibiades suggests that a jealous god divided man into two sexes, and that they have been trying to get together ever since. The psychologist Carl G. Jung, who explored the human love relationship in great depth, maintained that a person cannot be whole until he or she takes on another person wholly—until the man encounters and befriends his *animus,* his own inverted maleness, in a woman; and the woman meets and adopts her *anima* in him. In our society, as in many others, the necessity of settling down with one person and raising a family is instilled and promoted in so many ways that whenever an attempt at it fails, even though the choreography of

separation and divorce is by now thoroughly familiar and the
stigma of failure has diminished, "breaking up" is still almost always a traumatic experience.

And yet there is strong evidence that humans throughout
their history have not, in fact, been monogamous, but that they
have been, and continue to be, mildly polygynous.

Of the eight hundred and fifty-four societies in G. P. Murdock's *Ethnographic Atlas*, which claims to portray "the known
cultural universe" of the past five hundred years, only sixteen per
cent are strictly monogamous; thirty-nine per cent permit but do
not require polygyny, and forty-four per cent (including almost
every African society) are emphatically polygynous; only four, in
Tibet and India, are polyandrous. This breakdown is somewhat
misleading, however, because most of the people in the world belong to the strictly monogamous sixteen per cent, and because
even in the societies where polygyny is the cultural ideal, not
every man can afford an extra wife and many, if not most, of the
marriages are in fact monogamous. On the other hand, a good deal
of extramarital sex goes on in the monogamous societies; one has
only to read the Kinsey reports to be reminded that Americans are
not contented monogamists, at least in practice, and it is common
for sex partners of long standing to find themselves thinking of
other people while making love. The distinction between open
polygyny and having one wife with a woman or two on the side
(especially when children by mistresses can be made, by common
law, the man's legal heirs) or between having several wives at
once or in succession (particularly when there is some overlap to
the successive relationships) becomes largely a matter of definition
(should one call the latter, for instance, serial monogamy, or serial
polygyny?).

One thing, however, is clear: the nuclear family (also called
by some authors the standard, the primary, the elementary, the
simple, the independent, the traditional, the conjugal-natal, and
the conjugal-filial family) is not the universal building block (or
the basic association for enhancing survival, or the fundamental
normative entity) of every society, as the anthropologist Edward
Westermark originally proposed in 1891 and as anthropology and
sociology textbooks made it out to be until about a decade ago. It
is far from universal even in the societies where it is the pre-
scribed and dominant form. It is only one of several contingent

arrangements which happens to be common because in most of the world the sex ratio is about equal, and because most men can't afford or are unable to acquire more than one wife. In real primitive societies it is rare (as opposed to the multigenerational or "extended" family), except in ecologically precarious groups like Eskimos, who cannot live up to permanent commitments with greater numbers of kin. Those who like Lovejoy believe monogamy to be "the foremost adaptation of our species" have tried to explain polygyny as a later, cultural development, when human social evolution was "no longer under biological control"; or as a "composite family," a series of linked nuclear families with one husband in common; but the dynamics of polygyny are quite different, and this seems a forced, ethnocentric piece of reasoning, a projection of our Judeo-Christian bias toward monogamy (The Jews, of course, were initially polygamous. It was only by the time of Christ, as a result of urbanization and Roman influence, that the practice of plural marriage had largely died out among them.)

It is even harder to reconcile a universal one-female-per-male hypothesis with reproductive systems like the "ritualized access" of the Nayar, a caste in Kerala, on the Malabar Coast of southern India, whose men and women both have many spouses at once; or with the group marriages that crop up in a few other societies and result in offspring, but which have no resemblance to nuclear families.

In fact, the continued presence of the man who has made the mother pregnant is not strictly necessary for the child's survival; in many societies he plays no further role, and the mother manages quite well without him, especially when an extended family provides maternal uncles or other male relatives as father figures. This point, this seemingly slight shift of emphasis—that if there is any universal, basic association, any nucleus of human kinship, it is the mother-child unit—was first made by Robin Fox in his Kinship and Marriage, which was published in 1967, and it turned around a lot of anthropological thinking. "Fox's law of the dispensable male," as he recently described it to me—"if the mother-infant unit can possibly do without the male except for the simple purpose of insemination, it will"—seems to hold true particularly in the Third World and among minority groups in the West. In the United States, the mother-headed family (also

known as the matrifocal, the matricentric, and the matricentered
family), which lacks a resident husband but has a mother who
works or is on welfare and who often leaves her children with
her mother, is disproportionately common among "blacks" (Americans with African descent, whose gene pool is actually thirty per
cent Caucasian). According to the 1980 census, forty-seven per
cent of black families, compared to eighteen per cent of white
families, are headed by single women. The phenomenon is usually
explained in two ways: as a legacy of slavery, in which husbands
and wives were separated by sale, and the men, being slaves, had
little to offer as family heads, either economically or in terms of
real authority; as a product of urban poverty, unemployment, and
the welfare system (in many states, two-parent families are ineli-
gible for welfare, so the father is encouraged to shirk his family
duties).

Mother-headed families are also common in the Caribbean.
Some anthropologists, in fact, refer to the mother-headed family
as the "Caribbean-type" family. On the island of Dominica, for
instance, a woman who can keep a man has great status, and on
Jamaica, about two-thirds of the births to the poor are illegitimate.
The Jamaicans practice a delayed system of marriage, often waiting to take vows until they are in their forties. A group of children, some of whom may already be in their teens and all of
whom belong to the bride, is a common sight at Jamaican wed-
dings. Marriage is something couples work up to. The ceremony
is more than anything a legitimization of their relationship and
a sign of upward mobility. Caribbean men tend to be what the
feminist anthropologist Judith Bruce recently and perhaps a little
harshly described to me as "elusive reprobates." I know of one
man from Antigua, for instance, who fathered a total of thirty-
two children, no more than two of them by the same woman, and
lived with only one of the women, whom he ultimately married.

A considerable number of Caribbean men, on closer examina-
tion, are not that elusive; they can be found living with and giving
their primary allegiance to their mother (or to their grandmother;
while he was fathering most of his children, the man from Antigua, for instance, returned each night to his grandmother; they
actually slept in the same bed). A similar pattern obtains in
Brazil, where adult children traditionally live in the family home
until they marry (or all their lives, if they stay single). In Brazil

the great number of mother-headed families is partly a result of joblessness and male outmigration. In many cities and villages the men cannot afford to maintain their families, and they have to leave in search of work. Some of the men return periodically, but as often as not, the marriage dissolves and the woman is left to fend for herself. This is rarely tragic, however, because she usually has a large network of kin to fall back on, and there is a certain expectation among poor Brazilian women that this will happen. In practically every community there seem to be more women (although a check of the most recent statistics reveals that in 1981 the nationwide sex ratio was even, with about fifty-nine million males to fifty-nine million females), so there is little incentive for the men who do not go away to marry them. This situation adds to the number of mother-headed families.

In the poor states of northeastern Brazil the bond between a single mother and her son can be so strong that the son becomes his mother's surrogate "other half," and when he finally decides to get married, she can become bitterly resentful of her daughter-in-law for taking him from her. Devotion to the mother is a Latin, Catholic trait, related to the prominence given by the Church to the Virgin Mary; a mother's death is often taken by her children, particularly by her sons, as the end of the world. Yet there are equally strong polygynous tendencies in Brazil. One man I know of had a total of nine children by three women, each of whom lived in a different city and was unaware of the others' existence. He married the second while still married to the first. Another man, who lives in a suburb of Brasília, has had six children by twin sisters who live a few streets from each other. American blacks, Caribbeans, and Brazilians are all people with African polygynous traditions, and the connection between the mother-headed family (which is just as pervasive in black Africa) and polygyny is probably as important as its more frequently cited correlation with social and economic instability.

War, of course, is a wholesale creator of mother-headed families. After fifteen million Russian men were killed in the Second World War, for instance, millions of the Russian women who had been deprived of existing or potential husbands, rather than have no children at all, began to have them out of wedlock. The state tacitly encouraged this method of building up the population again—which was in effect polygyny—by relaxing its insistence on legitimacy and legal marriage and by providing, in 1949 alone, child support to 3,312,000 unwed mothers. (The only time polygyny has ever been legal in the West, however, was briefly in the German states after the Hundred Years' War, because of a similar decimation of the male population.) As that generation of Russian women came to the end of their childbearing years, in the nineteen-sixties, the laws about unwed motherhood in Russia tightened again, and social condemnation of illegitimacy resumed. In the past decade the mother-headed family has begun to spread among white American women for completely different reasons (their rising rate of divorce, their increasing economic independence from men).

⚜

While the father's role in his immediate family is, on balance, peripheral—he can be there or not, and either way, the needs of his "dependents" will be taken care of (with varying success depending on the type of family)—not only are men present at every subsequent level of social organization—bands, villages, tribes, chiefdoms, cities, states—but their role seems to be, on balance, dominant. "Amazon" societies, of women who do without men except for the simple purpose of insemination, exist in legends, but none has yet been found, and most of the societies that have been studied—even the matrilineal ones—seem to be constructed for the benefit of the men, to have followed, at least in terms of sexual balance of power, the general pattern of the male-dominated breeding systems of most of the other primates.

The development of human kinship may have proceeded this way: as the advantages of tools, weapons, shelter and fire, and ways of killing and outcompeting larger, stronger carnivores were discovered by trial and error, the early hominids may have learned to cooperate with each other and begun to form small bands of several families, whose males would go out and hunt, and whose females would take care of the children and look for edible plants. This division of labor, this exchange of meat and vegetables between men and women, may have been the basis of human economy. The sexes may have seen each other in a new light. "Men no longer needed women for sexual purposes only, and women no longer needed men for protection only, but each had a vested interest in the products of each other's labor," Fox suggests.

Another early trade item, as families and bands bartered and formed alliances with each other, was the women themselves. This was a human innovation: women became "objects of exchange," in Fox's words, as well as "objects of use," and it was from the need to draw a distinction between one's own women and other men's that kinship systems may have arisen. "One's own" women were blood relatives. It didn't matter how they were related, through mother or father; the point was that the women in this group—one's "clan"—were not for marrying oneself, but for marrying to other men, to acquire allies. In the most basic situation—a village divided into two clans—the men of either "moiety" might simply swap their sisters' children. Cross-cousin marriage (with the father's sister's child, or the mother's brother's child) is usually the ideal match, while parallel-cousin marriage, between the children of siblings of the same sex, is usually forbidden. Cross-cousin marriage forges an alliance between an uncle and his nephew, and the emphasis on this relationship—on the "avunculate," as it is called—is peculiarly human.

Another human innovation is our ability to form groups of patrilineal kin. Other animals do not seem to recognize their fathers consistently enough to do this. The male-bonded chimpanzees and hamadryas baboons come closest: some of the members of their groups of closely related males may be related through their fathers, but they don't seem to have conceptualized their paternal descent. Most traditional human societies, however, are consciously patrilineal. Forty-six per cent of the ones in Murdock's *Ethnographic Atlas* are, while only sixteen per cent are based on female descent. The United States, like the other Western countries, is a bilateral society with patrilineal tinges: anybody connected to you, in any way, even by marriage, is a member of your kinship group (which if it is bilateral is known as a *kindred* rather than a clan), but the names of the male ancestors are better remembered.

During the eighteen-sixties, when anthropology was emerging as a social science, there was great argument about whether humans had always been patrilineal. The Swiss jurist J. J. Bachofen, the Scottish lawyer John McLennan, and the American lawyer

Lewis Henry Morgan argued that we evolved from "promiscuous hordes" to groups ruled by women, and that patriliny was a later development, while the British jurist Henry Maine maintained that men had always controlled the reckoning of descent and everything else.

The question was impossible to settle, for lack of evidence, and in this century it has been rephrased rather than completely abandoned: What makes one society trace itself through its women, and another through its men? Several patterns suggest themselves. Hunter-gatherers (which humans have been for perhaps ninety-eight per cent of their history) usually have patrilineal, male-dominated societies. So do pastoral nomads; moving through arid expanses with herds of animals requires close cooperation between father and son. Feudal agricultural societies are male-dominated but are often bilateral. Industrial societies are bilateral and "male-dominated with androgyny"—women are just as good at many jobs, but there is still considerable stratification by gender in the work place. Kinship in these societies has atrophied to the nuclear family; the focus of loyalty and the responsibility for providing social services and something for the adults to do with their lives have shifted from the clan and the kindred to the work place and the state.

A belt of matriliny runs across Central Africa, through Zambia, Malawi, and southern Zaire, and is probably explained by the fact that until fifty to a hundred years ago, the men of the Tonga, the Bemba, and the Yao tribes, which reckon descent through their women, were gone much of the time, looking for slaves. At the middle level of agriculture—where there is plenty of fertile land, where women control the house and the garden plot, and men turn their attention to other things (slaves, gold, ivory, or other women, perhaps)—the society tends to go matrilineal. The mathematics for the rate of promiscuity needed to generate a preference for nieces and nephews have actually been worked out. (But the society may have *already* been matrilineal, Fox points out, and in a matrilineal society genetic fatherhood is irrelevant.)

There may have been a golden age of matriarchy just after the invention of agriculture, with which women have been plausibly credited. It seems reasonable that women would have discovered that roots or cuttings from plants they had gathered, if stuck in the ground, would grow. In Malaysia, in Indonesia, in Japan, in the Pacific Northwest, and along the Malabar coast of India, longhouses from this brief period of female supremacy have been unearthed by archeologists. Women past childbearing age in these societies often had the role of priestess in mother-goddess cults and fertility rites during which various inebriants and narcotics— perhaps also developed by women—were used. But then the plow was invented, perhaps more plausibly by men, and the men took back control of the descent-reckoning system. In the new seed-planting culture a new type of property was traded and fought over—fertile land—and men naturally became the proprietors.

The recently settled hunters of today, however, like the Yanomamo, the Ifegawa of the Philippines, and the BaLese of Zaire, who have taken up slash-and-burn agriculture in their respective rain forests but who still raid each other's villages for women, or did until recently, throw a little water on this theory, because they are patrilineal. There may be a correlation between patriliny and bellicosity. The !Kung bushmen of Africa are non-aggressive and bilateral, for instance, while in Australia neighboring groups of patrilineal aborigines are often chronically hostile. The warrior societies of East Africa and southeastern China, as well as the predatory hordes of the Mongols and the Tatars, were strongly patrilineal; the belief that they were all sons of a common ancestor fused them into a cohesive fighting force. In Western society, where the threshold of large-scale hostility is usually a national border, each sovereign state is like a great patrilineal clan, which the male members are obligated to defend. Both the words "patriotic" and "patrilineal" are, in fact, derived from the Latin word for father.

Many exceptions to these patterns can be found, however. The Iroquois, for instance, as well as various tribes of tropical headhunters, were warlike and matrilineal; the Navajo were nomadic herders who, after moving to the Southwest from Canada, adopted the matriliny of the local Pueblo. Chance historical factors and proximity to other systems—the sheer vagary of cultural drift—seem to have determined which way a society has gone as often as ecological appropriateness. The Plains Indians brought their kinship systems and subsistence strategies with them when they moved into the Great Plains after acquiring horses in the eighteenth century. The Sioux were already patrilineal, the Crow were patrilineal, the Kiowa-Apache went both ways. Some of them hunted buffalo, some had ritual sun dances, some had warrior societies. But before this new horse-riding culture could sort itself out, it was annihilated.

Other societies seem to have made either-or decisions: patriliny or matriliny would probably have served equally well. Still others use different modes of descent for different purposes; a growing number of societies, in fact, that had been classified as straight patrilineal or matrilineal are proving more complicated. One double-descent system which has been known for some time is that of the Yako, a tribe of about eleven thousand people who live mostly in the town of Umor, Nigeria. The Yako men inherit cattle and other movable property matrilineally, from their mothers' brothers, but their houses and their land pass from father to son. Their loyalties are divided between "patriclans," as Fox calls them, within which they cannot marry, and older, totemic "matriclans" whose members are obligated to stand by each other. The advantage of this system is that because the property is continuously being redistributed, no single clan can become more powerful.

The Mundugamor of New Guinea, whom Margaret Mead studied, also pass on land patrilineally, but "all other goods," Fox explains, "are passed from father to daughter and mother to son. These 'lines' of inheritance are called 'ropes' by the natives. Mead traces this to the hostility between people of the same sex."

Some societies, like the three hundred or so Cayapo Indians who live in the village of Mekranoti, deep in the forest of southeastern Amazonia, with no neighbors for hundreds of miles, have fictive kinship systems. When a boy in Mekranoti is eight years old, an older man who acts as his adoptive father admits him to the men's house—a thatched hut in the center of the village plaza which women are not allowed to enter on pain of rape or death. The men's hut is somewhat like the firehouse in a New England village: it is where the men go to be together, away from their wives, and to talk about what is happening in the community. The men belong to one of two groups, which are more like companies in a volunteer fire department (to continue the analogy) than clans or kindred groups, because membership in them is determined by choice rather than by descent, and each group has its captain and lieutenant. When I visited the village in 1976, these two "moieties" would usually play soccer against each other in the afternoon. The males also belong to four age-graded groups that hunt and take part in ceremonies together. One, for instance, consists of the bachelors between fourteen and twenty-two years old. When a young man wants to get married, he moves into the hut of the girl's mother and sleeps with the girl for a trial period of about a year, and if she hasn't become pregnant by then, the marriage doesn't take place. If she has, she must go into the forest to have the baby; her husband, the probable father, may not witness the birth. When she returns to the village with the child, her husband must go hunting, and he cannot return until he has killed something big. The villagers seem to know who is the father of whom, even though there is considerable promiscuity; most of them, in fact, can trace themselves on both sides to their great-grandparents. And yet they do not seem to have fully grasped the concept of paternity, or at least to have made the connection between sex and reproduction. One morning, while I was walking in the forest with one of the shamans and learning which plants were used medicinally, he showed me a plant among the fallen leaves whose four-inch brown stalk was leafless, and whose white head was covered with fine pink hairs. It looked, as some mushrooms do (although it was not a mushroom), very much like a penis. When a woman wanted to have a baby, he told me, she would eat one of these plants. Then one of the shamans would bathe her in the creek, wash her with a special leaf brew, and sing over her until midnight. Everyone in the village, he assured me, had been born through this process.

All sorts of ingenious variations on patriliny, matriliny, and double descent have been found. Among the Marubo Indians, for instance, who also live in the Brazilian Amazon, but near the Colombia border, children are born into their maternal grandmother's clan. This unusual, generation-skipping mode of descent has been discovered elsewhere only in Australia. The Murngin aborigines of Queensland, for instance, have a similar "four-section" system, each section being represented by a different grandparent. There are even eight-section systems in Australia, and tribes in which it is still not clear to structural anthropologists what is going on.

But however descent is reckoned, and even when it is not reckoned at all, the only real continuity in any society is between the woman and her children. Motherhood can be verified by witnesses, as has been the practice in most of the royal houses of

Europe, but paternity is the great unknown in genealogy. The more cautious, scientific genealogists do not use the word "fathers," they refer to "putative genitors" (as the Romans distinguished *pater* from *genitor*); while anthropologists distinguish between "biological" and "jural" fatherhood. The biological father of Tsar Paul I, for instance, is widely considered not to have been Peter III, Catherine the Great's husband, but her field marshal Peter Saltykov. If this is true, then the subsequent tsars were Romanoffs only in name.

Today an expensive battery of tests, which compare the blood type, the red-cell enzymes, the serum enzymes, the tissue-type antigens, and the histocompatibility loci of the putative genitor and his putative offspring, can come very close to establishing biological fatherhood by narrowing the field tremendously. Such a "leukocyte antigen" test recently freed the singer Paul McCartney from a 2.7-million-dollar paternity suit. But before these tests were developed, people had to rely on resemblances—unmistakable noses, distinctive dentition, specifically sited birthmarks—whose heritability is unpredictable (the inheritance of moles, for instance, is controlled by "autosomal dominant" genes with "imperfect penetrance"—genes located on the twenty-two chromosomes besides the X and the Y, which can pass directly from parent to child but do not consistently produce the same mole) and whose very existence may be impossible to judge objectively. There was no reliable method of proving fatherhood.

Societies have responded to this problem in different ways. The polyandrous Toda of India have solved it by simply being indifferent about who the real father is. Toda women usually marry several brothers, and when a woman becomes pregnant one of the brothers, in a ceremonial gesture called "presenting the bow," assumes jural fatherhood of the child, and perhaps the next couple of children to be born. After several years one of the other brothers presents his bow. The Trobriand Islanders of Melanesia, like the Cayapo Indians, deny that men have anything to do with reproduction. They believe that the male sex partner only enlarges the vaginal passage, so that the spirits of their ancestors can enter and be reborn; and yet they (also like the Cayapo) recognize the father as a kinsman of the child. As the anthropologist David Maybury-Lewis recently reminded me, it is a mistake to think that modern notions of biology exist "out there" any more than the jargon of anthropology does. Until early in this century even European medical textbooks denied the mother's gestatory role by portraying the fetus as a homunculus in the male sperm. A rejection of the father's biological role is implicit, of course, in the Christian doctrine of the Virgin Birth, and Jews, despite their ancient patrilineal traditions, have acknowledged the uncertainty of paternity by having Jewishness pass down matrilineally. This policy came into being after the Middle Ages, when many of their women were raped as the Jews wandered through Europe. In Israel today, citizenship is granted automatically only to applicants whose mothers are Jewish. The Arabs, whose equally strong patriliny derives from a similar history of pastoral nomadism, have a saying: "Tell me your mother's uncles, and I will tell you who you are." Even in our society, where confidence in paternity is generally high, the mother seems to be considered the more important parent. Masses of flowers and cards are sold on Mother's Day while Father's Day is not even celebrated in many households; and a recent, apparently serious study by some sociologists at the University of Michigan, which offered some three- and four-year-old children a hypothetical choice between giving up television or their father, found that only two-thirds of them preferred to keep their father.

Patriliny itself may be part of an attempt by men to "demean the woman's reproductive role," in Judith Bruce's words, to undermine the power that being the more important and verifiable parent gives her. In societies of every sort—this is one of the widespread patterns of genealogy—the female ancestors are not as well remembered. This female-line "genealogical amnesia" was first described in a paper by the anthropologist Robert Murphy about a tribe of Bedouin on the Arabian Peninsula. (The Bedouin are Arab-speaking nomads who herd goats, sheep, or camels, or combinations of the three; about a million Bedouin are scattered in small, mobile groups in the deserts between Mauritania and Iran.) Cutting off the women from their ancestry often enables the men to better manipulate the property and the affairs of the society, but not always. Not among the Batak, a farming tribe on the island of Sumatra, for instance. In 1980 a Mormon genealogist named Lyn Carson visited the Batak and recorded on tape the pedigrees that some of the old men chanted for him. The pedigrees were quite impressive—the men could go on for several dozen generations of

straight male-line descent—because of another global pattern in
genealogy: island pedigrees tend to be deeper than mainland ones.
Some of the most carefully remembered lineages are from the entrenched island societies of Iceland, Japan, England, and the
South Pacific. The main reason for this is simply that land on
islands is in shorter supply, and the hereditary right to it is more
jealously guarded (another reason, of course, is that it is harder
for people on islands to wander off and be forgotten). Carson discovered that the Batak had a curious patrilineal marriage taboo:
if two Batak wanted to marry, their fathers' male ancestors had to
be traced back, and if the same person was found within fifteen
generations, the marriage was forbidden. But the mothers of the
prospective bride and groom could be related much more closely,
and a good many of them were sisters. Property remained with the
mother's family, so the real continuity and power among the Batak
were obviously among the women. Yet when Carson tried to trace
the female lines, all he got was puzzled looks. The names of the
wives weren't considered important enough to be remembered.

The residence pattern can be as important as the mode of
descent in structuring the relationships within a society and in
determining status. The "matrilocal" pattern of the Navajo, for
instance, brings new males into the family of the women they
marry. So does "uxorilocality"; the distinction between the two
terms is that the uxorilocal man and his wife set up house near her
mother, and do not actually move in with the woman. A few
tribes in the Amazon, like the Mundurucu, the Akwe-Shavante,
the Cashinahua, and the Sharinahua, have patrilineal uxorilocality, which works much like a double-descent system, but this
is not a common arrangement; Lévi-Strauss himself, when its
existence was brought to his attention, doubted that it was even
possible. The Trobriand Islanders and the Tlingit and Haida
Indians of the Pacific Northwest are "avunculocal": newlyweds
live in watchful proximity of the husband's mother's brother, who
is the father figure in their matrilineal system. Each of these residence patterns focuses the society about its women, and it sets up
a proverbial situation which one anthropologist recently described
to me as "shlepping for the in-laws. Sons-in-law the world over
bend over with false courtesy and contorted deference, and par-
ents-in-law think the bums aren't good enough." The American
pattern, at least in the mobile middle and upper parts of the so-

ciety, is "neolocal": newlyweds generally start their life together
at some distance from their parents, seldom in the same community, practically never in the same house. The choice of residence is dictated partly by wherever the couple has found work,
but partly, too, by the tendency in our society for parents and their
adult children to disband.

To return to the notion that the real continuity in any society
is with its women, whatever its descent system: if humans throughout their history have been mildly polygynous and still are, and if
the mortality rate of men has been higher, then more women than
men have contributed to the human gene pool, and most of what
the geneticist Richard Lewontin has called our "mutational reper-
toire"—our ability to adapt and evolve—has been transmitted by
them. The female X chromosome itself, moreover, is three to four
times longer than the male Y chromosome, and contains much
more genetic information. In the 1982 edition of Victor Mc-
Kusick's *Mendelian Inheritance in Man,* a catalogue of every
clearly hereditary trait then known, a hundred and fifteen traits
unrelated to feminization are firmly assigned to the X chromosome.
But only a few traits besides the regulators for masculinity may
be Y-linked: greater relative stature, tooth shape, and hairy ears,
which are most prevalent among men in India. "The X chromosome has displayed particular stability in evolution," McKusick
writes. Everybody has at least one X chromosome, but only half
the population—the males—have a Y. Other genetic information,
from the mitachondrial DNA, which transmits critical instructions on cell respiration, is exclusively inherited from the mother.
But to claim that one sex alone has been responsible for human
evolution would be pushing the point ridiculously. "The same
genes pass through us all," a geneticist in Lewontin's lab reminded me.

🌳

Besides being a means of allocating the women—of distin-
guishing those who can be married from those of one's blood, however that is defined—kinship has had a number of other functions and characteristics for as long as there have been records of
human societies. One function has been to divide the community
into groups so that its resources can be efficiently exploited and
equitably shared. Another is to facilitate the orderly transfer of

property and authority between generations; and the various strategies of inheritance and succession which societies have come up with are no less ingenious than their methods of reckoning descent or their patterns of residence.

A third function is to keep the adolescent boys in line, to channel their newly awakened sexual responses and aggressive potential by initiating them through elaborate rites of passage, until at last, having proved themselves worthy of the honor many times over and not incidentally having been socialized in the process, they are admitted to the fraternity of the men. As members of this fraternity, kinsmen the world over, whether they say *ndugu*, as the BaLese do in Zaire, or *vlasnii*, as mountaineers do in Albania, call each other "brother." The use of the term by American black men may have carried over from Africa, where their ancestors lived in clans. In 1981 I found not only BaLese villagers in northeastern Zaire calling each other "brother," but also Pygmies using the word "bad" in an approving way and slapping each other's open palms, just as American blacks do—all of which I had thought was part of a routine which the members of an oppressed American minority had invented to support each other. On the other hand, the loose, fraternal way American blacks call each other "brother" may be an example of how the idiom of kinship is used to promote solidarity in groups of nonrelatives (union members and monks being other examples).

Another feature of traditional kinship is that it is "gerontocratic"—the older generations usually control the marital destinies of the young men and women, and decide who will inherit or succeed. In polygynous societies, where not every man gets to marry, the older men are especially powerful. Napoleon Chagnon has reported how the young Yanomamo, for instance, must curry favor with their elders in order to acquire a wife, and how the elders will often manipulate the kinship classification of a woman, changing it from "aunt" or "daughter," say, to "wife," so she can be married either to themselves or to a protégé. The same sort of maneuvering can go on when there is property to be inherited. The Giriama of Kenya, for instance, have no written land titles or cadastral records, and a young man can secure a coveted grove of wine palms, from which he can make a good living, only by getting some elders to verify his hereditary patrilineal right to it by testifying in the government court that the grove was his father's and his father's father's. In many African societies the rightful heir can be disinherited if rivals have him declared a witch by getting the elders to support their charge that he was responsible for somebody's death. When a Chagga man dies (the Chagga live on the slopes of Mount Kilimanjaro), the elders of his lineage appoint a "guardian" of his widow, who gains control of the house, the banana grove, and the woman herself.

Every society is governed to some degree by patronage, because those in responsible positions will naturally tend to favor those in whom they trust and believe, preferably their own kin. It is customary for each new mayor in Floriano, a city in northeastern Brazil, for instance, to fire everybody in office, even the school principals, and to install his relatives and friends. The system in rural Mississippi during the nineteen-forties, or at least in William Faulkner's fictional Yoknapatawpha County, was little different. In *Intruder in the Dust* Faulkner writes that "the one sole end of the entire establishment of public office was to elect one man like Sheriff Hampton big enough or at least with sense and character enough to run the county and then fill the rest of the jobs with cousins and in-laws who had failed to make a living at everything else they ever tried." In Ghana, the main purpose of working in the civil service is quite undisguisedly to get jobs for one's cousins. Failure to live up to this responsibility can provoke from a slighted kinsman retaliatory and sometimes fatal "magic" against oneself or one's children. It is only in meritocratic societies like ours that unconditional assistance to relatives becomes unethical and is condemned as nepotism, "a vice unheard-of in most other societies," as the anthropologist Jack Goody has written.

For most of human history, the rules by which people lived were made and enforced by their kinship group. Such rules as the sanctions against homicide, theft, adultery, and sexual deviation were enforced coercively, by threat of physical punishment; others were reinforced culturally, and gradually became internalized as "customs" which nobody would have thought of questioning or transgressing. Except in a few idiosyncratic societies like that of the Pygmies, who lead a comparatively insouciant, unstructured existence, coming and going as they please, with few rules, no formal descent groups or chiefs, but an all-embracing conception of the family and a reverence for personal freedom, most traditional societies have placed severe constraints on their members;

they have been tightly circumscribed, "controlling" environments, "life-term social arenas," as anthropologists describe them.

In many societies the notion that each person possesses rights as an individual has simply not existed. In ancient Rome, for instance, the *pater familias* had the power of life and death, or *patria potestas*, not only over his sons and their children but over his entire household, including adopted sons, clients, and slaves. "It was customary to lay the newborn baby at the father's feet," Stuart A. Queen and Robert W. Habenstein have written. "If he took it in his arms, he thereby acknowledged it as his own and admitted it to the rights and privileges of membership in the family. Should he refuse to do this, the child would become an outcast and would probably be exposed by the roadside. In that case it might perish or it might be taken away and reared by someone who wanted a foster child or a slave." The *pater familias* was free to put an adulterous wife to death, he could claim the earnings of his sons, he controlled their property, and he arranged the marriages of all his children. "In a sense," Queen and Habenstein write, "the members of the family were his chattel."

In ancient Judea, the patriarch, usually the senior male, had nearly as much authority over his household, or *beth*, which included his wives and his concubines, his grown sons and their children, his slaves and his bond servants, and sometimes strangers who had placed themselves under his protection. He too could put an adulterous wife to death, could sell his daughter, could even, if Genesis is to be believed, during the early nomadic period, which came to a close around 1200 B.C., offer his son in sacrifice, as Abraham came to the brink of doing with Isaac. But there were limits to his *patria potestas*: his daughter could refuse to marry a man to whom he had betrothed her as a child; if he beat a servant too severely, the servant could be taken from him; and after the Hebrews began to farm and to live in villages, he could not punish a disobedient son himself, but had to request collective punishment—usually stoning—by the community.

In the Middle East, senior males still have virtual *patria potestas* over the members of their kinship group. In 1977, for instance, a princess of Saudi Arabia's ruling House of Saud was publicly stoned to death for bringing dishonor to her grandfather, an older brother of the king. Her execution became the subject of a documentary film shown widely to shocked audiences in the

West; but even Muslims were shocked, because the punishment had not been applied for centuries. Stoning is the Shari'a, or Islamic law punishment for the crime of unlawful intercourse when it is committed by a married man or woman; there are only five such statutory punishments in the Koran.

The princess, who was married, had been having an indiscreet affair in London; the lovers had been seen in nightclubs kissing and holding hands. The proof of unlawful intercourse under Islamic law (the concept of adultery does not exist) is especially stringent: the couple must have been seen in bed together by four irreproachable male witnesses, who must be willing to testify that a string could not have been passed between them. If one witness reneges, the other three are liable to the penalty for false accusation—eighty lashes or "stripes"—and to the serious charge of impugning the man's and the woman's honor. Proof that the princess had committed unlawful intercourse was not even attempted, and it was unnecessary; that she had brought dishonor to her grandfather was already a capital offense—not in Islamic law, but in the customary law of Arabia—and he decided to exact the full penalty. When they learned what was to happen to them, the lovers tried to escape. The princess left her clothes on a beach one night, to make it seem as if she had committed suicide. But both were caught and brought to the grandfather. The lover was beheaded—which is not a Shari'a punishment at all.

Family honor (*'ird*) and personal honor (*sharaf*) are sacred, and crimes of honor—a father or brother beating or killing a kinswoman for bringing shame to him—are rarely punished; they are not, strictly speaking, even crimes. For a homicide to be punishable among some Bedouin tribes and in some of the more isolated and backward regions of the Middle East, there must be somebody more closely related to the victim than the murderer, who is placed under obligation to seek revenge or compensation. Thus in 1976 a man who belonged to a Bedouin tribe on the Sinai Peninsula, and who had killed his paternal first cousin, got away with the murder because the victim had no closer relatives in the male line; his father and brothers were all dead. In Kuwait, a member of the royal family has told me, women often go to the police for protection from the male members of their family.

One of the main obligations of kinsmen in traditional societies is to act together in cases of bloodshed. The aborigines of

Victoria, Australia, who believed that death was invariably the result of sorcery by somebody in another tribe, would go off on "bucceening" expeditions; the dead person's sons or other close kin would head in whatever direction the smoke of the cremated body drifted, or a fly or beetle placed on the grave flew, and they would kill the first people they met, which usually led to retaliatory expeditions by the people's relatives.

The "vengeance unit" of the Yanomamo is their village; Chagnon has estimated that something like a third of the men die raiding each other's villages. There is a strangely ritualized quality to their warfare. Truces are periodically declared so that the bodies of slain kinsmen can be collected and properly incinerated; cremation is the only way a person's immortal essence, which is thought to reside in his bones, can be released into the spirit world. After being cremated with his belongings on a pyre of logs in the center of the village, the dead warrior's charred bones are pulverized into a black powder, some of which is sprinkled into a soup of boiled plantains and is drunk on the same day by the man's shrieking, wailing kinswomen. The rest of the powder is transferred to hollow gourds and is saved to be drunk again on later occasions, to keep alive the memory of the man's unavenged death. Sometimes the drinking is spread out over several years, until at last there has been enough revenge. In particularly feud-prone societies, like those of southern Greece, Albania, Corsica, and Somalia, the female survivors play a similar role, improvising funerary dirges to incite their men to "wash the stain of blood from their house by spilling the blood of the killer" or of his close kin, as Jacob Black-Michaud has written. According to one source, before the First World War nineteen per cent of the adult males in Albania, with occasional local averages as high as forty-two per cent, became casualties of blood feuds.

Some of the earliest recorded laws are those that established the right to retaliate. The Hammurabic law of ancient Babylonia, which went into effect in 2100 B.C., demanded "an eye for an eye, and a tooth for a tooth." Very similar phrasing is found in Exodus; in the Twelve Tables which in about 450 B.C. set forth the Roman *lex talionis*; and in the Koran. The actual concern of these seemingly coldblooded statutes was not so much with punishing the crime, but with averting its possible consequences: in any society uncontrolled feuding is a great threat to order, and one way to prevent it is to limit the offended party to exact recompense, and nothing more. A number of societies have instituted monetary compensation as an alternative to exact physical recompense and uncontrolled feuding. The *vergelt* or "blood money" system of the ancient Teutons was paid out in diminishing order of relatedness, with the nearest patrilineal kinsman getting the most from the nearest relative of the murderer. The Anglo-Saxon system was similar, except that the widow's kin—the "distaff" side of the family—was also compensated, though not as much as the victim's "sword" side. (In England people still ask, "How is it going on the distaff side?")

According to later legal texts, the patrilateral kindred of the Irish, which was called the *gael-fine* and which included all paternal relatives, including females, until the sixteenth century was collectively responsible for both blood money (*eraic*) and "honor money" (*aire*), which had to be paid out when one of its members was found guilty of defamation, theft, or housebreaking. The Irish system contained an unusual clause: if the judgment was against a more powerful party, and the party did not pay up, the victim's next of kin, instead of having to seek revenge and standing a good chance of being killed in the process, could fast at the party's doorstep. The same strategy was traditionally resorted to in India, which may explain why fasting has been used as a political weapon in the struggle of both peoples for independence from the same greater power, England. The practice may once have been more widespread throughout Indo-Europe, and may have died out everywhere except at two of the region's outer limits.

The *baugr* system, which was practiced in Iceland from 900 to 1250, had perhaps the most elaborate payment structure. *Baugr* translates as "ring." When somebody was murdered, his kin became a "ring" of recipients. The ring went all the way out to the victim's fourth cousins, who were supposed to be paid *boot* (the source of our word "booty") by their counterparts on the killer's genealogical tree. The only party who was formally excused from having to pay was the killer himself, who was outlawed (like Eric the Red, Leif Ericson's father), or who himself became the victim of a vengeance killing. In certain cases, however, he could subsidize his kinsmen's payments, and the Icelandic sagas, which abound with tales of blood feuds fought or avoided, often show the killer making direct payment to the victim's kin, or paying through a mediator. The distribution of *boot*, however, does not seem to have settled the matter for good; it only bought peace for a time; and a derogatory remark which keeps appearing in the sagas, that a person who accepts *boot* instead of taking blood is "carrying his kinsman in his pocket," suggests that revenge was considered the nobler course of action. A man in the victim's clan could have been under conflicting pressure from those kin who wanted blood and distant kin who wanted a monetary settlement.

Because the Eskimos' kinship system (when they still lived in their traditional way, which has largely died out) was reduced to seasonally interacting nuclear families, the only person who could avenge a homicide was the victim's son. Although Eskimo men shared their wives freely, they killed men who took liberties with their wives without permission, or who stole them. Knowing this, the Eskimo with plans of adultery often killed the husband first. "Since it was the usual Eskimo custom for the killer to marry his victim's widow and to adopt his children," E. Adamson Hoebel has written, "a man might raise the boy who, when coming of age, could slay him."

Comanche law simply allowed the victim's kin to kill the murderer without further retaliation by either party. In cases of adultery the husband could kill or mutilate his wife, and he was honor-bound to seek damages from her lover, either in person or with the help of kin or friends (who would go along for a percentage), or, lacking kin and friends, by calling on a brave warrior, who would volunteer his services because dangerous deeds enhanced his prestige.

In old Arabia, as early as a thousand years before Christ, the souls of murdered men were imagined to flutter around their graves in the form of owls, crying with thirst and unable to find rest until vengeance had been taken. The burden of revenge fell on the victim's male next of kin—his son, his brother, his first cousin, his uncle, in that order. He was obliged to fast, to refrain from wine, perfume, and sleeping with women, and he could use any ruse except to kill the man in his sleep, because the souls of sleeping men were not thought to be present; and as he struck the blows he had to cry out the name of the person he was avenging. The practice of reaching a settlement by paying the *diya*, or blood money in Arabic, probably originated before the coming of the Prophet, with the Bedouin of the Arabian Peninsula. It was incorporated into Islamic law, and the standard fee—a hundred camels whose quality and sex depended on whether the murder was premeditated, "quasiintentional," or accidental—was possibly set by Mohammed himself. The payment of the *diya* is still an important institution among virtually all Bedouin. On the Arabian Peninsula, in Jordan, and elsewhere, jurists of the Shari'a law courts determine how much must be paid to a murdered man's heirs, often in yearly installments, by the culprit's *skila*, his nearest male relatives up to a specific number. The *diya* is the culprit's ransom from further retaliation by the victim's tribe. In Kuwait several years ago a first cousin of the king, who had accidentally killed a swimmer while backing his yacht out of a harbor, had to pay the *diya* to the swimmer's family, in spite of their difference in rank.

The Bedouin deal with antisocial behavior locally, with their own traditional methods. In one Sinai tribe, for instance, if a man kills or severely beats a woman he has married from another lineage, complicated legal proceedings begin between the members of their two lineages, often with the help of a third party whom both sides trust or who has recognized talents as a mediator. The members of this tribe are very talkative and legalistic. They are also great raconteurs, and a high proportion of their stories are about involved legal settlements of the past. Like all the Bedouin, this tribe has what is known as a "segmentary" system of kinship. Broadly speaking, four kinds of group exist. The smallest is the *bayt*, the tent, home, or family, consisting of a man, his wife, and their children. About one man in ten has more than one wife. In contrast with most other societies, a man does not need wealth to become a polygynist; rather, he must have a kinswoman (daughter, sister, or paternal cousin) whose hand in marriage he controls and whom he can exchange for a wife.

Each family can camp wherever it wants; its movements are determined by a variety of factors, notably by the availability of water and pasture. The camps of these Bedouin are nowadays very small—sometimes made up of just a single family. Rarely do more than five families camp together, and these often belong to the same lineage, or *rub*ᶜ.

The genealogical chart of a *rub*ᶜ would be shaped like a pyramid, with everybody descending in male line from an "apical ancestor"—the man who founded the lineage as many as eight generations back. There is usually at least one person in the lineage who knows just how all its members—living and dead—are related to each other. Half a dozen or so of these lineages make a larger pyramid, or "clan" (also called rub⁣ᶜ), with its own apical ancestor, and the ancestors of the clans are in turn all descended in male line from the legendary founder of the whole tribe, who is said to have come into the Sinai long ago after leaving his own tribe and wandering through the desert. In some segmentary systems there is one more level of descent, the ultimate pyramid— the nation. The Somali, for instance, a nation of Hamitic blacks below Ethiopia, all claim to be descended from a common ancestor named Samaale, who lived some thirty generations back. A considerable number of Somali are serious genealogists and can trace the intervening connections.

If a man in this Bedouin tribe kills or injures another, the other men in his lineage are all liable for the *diya,* and all become potential targets of vengeance. The negotiations between the two lineages, with emissaries going back and forth, can continue, intermittently, over a period of months or years. Many factors can influence the outcome—the relative strength of the lineages, whether the victim is perceived to have brought the assault upon himself, how strong the emotional ties were between him and his kinsmen. There may be a practical reason for choosing revenge over *diya:* it is a better deterrent against future aggression. But more often than not, a settlement is reached. When a payment is made to a lineage for a killing or a wounding, the members of the lineage who receive the money decide among themselves how to divide it up. Normally they have a standing agreement that the victim (or, in the case of a homicide, his closest relatives, say his father, his brothers, his sons) receive a third of the sum, while the rest is divided in equal shares among the other members of the lineage. The Bedouin, in general, are more prone to settle than the sedentary agricultural societies of the Mediterranean, whose vendettas can last for generations, flaring up and subsiding like an incurable recurrent illness. The tendency of Albanians and Corsicans to become embroiled in interminable blood feuds may be related to the relative shortage of fertile land, and to the fact that the parties are less able than seminomadic Bedouin to avoid each other.

The Alencar and Sampaio-Saraiva families, who come from

a remote farming community in northeastern Brazil called Exu, have been feuding on and off since 1949, and as of 1981, when there still seemed no prospect for a settlement, thirty-eight members had been killed. According to one account, the feud was precipitated by a quarrel over a woman. "Unhappily married to an Alencar, Maria Monteiro fell in love with a Sampaio. The couple moved in together, and tried to get rid of her husband by feeding him strychnine. The attempt failed and the jilted husband sued for divorce, sending his lawyer to Maria with the legal papers. Maria's lover forced the lawyer to eat the legal documents and wash them down with his urine. Several days later, the first Sampaio was gunned down in Exu's main square. In turn the mayor, an Alencar, was shot dead." The man who committed the first murder, José Arias Alencar, left Exu and (according to another account) did not return until 1976, to become the mayor. Two years later, he was gunned down on a street named after his victim, and the vendetta was renewed. After most of the local Alencars and Sampaio-Saraivas had been killed, hired *pistoleiros* began to hunt down branches of the families in Rio de Janeiro and the sprawling city of Recife, and to assassinate remote cousins. In July 1981 the thirty-third victim, sixty-seven-year-old José Roberto Sarto Alencar, a caretaker of the City Park in Rio de Janeiro, was kidnaped; the next day his body, shot four times, was found. The man had left Exu in 1939. After the thirty-fourth victim had been killed, the archbishop of the city of Salvador managed to negotiate a "moral pact of nonaggression," which heads of both families signed on national television, but it lasted only a year.

An even more harrowing example of how irrational and destructive the duty to take revenge can be in some societies made headlines in Egyptian newspapers in 1966. It involved two brothers who were taking trucks across the interior. One of the brothers, as he was driving through a village, struck a child playing in the street and stopped his truck—ill-advisedly, because the crowd that had gathered at the scene pulled him out and beat him to death. The second brother, who followed about ten minutes later, quickly realized what had happened and, backing up his truck, accelerated into the mob and ran down as many people as he could.

❦

Perhaps the most onerous demand of traditional kinship is to have to kill an innocent stranger because of an inherited feud or because of deeply ingrained notions of honor. "No man can cause more grief than that one clinging blindly to the vices of his ancestors," Faulkner has written. But there has usually been no way to escape from one's kinship group, even when the hatefulness of its obligations exceeds the value of its services. To be banished from the group is often an even worse fate, because there seems nowhere to go; one loses almost every point of reference, the entire cooperative structure upon which one has learned to depend for social reinforcement and physical survival. To be expelled from one's clan in ancient China, for instance, and to be deleted from its genealogical records was, and in remote rural parts of the country may still be, considered worse than death. Only terrible offenders, who had failed to perform rituals in the ancestral hall, who had achieved notoriety in their public career, who had committed adultery with their own kin, or who had sold a wife into servitude, were cast out upon the sea of kinless oblivion.

Several societies have allowed men to renounce their kin or to transfer to another group. This was generally easier for younger sons, who had fewer obligations; daughters in every exogamous society, of course, *have* to leave their group. The Romans had a ceremony called *emancipatio,* involving a fictitious sale whereby a son could detach himself from his family and free himself from the *patria potestas.* Adoption not only of boys but of grown men was common in both Rome and China, especially when the head of the household had produced no heir. Joining the family of a rich, powerful godfather was also, in Rome, an important method of rising socially. The great general of the second century B.C., Scipio Africanus Minor, for instance, was also known as Scipio Aemilianus because he had been adopted into the Scipio family from the Aemilian clan. The partly fictive crime "families" of Sicily, Colombia, and the United States use the old Church system of *compadrazgo* to recruit new members: they are made up of a core of close kin and an entourage of unrelated protégés, who are "adopted" by the head of the family, the "godfather."

The Bedouin tribe just described has complicated, rarely used procedures by which a man can transfer or be expelled from his blood-money group. A habitual troublemaker can endanger—

physically and financially—the others in his group. To expel him, however, his group must first clear all the obligations that have become incumbent on it as a result of his misdeeds. Or there may be bad blood in the group, and a member and his group may mutually disown each other. But this is a traumatic step, like getting divorced or renouncing national citizenship, and the first thing a person who finds himself on his own tries to do is get into another group, because it is even harder to survive in the desert alone.

There is some evidence that the Anglo-Saxons and the Normans broke with their kinship groups when they sailed to England and continued to go off to live by themselves fairly often, with just their wives and children, after they had settled in their new land. The Franks had a provision in their laws which permitted somebody who didn't feel like taking on the responsibilities of kinship, who perhaps wanted to bow out of a feud, to go into the folk court and repudiate his kin. This may have been one of the seeds of Western individualism.

☘

A final feature of traditional kinship is that it usually doesn't end with death. Again, possible evolutionary precedents are found among animals: elephants have been known to pick up the bones of other elephants killed by poachers, and to carry them a distance; to visit repeatedly at dusk the skeletons of members of their herd which had been overtaken and smothered by lava flows, and to defecate copiously beside them (I have seen this myself on the slopes of the recently erupted Mt. Nyiragongo, in eastern Zaire); to cover with grass both buffaloes killed by tigers and dead humans. Elephants seem to have a response to death, and they may even attempt to communicate with the dead, although this is beyond the present ability of scientists to verify. Mountain gorillas too, Schaller has told me, drag around moribund members of their troop and try to get them to stand, and after they have died, masturbate on them and try to get some reaction from them.

Just as most societies have assigned new functions to their members as they pass through the various age grades, they have tended to give continuing roles to their dead, making them into role models to be emulated and consulted, supernatural beings to be feared, or at least into points of reference from which descent could be reckoned. No society seems to have been willing to accept that its dead do not survive in some form. The belief in immortality persists even behind the Iron Curtain, where religion is not encouraged, and it seems to have been in circulation since the Paleolithic, when the dead were already being buried ritually, with personal effects that might be useful in the life to come. About sixty thousand years ago, for instance, in a cave in the Zagros Mountains of Iraq, an adult male *Homo sapiens neanderthalensis* was buried not only with an ax, presumably his, but with an arrangement of flowers identified by pollen analysis as yarrow, cornflower, St. Barnaby's thistle, ragwort, grape hyacinth, hollyhock, and woody horsetail. Most of these plants have known medicinal properties and are still used by herbalists in the region, so it is possible that the man was a shaman. He had been drawn up in the fetal position, perhaps because his society believed in rebirth. At several other Paleolithic burial sites where similarly "flexed" bodies were found, the bodies were also tightly bound, perhaps to prevent them from springing out of position during rigor mortis, perhaps to keep them from going abroad and harming people. Most societies have been equally careful about how they dispose of their dead. The aborigines of Australia have for centuries provided theirs with huts, food, water, fire, clothing, tools, and weapons. In China the wives and retainers of kings were buried alive with them until the Chou Dynasty (1122–256 B.C.), when they were replaced by life-size terra-cotta effigies. The Mongols, the Scythians, the Egyptians, the Shoshone, the Comanche, and the Dahomey of West Africa had similar practices, and as late as the nineteenth century the widows of Hindu princes were killed and immolated on the same pyre as their husbands. When an early Tibetan king died, his ministers had to become for the rest of their lives the custodians of his mausoleum. They lived off the leftovers of feasts periodically held at the mausoleum in the king's memory. In Tibet today the dead are recycled back into the ecology by "sky burial." They are taken at dawn to isolated hilltops and left there for vultures.

The cosmologies of tribal people are often very intricate. The Yanomamo, for example, who seem not to distinguish past, present, and future, or to recognize the existence of a world apart from themselves, believe they each have a second existence, an alter ego called a *rishi*, which may be an animal, a rock, wind, or thunder. The men's *rishis* tend to be fierce predators like jaguars or harpy eagles, while the *rishis* of the women are often butterflies or other gentle creatures. At death, some climb a vine ladder to heaven; others are transformed into animals for their misdeeds. In the village of Wakatauteri, which I visited in 1977, there was a local taboo against hunting deer, which were thought to be reincarnated ancestors. A man who killed a deer had to undergo the same ritual of purification as if he had killed a human: to lie in his hammock for a week without touching his body or speaking to anybody.

The Delaware Indians, who now live in Oklahoma and Ontario, believe that some of their dead remain on earth as ghosts, while others rise as sparks to the heavens. Many tribal people have thought the stars were transfigured ancestors. The peasants in the mountains of Michoacán, Mexico, believe that the millions of overwintering North American monarch butterflies who begin to descend on them around All Souls' Day are the souls of the dead.

Many traditional societies have an ancestral-name taboo; the people are afraid that speaking the name of a dead relative will disturb and anger his ghost. Delaware traditionalists, for instance, do not mention their ancestors by their real, non-Christian names until after three o'clock in the afternoon. Eskimos do not mention dead relatives' names until they have children, in whose bodies they believe the relatives are reborn. Then they give the children the relatives' names, and do not spank or mistreat them, lest the relatives decide to leave and take their souls away. The Cherokee believed that dreaming or even thinking of a dead relative could result in severe illness. The women of the Warramunga tribe of central Australia refused to lay an ax to the gum trees that lined the local creeks because they feared that by doing so they might set free the ancestral spirits of their blacksnake clan, who would immediately dart into their bodies and try to be reborn in them. The two young BaLese tribesmen with whom I walked through a hundred miles of forest in northeastern Zaire, in 1981, always barred the door of each hut we slept in because they were afraid that ghosts called *mbolozi*, which could change into leopards, might break in.

The Tukuna Indians in the village of Vendavel, about fifteen hundred miles up the Amazon River, were in spiritual transition when I visited them in 1982. They still held to their traditional cosmology, still believed, for instance, that they all were descended from a fish named Maquita. But about ten years earlier a man named José Cruz had converted them to a messianic cult he had founded, so they were also Christians. I asked an old man in the village what he thought happened after death, and he said that if you were baptized, you went to heaven, but if you weren't, you went to the forest and became an animal.

Many tribal people, with their animism and their reverence of totemic ancestors like the fish of the Tukuna (or the kangaroo, emu, rat, bat, hawk, cockatoo, bee, fly, yam, grass seed, sun, moon, fire, water, lightning, and wind of the central Australian aborigines), have felt a strong kinship with every form of life. The famous Sioux leader Sitting Bull said in a remarkable address to his people in 1877:

> See, Brothers, spring is here.
> The earth has taken the embrace of the sun,
> And soon we shall see the children of that love.
> All seeds are awake, and all animals.
> From this great power we too have our lives.
> And therefore we concede to our fellow creatures,
> Even our animal fellows, the same right as
> Ourselves, to live on this earth.

This intuition—that all life is interrelated and ultimately derived from the sun—was probably one of the earliest and worthiest ones humans have had. In the past century and a half scientists have confirmed its soundness by placing every species on the same phylogenetic tree, with animals branching off from plants near the base, then ascending through primitive phyla and finally becoming vertebrates; by tracing food chains that originate as solar energy and pass from lowly algae all the way to the higher carnivores; and by discovering that all life ultimately consists of the same twenty amino acids.

Buddhists feel kinship with every "sentient being" because they believe they have been reborn so often that every animal has at one time been their mother. A few high-ranking Buddhists, like the Tibetan *tulkus,* who are considered reincarnations of ancient holy men, can even trace their previous lives. The sixteenth Karmapa, for instance, was recognized when still a child as a reappearance of the first Karmapa, a "fully enlightened being" who lived from 1110 to 1193, and before he died, in 1981, he left instructions to the keepers of his lineage—themselves *tulkus* reincarnating other ancient sages—about where the seventeenth might be found. Similarly, in Senegal there are Islamic scholars who trace their teacher, and their teacher's teacher, all the way to the Prophet. This is *their* pedigree, even though the previous generations are neither relatives nor reincarnations.

Many human societies have tried to establish lines of communication with their ancestors, and some have been convinced that they succeeded. Emperor Hirohito still makes ceremonial reports on the state of Japan at the shrine to his Yamato forebears, and in Dahomey, whenever the king had something important to relate to his ancestors he would simply execute a couple of messengers. "The king, wishing to send a message to his father, summons a captive, carefully primes him with the subject of his errand . . . and strikes off his head," the Victorian traveller and ethnologist Sir Richard Burton reported after visiting Dahomey in 1863. "If an important word be casually omitted he repeats the operation, a process which I venture to call a postscript." All the messengers were intoxicated, "the object being to send them to the other world in the best of tempers." The practice "originates from filial piety, it is sanctioned by long use and custom, and is strenuously upheld by a powerful and interested priesthood." Burton doubted that it could be abolished any more easily than prayers for the dead could be done away with in England, and he estimated the total annual slaughter of messengers at five hundred.

The conviction that one's dead relatives are always watching and taking an active interest in one's affairs, and that one is responsible to them for one's actions, has been especially strong in China, where ancestors have been venerated almost as private deities for more than three thousand years. Up to the first century B.C., when Confucianism became established and shamanism began to be looked down upon, at least by the governing classes, professional necromancers would often be invited to dinner, where they would gyrate themselves into a trance and begin to speak in the voice of whichever ancestor they had been asked to put the family in touch with. Recognizing that some ancestors could be manipulative and even malevolent, Confucius had preached that it was also a good idea sometimes to keep one's counsel. "One must respect the spirits and keep them at a distance," he said. Yet even today, on Taiwan and in parts of the mainland, the Ch'ing'-Ming Festival is still celebrated, usually in the first week of April. The graves of the ancestors are swept clean, and food is set out for their "hungry ghosts," a practice with parallels in many societies: All Souls' Day in Mexico, when food is taken to the cemeteries; the midnight service of Orthodox Russians on the eve of Easter, when painted eggs and candles flickering in little red *lampadas* are placed by each grave; the *kaiko* festival held once every twelve years or so by the Maring tribe of New Guinea, who slaughter and spit-roast most of their adult pigs over their ancestors' graves; the great annual feast, *id al-gurban,* of the Bedouin of Najd, Arabia, at which each family slaughters as many camels as it has lost members during the past year. The Arabs of Tripolitania during the mid-1800s, however, did just the opposite: when short of food and passing by the grave of a sheik named Shahwan b. Isa, they would call out his name, and through his intervention, they believed, it was usually possible to hunt up something to eat in the vicinity.

Sometimes concern for the well-being of dead relatives has been carried to curious extremes. In Singapore a few years ago a "ghost marriage" took place between a Miss Cheeh, who had actually been born dead, prematurely, twenty-seven years earlier, and a Mr. Poon, who would have been thirty-six if he had not also been stillborn. Their parents, who had been repeatedly bothered by their ghosts in dreams, had independently consulted the same spirit medium, and the medium, diagnosing the ghosts' problem as loneliness, had acted as their marriage broker. The Cheehs and the Poons, who were not previously acquainted, had met to discuss the arrangements. A bride price of US $22 was agreed upon, and dolls representing the couple, a miniature one-story house for them to live in, complete with a manservant, a car with chauffeur, a bed with a bolster and pillows, and a table set with teacups and a teapot were cunningly fashioned out of paper, at a further cost to the groom's family of US $130, so that the marriage could be performed and Jealous Sister and Neglected Son could have a comfortable start in their life together.

The various spiritualist cults in Brazil—*espiritismo, umbanda, candomble, macumba*—have attracted millions of followers from every walk of life, and a séance with a dead relative can be arranged quite easily. The cults evolved from the belief of West Africans, particularly Ashanti tribesmen brought over as slaves, that the spirits of the dead can possess the bodies of the living and speak through them. The ability to be a medium, to be possessed or to be receptive to transmissions from the dead, is regarded as a special gift. Some are *videntes*, who see the dead; others are *ouvintes*, who hear them speaking. Quite often even Brazilians who don't belong to one of the cults have experiences that seem to them as if somebody close to them who has died is trying to get in touch. Such an experience happened to a schoolteacher I know, who was watching television in her house outside Brasília one Sunday afternoon at about two o'clock, when there was a sudden knock at the door. The woman opened the door but nobody was there. The next day a telegram arrived from a city about four hundred miles to the north, with the news that her father had died at about two o'clock the day before. Although a devout Catholic, she was willing to believe that the coincidental knocks at her door represented an experience of the *ouvinte* type.

Professional mediums are often consulted in Brazil when there has been a death in the family. A nurse I know, who lives in one of the ultramodern apartment complexes in Brasília, went to a medium a few days after her oldest daughter had been killed in a car accident. After the séance had begun, she was sure she heard her daughter's voice coming from somewhere in the darkened room. It said that the daughter was happy to have been reunited with her grandmother, who had died a few months earlier, and asked her mother to forgive her father (her parents were going through a nasty divorce) and to pray for her. The séance consoled the mother greatly. The interest of these experiences is not only whether they are figments of autosuggestion, completely in the minds of the people who have them, or whether the dead do survive on some plane and can get through to some of us, but that they demonstrate in one more way the strength of the bonds that can exist between kin, sometimes even seeming to defy extinction.

3

Stratification and Pedigrees

MOST TRIBAL PEOPLE—MOST PEOPLE, IN FACT—HAVE NOT KNOWN
their ancestry in great detail. For either an "elementary" or a
"complex" system of kinship—the two systems which almost all
societies have had—to work, it is only necessary to know who
one's grandparents were (and if the society has formal descent
groups, what group they belonged to)—*if that*. An elementary
system, in Lévi-Strauss's paradoxical definition, tells you both
whom you can and whom you can't marry, and is thus more re-
strictive than a complex one, which tells you only whom you can't
marry. Most of the tribes of Australia and New Guinea have elementary systems, while most of the systems in Africa are complex.
Western societies, including ours, are complex; essentially, Americans can marry whomever they want to, as long as the person isn't
a close blood relative. "In our system, to use a crude metaphor,"
Robin Fox explains, "we cast our bread upon the water; we release
our sisters and daughters to the world at large in the expectation
of receiving someone else's sister or daughter similarly released.
Many other societies . . . do not leave such things so much to
chance."

Most Americans do still tend to marry within their class and
ethnic and economic group, but there is no rigorous genealogical
input into the actual selection of the mate—even the vaguely and

variously defined requirement that he or she come from a "good family" is becoming less important—and the average American is as hard pressed to come up with the names of all eight of his great-grandparents as the average tribal person. In fact, according to van den Berghe, our genealogical awareness may be even shallower. "Grandparents are rather shadowy figures for many Americans," he writes. "Roughly three-fourths of American undergraduates whom I ask to give the first and last names of all four of their grandparents flunk the test." Although this seems scarcely believable, a number of professional genealogists in different parts of the country have told me that they have had the same experience. The first to be forgotten is usually the maiden name of a maternal grandmother who died before the grandchildren were born.

Pygmies have a still looser system of kinship and marriage: they are "agamous"; they are told neither whom to marry nor whom not to, although they usually have the good sense not to mate with primary kin—parents, children, siblings. Since they lack formal descent groups, they have no particular reason to be interested in their ancestry, and few of them, either, can go back for more than three generations. The pedigrees of the Bantu and the Sudanic villagers with whom some of them trade are no deeper, even though the villages have patrilineal clans. The tribal people of the South American rain forest have similarly short memories (which is not to say that genealogy is not important to them: recitation of the pedigrees, along with telling of the Creation Myth and exhortation to follow the norms, is an integral part of the initiation rites of the Desana, who live on the Vaupés River in northwestern Amazonia, for instance).

There are several reasons for this general pattern. If a family has been prolific, after four generations its tree can go wild; there can actually be too many names to remember unless they have all been written down; and many tribal people haven't had writing. A Brazilian woman I know probably has close to a thousand living relatives through only one of her great-great-grandfathers, who had sixteen children and eighty-six grandchildren, and lived to see seventy-two of his great-grandchildren and two of his second great-grandchildren before dying in 1959 at the age of a hundred and twenty. Several hundred of his descendants are known to two of his daughters-in-law, now in their seventies, who live in different states of Brazil; the others might well take years to track down, because the family is scattered all over the country, the vital records of Brazil are far from comprehensive (many births are registered years afterward or are never registered at all), and several of the old man's sons and sons-in-law, for reasons known only to themselves, gave their children different surnames.

A man with more than one wife can have prodigious numbers of offspring in four generations. The late king of the Akan, a tribe in eastern Ghana, Nana Sir Ofori-Atta (he was knighted by Queen Victoria), for instance, had about a hundred children by "a range of twenty to twenty-five wives, and some mistresses," one of his sons, Kari-Kari Ofori-Atta, has told me; while a recently surfaced claimant to being the world's oldest living person, Sayed Abdul Mabood of Pakistan (whose passport showed him to be a hundred and fifty-nine in 1983), had more than two hundred grandsons by only fourteen sons (the women who gave him all these male offspring were not credited). The Mormon patriarch Brigham Young had by nineteen of his twenty-seven wives fifty-three children "all sound in mind and body and with no blemishes," according to a chart of his pedigree, who in turn produced three hundred and one grandchildren. No one has tried to count the great-grandchildren, and while the Mormons are among the world's most conscientious genealogists and have kept excellent records of their families, the task of tracking down all of Young's living descendants, who are already in their seventh generation and number well into the thousands, may not even be possible. One of his innumerable third great-grandchildren, Steve Young, played quarterback on the varsity football team of Brigham Young University and in 1984 signed a forty-million-dollar-plus contract with the Los Angeles Express—more money than an athlete has ever received for his professional services.

Another reason why the pedigrees of tribal people are generally shallow is that in a small, isolated community there may be a shortage of marriageable people outside one's kinship group, and a certain amount of plasticity with respect to what group one actually belongs to, often helped out by an ancestral-name taboo, may be desirable.

The Indians of North America didn't go in for deep pedigrees because they didn't need them either. Most of their kinship systems are of the matrilineal Crow or the patrilineal Omaha type, which Fox has described as "really halfway houses, transitional systems—technically complex, but with elementary overtones." A six-generation pedigree in native North America was quite exceptional. Only two of that length are collected in the ethnological bulletins that the Smithsonian Institution published early in the century, when the Indians' oral traditions were more nearly intact. One is of some Okanaga chiefs in the state of Washington; the other, also chiefly, is of the Oshkosh family of the Menomini.

Most Indian societies were egalitarian and nonmaterialistic. It was a huge continent, with plenty of space and game for everybody; resources and possessions were shared, and the notion the European colonists brought with them, that land, with all the tree-beings and the animals it contained, could be privately owned, was initially baffling. It is doubtful whether the Tanketeke Indians, for instance—who in 1680 were relieved of their ancestral home in the present-day township of Bedford, New York, by twenty-two Puritan families who came up from Stamford, Connecticut, and offered them forty-four pounds' worth of merchandise, including "twelve cotes and three hundred gilders wompom"—understood what the transaction was all about. Within the hundred years that followed, most of the displaced Tanketeke died from smallpox, measles, influenza, plague, and rum, and they have no known living descendants, although descendants of the Puritans still live in town.

None of the factors that induce people to keep track of their ancestry over long periods of time were present in native North America, and several beliefs made it very hard for an Indian to remember whom he was descended from. Many tribes had the ancestral-name taboo. Several in the Northwest even required that after a death all the dead person's relatives change their names. Indians were traditionally named for personal qualities, natural forces, animals, plants, brave deeds, memorable events, or dreams. "The North American Indian regards his name, not as a mere label," James Frazer, the great Victorian anthologist of indigenous customs and beliefs, wrote, "but as a distinct part of his personality, just as much as are his eyes or his teeth, and believes that injury will result as surely from the malicious handling of his name as from a wound inflicted on any part of his physical organism." In some tribes a man could have up to a dozen names as he passed through the different age grades or achieved increasing political or religious stature. The name gave no clue to descent, however; it had no hereditary component, no surname; no patronymic, as the Russian and the Scandinavian names have, which gives the genealogist an automatic one-generation head start; no *nomen* or *cognomen,* as the Romans had, which revealed their clan and family branch. The adoption of clan names as surnames in some tribes is a recent compromise with "Anglo" practice.

☙

As long as people lived as hunter-gatherers and made decisions affecting the group collectively, there was no need for anybody to know his ancestry in depth. It was only as some people became richer or more powerful than others, and their higher status became hereditary, that pedigrees became important. The first stratification may have been of a tactical nature: a group in which a talented leader had naturally emerged and had begun to give orders might have been more successful at exploiting its resources, or at stealing women from its neighbors and defending itself against reprisal, than an "acephalous" group in which everybody did as he pleased. Or somebody with special spiritual qualities may have been appointed the religious leader of the group, and the others may have harvested his fields so he could have more time to pray—which is what happened among the Pueblo. Such societies are still like egalitarian bands in that nobody has more land or a bigger house than anybody else—but a few enjoy greater prestige, and goods are funnelled through them; they act as the central figures of a redistributive economy. Many of the tribes in Africa have "rank societies" of this sort, and many of the Bedouin tribes, while remaining essentially democratic, have *shaykhs,* leaders whose power and prerogatives have passed down patrilineally for centuries, though not always to the oldest son. The *shaykhly* families are indistinguishable from other Bedouin in dress and behavior, and they are treated with no special deference, yet they have a certain cachet as "the first among equals," as the noblest of a tribe that considers all its members noble.

Real stratification, however, is found only in societies that have made the transition to agriculture. Wheat and barley were first domesticated in the Middle East about ten thousand years ago, rice in Thailand about a thousand years later, corn in the highlands of Mexico about two millennia after that, and from these three principal centers the practice of settled agriculture spread, completely recasting the life of everybody who came in contact with it. With a dependable food supply, people were able to have more children and more of the children were able to survive and reproduce; communities grew denser and more complex; they became cities, and the cities fathered civilizations. Because food could be produced in surplus and preserved—and thus converted into a durable form of wealth—prestige and power began to attach to those who accumulated instead of shared, and a gap opened between the rich and the poor. The first rich probably included those who operated irrigation ditches or owned granaries. In time an exalted class, almost a pseudospecies, arose, whose members had distinctive dress and other emblems of status; who lived in big houses in a separate part of the city and were laid to rest in other big houses; who were waited on by servants and became increasingly nonproductive; who married only among themselves and got the priests and the lawmakers of their society to sanctify and institutionalize their hereditary right to the wealth and power they or their ancestors had accumulated. It is at this point of social evolution, wherever it has occurred, that pedigrees begin to deepen dramatically.

Some of the earliest known writing contains the names of people who belonged to the hereditary elite of Egypt; this is usually the first information that gets recorded in any stratified society. Already by Dynastry 3 of the Old Kingdom—by roughly 2700 B.C.—monuments to the dead listed the surviving kin—wife, children, parents, siblings, sometimes even in-laws; but often not everybody was commemorated, apparently only those with whom the dead man felt a real bond, just as in our society not everybody in the deceased's family is necessarily included in his will. The Palermo Stone, chiselled during Dynasty 5, between 2500 and 2350 B.C., lists early kings and important events during their reigns; and inscriptions in the temple of Seto I, who ruled during Dynasty 19, around 1320 B.C., break up Egyptian history before that point into the dynastic divisions that are used today, and contain long lists of early kings. Some of the kings, however, were apparently not thought to have made a positive contribution, and were left out. "Ghost stories," in which the hero goes to a cemetery and spends days reading grave inscriptions until at last he finds couched among the hieroglyphics the one he is looking for—the secret name of the god Thoth, say—appear on papyri from 1100

B.C. on. In Dynasty 26, around 664 B.C., the epitaph on a tomb in Thebes containing the body of a man named Aba claims that he was descended from another Aba, who lived two thousand years earlier, but the intervening ancestors are not named. In Dynasty 27, around 525 B.C., when the country was ruled by Persians, the native aristocracy, perhaps to show that although it had lost power its credentials were still impeccable, made a concerted effort to trace itself back as far as it could, which was about twenty generations.

The pedigrees of the early Asian kings were no less venerable. In 1819 a British traveller named Moorcroft, passing through the Punjab Hills of northern India, discovered that his host, one of the Katoch rulers of Kangra, could trace his principal male line back for more than four hundred and fifty generations. This is the deepest pedigree, by a long shot, that I have run across. The historian B. N. Goswamy mentions it in passing; I have written him asking for the reference but have had no reply—it would be nice to know how authentic this apparent front runner for the world record is (or was) and whether it still exists. The pedigree presumably started with the sun, the moon, or at least a demigod; most of the Hindu royal houses claimed either solar or lunar descent. Between the fifteenth and nineteenth centuries every important Hindu ruler had a retainer, called a *bhat* or a *chaman*, whose job was to chant his patron's pedigree on ceremonial occasions and to burst into paeans about his glorious ancestry. In miniatures of the sumptuous durbars, or courts of the period, the *bhat* can often be spotted. He is usually an old man, steadying himself with a stick and holding out his free hand in the act of declaiming.

Some Chinese clans, which have maintained records for more than a hundred generations, have ancient genealogical traditions. Several claim to have been started by the Yellow Emperor, a semilegendary figure who is credited with domesticating rice and is thought to have lived around 2600 B.C.; but the beginning of each of the genealogies is the same, and probably only one of the descents, or perhaps none of them, is authentic. The earliest surviving record from China dates from 770 B.C., but it was not until five centuries later, during the Han Dynasty, when China was unified as an empire, that genealogical scholarship began in earnest. One historian, Ssuma Ch'ien (145–85 B.C.?), traced several high officials of the early Han back for twenty generations, but even he admitted that the pedigrees were conjectural until the Chou Dynasty (1122–256 B.C.). The tradition of ancestor veneration, which is at the core of Chinese culture, began in the Chou, when patrilineal clans replaced the fratrilineal structures of the Shang. Feudal lords began to burn incense as an offering to their forefathers, to give themselves elaborate burials, to keep track of their descent, and to observe rites of succession in which the eldest son was presented with a piece of sod as a symbol of the fief he was inheriting. In the sixth century B.C., Confucius, preaching the need to return to the old virtues of the Chou, gave greatest importance, of the five basic relationships in his social code, to the one between father and son. One's parents, he said, personified the powers of the universe. "He who loves his parents hates no man; he who reveres his parents is discourteous to no one."

There were other traditions of filial piety besides Confucianism. Among the common people in northern Shantung around the time of Christ, for instance, the oldest daughter was known as the "shaman-child" (*we'erh*); she was not allowed to marry, and was in charge of the family's religious rites. By the Sung Dynasty (960–1279 A.D.) most clans, and some rich families in the South, had ancestral halls, in which wooden tablets with the names of the founder of the house, the first ancestor of each branch, widows of distinguished chastity, and other particularly meritorious forebears, as well as the four most recent generations, were displayed. The eldest son of each branch was expected to pay daily homage to the tablets. Ingratitude to the ancestors was almost as serious as the greatest shame which could befall a family head: to end his line by producing no heir. As a last resort, a childless man could adopt an extra son of his brother's, or try to beget an heir with a concubine; if these failed, he could skip a generation and designate a grandson, or he could choose a "son" from the nearest line of collaterals—a first cousin once removed, perhaps. During the Communist revolution many ancestral halls were burned or turned into recreation halls, and the social-service role of the clans was largely taken over by "production brigades," but a good many of the genealogies were spirited underground, or taken abroad (where they would become the uprooted family's most treasured possession), and they survived because many copies had been printed. The tradition of ancestor veneration is still strong on Taiwan and

in rural parts of the mainland, where people have been returning
from the production brigade to the nuclear "farm" family as the
basic unit for working and accounting, and are having lots of
children again, even though couples in the cities who have more
than one child are heavily penalized.

The Chinese have a segmentary patrilineal system of kinship
like the Bedouin, except that their clans are exogamous: marriage
among male-line relatives is forbidden, while the best marriage
a Bedouin can make is with his father's brother's child. The Chinese genealogies start with Beginning Ancestor, Shih-tzu, and
from him a pyramid of descendants rains down, with oneself
among thousands at the base; the approach is group-oriented, unlike Western pedigrees, which begin with Ego and work back,
seeking names that rise in an inverted pyramid. Until the T'ang
period, which began in 618 A.D., only the "esteemed clans"
(Wang-tsu) had genealogies, and these were distinct political
assets, because only people of proven lineage were entitled to high
office or rank. Gradually the practice spread, though never to the
point of including anything close to the entire Chinese population. The listing of names, with glowing *vitae* of the more illustrious ancestors (some even gave the hour of birth and death, and
the location of the grave), became a genre of literature and of
calligraphic art. The clan genealogies that have survived range
from a few handwritten pages to a hundred pages of block-
printed Classical Chinese, on rice paper folded over to reduce
"bleeding." One of the longest, most elegant ones lists the generations of Confucius, which continue on some lines right up to
the present. Soong Ai-ling, for instance, whose sister Mei-ling
married Chiang Kai-shek, married a man named H. H. Kung,
who allegedly stood seventy-fifth in line of descent from Confucius.
Most clans used the five-generation format developed by a scholar
named Hsiu Ou-yang (1007–1072 A.D.). On these tables the eldest sons' line descends, generation by generation, along the right-
hand margin, and the other children and their lines appear to the
left. Women are peripheral. If they appear at all, it is only by
surname ("Miss Wu," for instance), and only to show that a man
did not marry a woman with the same surname, which was unthinkable. Sons who died before puberty were not recorded, and
those who had been expelled from the clan were ignominiously
deleted from its tables.

The Chinese have had patrilineally transmitted surnames since around the time of Christ, and D. J. Steel writes that "It was customary for each family to have a series of thirty-six names . . . each child was given its correct generation name. After thirty-six generations the series would start again. Thus in the Khoo family the twenty-first name might be *Lim* followed in succession by Lam, Hock, Lee, and Loo. Khoo Lim Chang's son might be named Khoo Lam Wen. There was no objection to the generation names also being used as personal names. The latter's second cousin might be Khoo Lam Lee. Regrettably, this interesting Chinese custom is dying out."

The preoccupation with ancestry permeated every part of Chinese life. If a man passed the stiff entrance exam for the civil service, for instance, he was considered to have brought such honor to his family that his parents and sometimes up to ten generations of his forebears were listed after his name on the roster of successful competitors. The local histories and gazeteers (*fang-chih*), which originated in the T'ang period, are full of genealogy. They were kept at several levels—village, town, subprefecture, province—and are much better on women than the clan genealogies. During the Ch'ing Dynasty (1644–1912 A.D.) the writing of minutely detailed *fang-chih* became very popular. Tens of thousands of them were produced.

The Koreans adopted the Chinese system of genealogy and used it to legitimize the hereditary privileges of their *yang-ban*, or prominent land- and officeholders. Some clans can go back for thirty generations or so, quite accurately from the Yi Dynasty (1392) on. The ruling class of Japan was even more obsessed with lineage and descent. Early on, in the third or fourth century, the imperial clan, the House of Yamato, gained ascendancy, and the other clans devoted their genealogical energies to establishing a connection with it instead of to extending their own lines. (The Yamatos are still in power; the aged Hirohito is the hundred-and-twenty-fourth emperor of the dynasty, which has enjoyed the longest run of hereditary rule in world history.) A lot of *nisekeizu*, false genealogies, were perpetrated, especially ones with doctored connections to the Sewangezi line of the Fujiwara family, which had married into the House of Yamato. This connection had the added advantage of qualifying one for the office of Sei-i-tai Shogun, the military dictatorship established in the eighth century;

the Shogun had to belong to one of four families, and the Fujiwaras were among them. Since "high birth" was the only prerequisite to practically every position of importance in Japan, in the year 815 alone a thousand one hundred and eighty-two noble families had their genealogies done. Samurai warriors and Shinto priests also had to meet specific genealogical requirements, and the preparation of their pedigrees was done by professionals, who knew enough genealogy to make them convincing, and who had a higher level of literacy than most of their clients.

At the same time the lower classes were kept ignorant of their descent, in an important aspect of the larger effort to keep them in their place. During the repressive Tokugawa Shogunate, from 1634 to 1871, the peasants were not even allowed to use surnames. When the "privilege" was given back to them, a terrific explosion of onomastic creativity took place all over the island. Some chose surnames at random, but many took them from family traditions that had been kept alive orally. Today the Japanese use as surnames roughly seventy-one thousand combinations of characters; with regional variants, they have a hundred and seven thousand distinct surnames. The Chinese, who currently number a little over a billion, have only about five hundred surnames, and the Koreans have barely half that many. Some European countries have, if variant spellings are counted, about ten thousand native surnames, but no country has such a flourishing cornucopia as Japan. The Japanese take great interest in the provenance and the iconography of each other's surnames—in knowing what plant or animal, or feature in the landscape, what title or position held by some ancestor long ago, inspired them. Some, like Sato and Suzuki, are borne by millions of people. Others occur only in remote villages.

One means of being remembered after death has been available to everybody in Japan: the *kakocho,* or necrologies, which Buddhist priests have kept of their parishioners since the thirteenth century. The listing of the posthumous "vow name" of the parishioner who had died, along with the name of his chief mourner, became widespread in the seventeenth century, and rituals for the dead—a proper funeral by burial or cremation, sale to the survivors of the *kaimyo,* as the vow name is called, and keeping incense burning and candles lighted, in some cases for as long as fifty years—are now the main business of Japan's eighty thousand or so

Buddhist temples (much as the sale of dispensations for marrying within the forbidden degrees of consanguinity was for centuries an important source of income to the Catholic Church). Hawaiian Buddhists have the same type of *kakocho,* and even some of the Ainu aborigines, who live on northernmost Hokkaido, follow the tradition. The necrologies are not restricted to humans. In the city of Hokkaido, for instance, on the sixteenth day of the ninth month of the third year of Binkyu, which translates to 1863, a swan was registered. First its *kaimyo,* "the great luminous god of the white bird," symbolizing commitment to a pure life in the hereafter, was entered, then the name of its chief mourner, a man named Heikich.

In India, too, genealogical knowledge is stratified—the higher the caste, as a rule, the deeper the pedigree—but the reverence for ancestors is pervasive; B. N. Goswamy has described Rajasthani peasants prostrating themselves as the names of their dead relatives were being recited. Some of the oldest Indian records are the pilgrim registers that have been kept for centuries at Hindu shrines, mostly in the northern part of the country, by a subcaste of Brahmans called *pandas.* Twenty-seven of the one hundred and forty-two shrines draw great numbers of pilgrims from all over the country. Some have been in operation since 1000 B.C. By the second century A.D., some of the *pandas* had begun to keep oral track of the more prominent families of pilgrims who had been coming over the years. The practice spread to other shrines and it eventually embraced pilgrims of every caste. By around the year 1000 there were too many names and too many generations to remember, and the *pandas* started writing them down. The registers are called *bahis.* Most of them go back at least three hundred and fifty years, or about twenty-five generations.

⚜

In 1980 an agent of the Genealogical Society of Utah named Monte McLaws went to Haridwar, the second-most-visited shrine after Varanasi (the former Benares), to see if the *bahis* there could be microfilmed for the society's archives in Salt Lake City. McLaws had read about them in an article by Goswamy, and the Ford Foundation representative in New Delhi had given him the name of a *panda* in Haridwar named Kirparam Sharma. "Every Hindu would like to go to one of the hundreds of sacred places, most of

which are on the Ganges, at least once in his lifetime," McLaws
explained. "Some of the pilgrims go to do penance for a sin.
Others bring the ashes of a cremated relative to immerse in the
sacred river, which is thought to release the soul for reincarnation.
Solar eclipses draw hordes of pilgrims. The *panda* finds them food
and lodging, helps with their travel arrangements, and provides
religious support, performing whatever ceremonies they require.
He is part priest, part businessman. Over the years the *pandas*
have divided up their customers by geographical area, and each
has developed a specific clientele. In Haridwar the *pandas* sometimes meet their clients as they get off the morning train. Goswamy has described the chaotic scene beautifully. As the pilgrims
step down, the *pandas*, most of whom have checked red cotton
cloths over their shoulders, call out 'Kahan ke basi? What is your
native place?' Those *pandas* who have records relevant to the pilgrim's native place draw near and ask, 'What is your caste?' 'What
is your subcaste?' When they hear the answer, the *pandas* thin
out to maybe two or three, who start asking, 'Who is your father?'
'Your grandfather?' etc. If the pilgrim doesn't volunteer the information, the *pandas* begin to make suggestions, reciting from memory the names of families in the pilgrim's caste and community,
and looking for a flicker of recognition. When a *panda* hits on the
right name, the pilgrim knows he has found the *panda* of his
ancestors, and they go off together in a cycle rickshaw to see the
panda's registers, which have the names of the pilgrim's family for
as long as it has been coming to Haridwar.

"In New Delhi I rented a car with a driver and went to
Haridwar to find the *panda* named Kirparam Sharma. I had the
panda's name, so I thought I could find him. But there must be a
thousand *pandas* in Haridwar, and half of them are called Sharma.
The name is like Mohammed in the Middle East. We must have
spent half a day talking to *pandas* and explaining who we were
looking for. Haridwar is in the plains, and it was broiling—about
a hundred degrees. Finally we found him. He was in a small dark
room with a sign above the door: 'Prof. K. R. Sharma, palmist
and spiritual technologist.' I went in with my tape recorder.
Sharma spoke English. He was a sort of self-appointed international *panda*. He received the dignitaries. He showed me a book
with the names of some people from California. His son-in-law
was with him, picking up the business. When a *panda* has a son,

he starts training him early, making him learn pages of *bahis* by heart to stretch his memory. About thirty long, narrow books—maybe two and a half to three feet long by eight to ten inches wide, with burlap covers and looseleaf pages that could be replaced if water or worms got to them—had been rolled into bundles and placed on shelves behind him. These were the most frequently referred-to *bahis*, the ones that went back a hundred years. The earlier ones were kept in a large wooden chest.

"Sharma was a shrewd businessman. He wasn't going to show me anything until I had given him some rupees and convinced him that I wasn't interested in breaking into his business or in making the information available to his competitors. He unrolled one of the registers and read me entries for one family, who had been coming to Haridwar for eighteen generations. The entries were in Hindi and went on for ten pages. The women were left out, except when their deaths were referred to indirectly, as when a man had come with the ashes of his wife. The *bahis* are considered to be sufficiently authentic to be used in courts of law as proof of heirship, and Goswamy has pointed out their value for reconstructing village populations, caste structures, and migration patterns."

In the Arab world, genealogy had already become important well before the time of the Prophet: nobility, a man's proudest attribute, was a function of his tribal affiliation. Mohammed belonged to the Quraish tribe of Mecca, and his membership in it later elevated its prestige tremendously. Until the middle of the sixteenth century, the Caliph of all Islam had to be a descendant of the Quraish. Among Arabs today, traceable descent from the Prophet has cachet, something like being a member of the royal family of England. The descendants can proclaim themselves by wearing a green or black turban and sash (Shiite descendants, like the Ayatollah Khomeini, prefer black), although the idea of hereditary succession to political office never took hold in Islam. Queen Elizabeth has a descent from Mohammed, through the Black Prince, Edward Prince of Wales (1330–1376), whose mother had Moorish blood on her mother's side; but as will become evident later, when the mathematics of descent are gone into, so does practically everybody, although few are able to trace it. The

Prophet had many children, but only one, a daughter named Fatima, had issue. Fatima married her first cousin Ali, and they had two sons, Hasan and Husain. Male-line descendants of Fatima through Hasan are known as *sharifs*, while those through Husain are known as *sayyids*. King Hussein of Jordan is a *sharif*. He is also the thirty-ninth head of one of Arab Islam's leading families, the Hashemites, who were for thirteen hundred years the guardians of the holy cities of the Hejaz, Mecca and Medina. His distant cousin, King Hasan of Morocco, is also a Hashemite *sharif*, a thirty-fifth great-grandson of the Prophet.

Besides the descendants of Mohammed, there are long chains of "guarantors" of traditions about what he did or said, which can be traced back to his disciples. Although some of the links are between father and son, the chains represent intellectual rather than biological transmissions. The major orders of Sufism, which practice Islamic mysticism, all have "spiritual pedigrees" dozens of teachers deep. The Musa-al-Kazim family, Arkon Daraul writes in his book *Secret Societies*, "who have ruled Paghman [in Afghanistan] for seven centuries, are directly descended from Mohammed and are the traditional heads of the Nakshbandi Order [of Sufism]. They are also said by some to preserve a special training system which is granted only to a very few initiates. It is by means of this system that they have been able to produce an apparently endless succession of princes, military leaders, savants, and successful men in many walks of life." Musa-al-Kazim was the seventh *imam*, the seventh descendant of the Prophet in the line of Husain. His descendants, who are known as *musawi sayyids*, are only one of the many Muslim elites.

During the Middle Ages the Islamic royal houses and noble families had deep pedigrees constructed by professionals who were adept at summarizing the characteristics of a tribe or the deeds of an eminent forebear in a pithy sentence or two, and who were often portraitists and calligraphers as well. I was shown by an Islamic art dealer in London not long ago an illuminated genealogy of the Turkish house of Uthman, for instance, with an exquisite miniature of a bearded moghul beside each name, and a scroll with the father-to-son lineage of a noble family from Jerusalem which started in the fifteenth century and ended, about thirty feet later, with the Prophet. Because descent from Mohammed was so socially desirable, a lot of spurious genealogy was produced. There was also a lot of genealogical infighting among rival groups, which tried to thwart each other by raising doubts about each other's ancestry. The historian Haythan b. Adi, for instance, who died *in anno hegirae* 207 (829 A.D.), proved that a man named Abu Amr b. Omayya was not a true son but had been adopted, and thus impugned the nobility of all his descendants, while Abu Ubayda, the grandson of a Persian Jew, damaged the credibility of the pro-Arab party and ridiculed the racial vanity in the highest circles of pure Arab society by showing that their descent was nowhere as uncontaminated as it had been made out to be.

In the Arab world today, and wherever Islam has taken hold, people tend to be keenly aware of their ancestry. "Learn of your genealogical tree as much as is needed for the practice of active love toward blood relatives," the Prophet is said to have preached. In some of the Muslim tribes of West Africa, boys passing into manhood are required to compose a praise song about their forefathers, and most family heads can take their principal male line back for seven or eight generations, which in a polygynous society can represent quite a time span, since a man may well father children until he is seventy or older and a generation may run fifty years. The Shiite Muslims, who make up about twenty per cent of the followers of Islam, tend to be particularly interested in genealogy. They believe that the truth resides in the descendants of Ali, as opposed to the majority of Muslims, the Sunnis, who maintain that Mohammed left the direction of Islam to the community. Shiite scholars, including the Ayatollah Khomeini, regard themselves as interpreters of the will of Ali and the twelve *imams* in his line, the last of whom went into hiding and will reappear.

⚜

The deepest oral pedigree on record, as well as I have been able to determine—at least seventy generations—was chanted for Lyn Carson on the island of Nios, off Sumatra, in 1980, several weeks after his previously described visit to the Batak.

"I had been hiking with a guide for hours through muddy jungle," Carson reminisced. "Finally, after dark, we reached a hut on posts, with a high-peaked, thatched roof. Inside, seated on a straw mat, was a man in a T-shirt that said HIS on it. He must have been in his late seventies. His teeth were red from chewing betel nuts, and he kept spitting the juice through a gap in one of the plank walls. I was glad I had my antihistamines. He invited us to sit with him. I handed him the traditional gift." Carson, a Mormon, is forbidden by his religion to drink alcohol, and it was with some embarrassment that he confessed what the "traditional gift" was—a bottle of some kind of liquor he had picked up locally. "The old man seemed grateful that we were interested in his people, and he began to chant the names of his forefathers on a straight-line basis. One of them had had a wife in the high jungle and another on the coast, and when he got to the sons of the two women, he stood in the kerosene light and acted out a spear-throwing contest they had had. When he finally came to himself, he had to call in his wife to make sure he hadn't left out any of his grandsons or great-grand-sons. Some of them were there, and he made them sit through the recital; he was concerned that they learn the pedigree. We taped the whole thing—it went on for over an hour—and played it back for him, as he listened intently, nodding and smiling from time to time."

The old man was a chief in a society whose modes of in-heritance and succession had been settled perhaps thousands of years earlier and had been strictly adhered to ever since; he be-longed, like many tribal people in Indonesia, to the sort of island society that generates deep pedigrees. The oral-genealogical tra-ditions of the South Pacific are equally venerable. Some extend to before the time of Christ. But by 1970 they had died out on many island groups. Several of the surviving pedigrees have the same ancestors in the early generations and link people on distant islands, who have not been in contact for perhaps five centuries. The islands of Hawaii, New Zealand, and French Oceania all have in their legends the same founder, Maui, who lived between 200 and 600 A.D.; the date of his existence varies from archipelago to archipelago, but his superman deeds are much the same.

On the island of Savii, in western Samoa, there are still family chiefs, called *matais*, who can chant twenty-five generations of straight-line descent through their mothers or fathers. Each village on the island, though it may have hundreds of inhabitants, is considered a "family" (*'aiga sa*), whose members trace their de-scent, through either mother or father, by blood or marriage, or sometimes fictively, from a common ancestor. (In anthropological terms, the *'aiga sa* is a "ramage" as opposed to a kindred. A ramage is like a kindred except that it is more ancestor-oriented; the relative everybody in the group shares lived at least four generations back.) Parents often have, besides their own children, "feeding children" from other, broken families, and there is a tradition of giving the first son to be raised by his grandparents, so the actual biological relationships can be hard to disentangle.

At meetings of the village council, *matais* representing different branches of the family sit at specific posts of the round community house. Women are excluded unless they are *matais*. A ceremonial beverage, an opiate of the kava root, is passed around, and one of the *matais*, usually the "talking chief," who is the staff administrator of the high chief, will start things off by reciting the generations of the family's ancestors, which establishes who everybody is and his right to the land he owns. Special, lengthy coverage is given to the more politically important branches with *matais* on them. Then the high chief gives work assignments for the village's taro, banana, and coconut plantations. Each parcel of land on the island is allotted to a *matai*. When a parcel becomes available, title does not automatically pass from father to son; the village council nominates a new titleholder who must, by reciting his pedigree, satisfy the district land court that he is the rightful *matai*, as other *matais*, proposed by other councils, may be after the same land. The land court is made up of old *matais* who are versed in genealogy and can spot a fabricated pedigree. Its sessions may go on for days. The *matais* on rival councils try to predetermine the outcome by supplying the candidates with correct or incorrect information.

John Laing, a colleague of Carson's and McLaws's at the Genealogical Society, made twenty trips to the South Pacific between 1971 and 1979, going from island to island and collecting Polynesian pedigrees. Laing was distressed by the "progress" that was reaching Western Samoa when he visited the island. "Under the old system," he told me, "there were no hunger or behavior problems. As Fetaui Mata'afa, a member of the Western Samoan Parliament, has written, 'The stress involved in providing for the welfare of the Samoan family is dispersed and shared by many persons, whereas in the European nuclear family, it is usually concentrated on one person.' Now European ideas and products—

cars, beer, Kung Fu movies—are coming in and bombarding the traditional family life. At night everybody lies seminaked in the community house before a color tv set, watching programs broadcast from American Samoa, seventy miles away. I had never seen such a dichotomy. In the last couple of years there has been a terrible rise in the number of rapes and other violent crimes, and the suicide rate among Western Samoans between the ages of fifteen and twenty-one is said to be the highest in the world."

On the island of Tonga, Laing found "seven generations max." On Tahiti and the Society Islands, which are quite thoroughly westernized, Laing and his associates interviewed several hundred family heads. Only a handful had information, although those who did gave him several long male and female descents. On the Tubuai, or Austral, Islands, and the seventeen Cook Islands, the pickings were even slimmer, but on the Tuamotu Archipelago in French Polynesia, which consists of about eighty small atolls ten or fifteen miles in diameter, some of them rim islands with a lagoon in the center, there are still a few old men who go in for the traditional evening entertainment, chanting their pedigrees, and there are large, impressive stone statues of defiled ancestors, chiselled years ago by people who had only stone tools. Some of the pedigrees are sixty generations deep, and begin as long as fifteen hundred years ago, with founders of clans who may not even have lived on the archipelago.

On the Hawaiian Islands, the oral-genealogical tradition has been extinct for several decades. About a hundred pedigrees, including the twenty-six-generation one of a famous chief named Kuali, have been transcribed and deposited in the Bishop Museum in Honolulu. Several families trace themselves to Hawaii-Loa, the leader of a group who arrived in a canoe from somewhere, perhaps the Pacific Northwest, in about 58 B.C.

The indigenous people of New Zealand, the Maori, have lost their oral tradition, too, but since 1848 somebody in each extended family has been responsible for keeping the *whakapapa* (pronounced *fakapapa*), or written record of its genealogy. The Maori land system is like the Western Samoans'. Every parcel must be adjudicated in one of seventeen native land courts; a prospective titleholder must produce his *whakapapa* and demonstrate his relationship to a certain *tohunga*, which is the Maori equivalent of a *matai*. There is a problem of European encroachment. About thirty per cent of the two main islands is still owned by the Maori, but individual titles are constantly disputed. One title defense, by the *tohunga* Tamarau, involved more than fourteen hundred names, spread over thirty-four generations. A few *whakapapa* go back to the original settlers of the island, who arrived in at least seven canoes between seventeen and thirty-three generations ago, in about 1300. Who these settlers were, and where they came from, is still an open question.

Types of Inheritance

BEFORE PROCEEDING TO THE WEST, WHERE THE SAME PATTERN will be found—deep genealogy in the upper classes, often with fanciful connections to gods or important mortals of the past— perhaps one should ask if there is any point in knowing one's ancestry in such detail, other than for the purpose of shoring up hereditary status. Does kinship have any long-term significance, in other words? What aspects of us can live on in our descendants, and for how long?

There are three basic types of inheritance—genetic, cultural, and psychological—which often act together so closely as to be indistinguishable. The short-term importance of these transmissions is inestimably great. One has strong affinities with one's grandparents and with one's grandchildren; but over longer spans of descent the similarities begin to dissipate rather quickly: the connection between one of your grandchildren and one of your grandparents, for instance, is already a good deal more tenuous.

Because of the dissolving effect of sexual reproduction and because the number of ancestors doubles each time they are taken back another generation, individual lines of descent quickly lose their biological importance. Only seven generations back, for instance, at roughly the time of the American Revolution, one already has in theory a hundred and twenty-eight ancestors on a hundred and twenty-eight separate lines. In fact the number is almost always smaller because of cousin intermarriage; when people who are already related marry, they occupy a second slot on the pedigree of their descendants; duplication and "pedigree collapse"—a fascinating and important phenomenon that will be discussed later—occur. But even when there has been a lot of collapse, the chances of inheriting a particular trait from any one ancestor seven generations back are very slim. If one of the six people on the line between the ancestor and oneself was not a biological parent (which has not been an unusual occurrence), the chances are, in fact, zero.

The proportion of your genes that you share with a given ancestor (besides those that are common to everybody) is, on average, one half squared by the number of generations that separate you. Thus only $\frac{1}{2}^7$, or $\frac{1}{128}$ of the genes of an ancestor seven generations back, will reach you. The fraction is usually greater because of cousin intermarriage, but even if there are about a hundred thousand genes in the human genome (to go with one of the higher estimates), less than a thousand of your genes will probably have descended from him. The genes that compose his legacy to you are chosen completely at random, as if they were cards dealt from a deck that had been cut in two, shuffled, reshuffled, and half replaced by new cards—six times. The shuffling and reshuffling take place—to review the fascinating process by which a good deal of the genetic part of individual variation is achieved—during the stages of sex-cell division, which are called meiosis and gametogenesis. Before they mingle and two of them fuse, the egg cells of the female and the sperm cells of the male split into two smaller cells called gametes, which contain only half the usual number of chromosomes—twenty-three instead of forty-six—along which genes are sequenced. Which twenty-three chromosomes—the forty-six come in two sets, one from either parent—is determined by pure chance. As a consequence of this "random assortment," the probability that two siblings will inherit from either of their parents the same twenty-three chromosomes is very remote—only $\frac{1}{2}^{23}$, or one in eight million. The fraction is actually even smaller because of a process known as recombination, or "crossing over." As the forty-six chromosomes are segregating into the two groups of twenty-three, and before the groups are sequestered in separate gametes, bits of DNA fly off one chromosome and exchange themselves with "homologous" bits on the corresponding chromosome from the other parent, so that while you might inherit through your father your paternal grandfather's thirteenth chromosome, part of it—its "short arm," say—may have actually been his wife's. Usually the segments that are exchanged are relatively large—five-eighths of the chromosome, or a whole gene—but genes are fragile strands that can snap off anywhere, and sometimes small genetic subunits are transferred. The breaks occur entirely at random, and sometimes recrossing over even takes place. Crossing over reduces the probability that two siblings will inherit an identical set of chromosomes from either parent (unless, of course, they are identical twins, in which case they both get perfect clones of each set) to much less than $\frac{1}{2}^{88}$ (which would be the fraction if the breaks always occurred at the same place), to a fraction of such infinitesimal smallness—something like one over one followed by ten billion zeros—that it may as well be zero. And the genetic gap between siblings, only half of whose genes are "identical by descent" if they are full siblings, quickly widens along *their* lines of descent: their children, who are first cousins, share only an eighth of their genes.

Which of the millions of sperms ejaculated by the male during coition, each with its own virtually unique blend of chromosomes, will end up penetrating and fertilizing one of the female's ova after mating is also entirely a matter of chance. There is a very remote possibility, moreover, that the gene or one of the genes involved in producing the trait which this ancestor seven generations back, this hypothetical fifth great-grandparent, is trying to perpetuate, will suffer a mutation. This happens rarely—in the replications of a single gene, only once in a million times, on average; and only once, on average, in the replication of every million genes. Only the mutations that take place in sex cells matter for future generations; a mutation that happens during the development of a toe, say, has only local one-time significance. Yet each of us inherits on the order of twenty potentially deleterious recessive mutations, from which we are usually protected by also getting, from our other parent, a normal, dominant copy of the same gene.

Whether the trait will survive all these winnowing processes for seven generations, or six acts of reproduction, depends a lot on what sort of a trait it is. A complex trait, governed by many genes, is more apt to be broken up by crossing over. A trait controlled by only one gene has three basic modes of inheritance: autosomal dominant, autosomal recessive, and sex-linked. Each mode has its own transmission pattern, its own odds. Most of the known "monogenic" traits are autosomal dominants, whose inheritance works like this: if one parent carries the gene, and the other does not, each of their children has a fifty-per-cent chance of inheriting the gene and expressing the trait; but if both parents have the gene, the probability that it will be inherited rises to seventy-five per cent. Partly because dominant genes tend to encode structural proteins and developmental patterns, while recessives tend to regulate metabolic enzymes, and partly because dominants are expressed more readily—only one copy is needed to produce the trait—they tend to pass on more "phenotypic" or visible similarity from generation to generation than recessives do. Autosomal genes are more common than sex-linked ones, mainly because they are distributed over almost sixteen times more chromosome length, but also because the heritability of a sex-linked trait depends on the sex of the person who carries the gene and on the sex of the person in line to receive it. Another class of genes is "sex-limited"; they determine secondary sexual characteristics but are not necessarily on the sex chromosomes, and their expression depends on the sex of the person who carries them. A woman may carry the gene for male baldness, for instance, without losing hair.

Much of our heredity does not have a straightforward Mendelian pattern of inheritance or odds that can be readily calculated. Many traits fall into gray areas of "incomplete dominance" and "imperfect penetrance," and the probability that they will be transmitted can only be estimated empirically. There are "polygenic" traits, controlled by many genes, and "multifactorial" ones, whose genes are modulated by internal and external environmental factors. There are "threshold characters" like diabetes and schizophrenia, which seem to require for their expression a certain quota of genes, but which genes, and how they interact with their environmental catalysts, are not yet known. At this point, far less than one per cent of our heredity has been elucidated, and most of the traits whose progress through the generations of a family has been tracked, whose gene has been assigned a specific locus on a specific chromosome, or whose code of nucleotide base pairs has been sequenced, are deleterious recessives and other "bad stuff." The socially important aspects of our heredity about which one would most like to know—which genes are involved in the transmission of behavior and intelligence, how, and to what extent—are still a long way from being understood. But it is already clear that these traits are the most complex and the least likely to persist in a family for any length of time.

And yet certain things obviously do run in families. The gene for night blindness, for instance, an autosomal dominant (to pick a genetic disorder almost at random), was traced for eleven generations of descendants of a butcher named Jean Nougaret, who lived during the seventeenth century in a small village near Montpelier, in the South of France. Eighty-six of the six hundred and twenty-nine descendants Nougaret had by 1838 were afflicted with the condition. Facial resemblances can be consistently heritable, although their genetics are not well understood. They are still for the most part "anecdotal" traits—virtually impossible to measure scientifically or to verify objectively—but the fact that certain recognizable similarities keep showing up in generation after generation suggests that they are controlled either by very few genes or by closely linked clusters of genes (a pattern known as pleiotropy), and Victor McKusick has catalogued as simple dominants a few features like cheek dimples, whorls in eyebrows, odd-shaped teeth, and the asymmetrical lower lips of people who lack on one side the depressor muscle for their mouths—a trait that reveals itself when they are crying.

Perhaps the most famous facial resemblance is the Hapsburg lip, an underslung lower labium that has kept cropping up— on the sixteenth-century Holy Roman Emperor Charles V; on Philip of Spain, in the next century; on Emperor Josef of Austria in the next; on Franz Josef in the next; on Alfonso XII of Spain in this one. The Bourbon nose has proliferated in the royal houses of Europe, while Tsar Nicholas II and King George V, who shared a Danish grandmother and a good deal of German ancestry through their fathers, looked almost like identical twins.

Inbreeding and assortative mating—the tendency of people who look alike (or belong to the same class, or both have the same affliction) to marry each other—favor the perpetuation of physical resemblances. The frequent intermarriage among the aristocracies of Europe, for instance, has been self-reinforcing not only politically but genetically; the members of the various nobilities have not only thought and acted alike, they have *looked* alike because they have received the same "aristocratic" features from the same comparatively limited gene pool.

One of the earliest attempts to trace how complex traits run in families was made by the Victorian scientist Francis Galton, who pored over the pedigrees of eminent (mostly British) judges, statesmen, military commanders, literary figures, scientists, poets, musicians, painters, divines, Cambridge classicists, oarsmen, and North Country wrestlers, and discovered definite hereditary patterns of what he called "eminence." In *Hereditary Genius,* published in 1869, he reported that Charlotte Brontë "was the most conspicuous member of a family remarkable for their intellectual gifts, restless mental activity, and wretched constitutions"; that "the descendants and antecedents of Sir Philip Sidney were men of parts and minions of their time"; that eight males in the family of Samuel Taylor Coleridge were "gifted with rare abilities"; that the descendants of Erasmus Darwin, including his grandson Charles and Galton himself, had "a taste for natural history"; that the family of the German chemist, naturalist, and physician Johann Friedrich Gmelin "gave five names to science"; that there were "eight or nine good painters" in the family of Tiziano Codoro Vecelli, better known as Titian. The one exception and "apparent perversion of the laws of heredity" was the "divines," who his studies revealed were "not founders of influential families" and "on the whole an ailing lot of men." The children of religious parents, he reported, "frequently turn out badly."

Galton's interpretation of his data, however, was dated. He assumed that the inheritance of "eminence" was entirely biological (although the word "gene" did not yet exist) and that because the sort of eminence which flourished in upper-class England was much less evident in the tribes of black Africa, a valid comparison of the innate capacities of the white and Negro races could be made. The notion of multifactional inheritance did not yet exist, either, so Galton did not consider in his discussion of the Bachs, for instance, how much the high number of musicians (forty out of sixty of the descendants of Veit Bach in the five generations after him—including Johann Sebastian—are known to have been competent musicians) may have been due to a supportive environment, and how much to genes they may have shared.

In spite of his belief in the innate superiority of the English upper classes and his blindness to the cultural aspects of inheritance, Galton concluded that deep pedigrees, except for the prestige attached to them, were meaningless. "A man who has no able ancestor nearer in blood than a great-grandparent is inappreciably better off in the chance of being himself gifted with ability, than if he had been taken out of the general mass of men," he wrote. "An old peerage is a valueless title to natural gifts, except so far as it may have been furbished up by a succession of wise intermarriages. When, however, as is often the case, the direct line has become extinct and the title has passed to a distant relative, who had not been reared in the family traditions, the sentiment attached to its possession is utterly unreasonable. I cannot think of any claim . . . that is so entirely an imposture."

❧

In the past decade a number of geneticists, notably Luigi L. Cavalli-Sforza and Marcus W. Feldman of Stanford, have explored the role that "culture"—which they define as "anything which is transmitted through communication and learning"— plays in inheritance. "In addition to their genes, parents pass on to their children an environment in which they develop physically and of course mentally," they have written. "Culture is transmitted in ways that can be indistinguishable from those of genes." As a result of their work and that of colleagues like S. Scarr and R. A. Weinberg—whose research in 1976 showed "that black children adopted in good white homes reach an IQ practically indistinguishable from that of white children reared under comparable conditions, and much higher than that of black children raised in poorer black environments"—Cavalli-Sforza and Feldman have lowered their estimate of the genetic component in the variability of intelligence from the average of seventy per cent which earlier statistical treatment had proposed, to thirty per cent, with a value of forty-two per cent for the cultural component (and the balance for error in testing). The thirty-per-cent estimate was first suggested by scientists at George Washington University. Cavalli-Sforza and Feldman find it "a proportion which seems nearer to that suggested by common sense."

Of the three types of inheritance, cultural inheritance is the most tenacious. The preservation of the cultural identity of the Jews over two millennia of repeated persecution and displacement offers a remarkable example of the ability of a "mental order," to use Thomas de Zengotita's term, to persist. One's religious beliefs are part of what Freud called the superego, one's conscience and moral values, which are perhaps the most important and readily traceable things of an immaterial nature one gets from one's parents. Cavalli-Sforza, Feldman, and two colleagues, who distributed a questionnaire to undergraduates at Stanford University and then interviewed them, found "strong vertical cultural transmission for political tendencies and religion." "We examined the proportion of children who pray as a function of one or both parents praying and found that religiosity is largely determined by the parents—the mother is very important" (something that Judaism seems to have recognized by having Jewishness pass down matrilineally). "It is not likely that the transmission is genetic."

Some cultural traits gradually become reinforced biologically, while some biological traits may be reinforced culturally, so that it is impossible to sort out or assign a relative degree of influence to either component. The eyes of Indian women may offer an example of such joint cultural-biological inheritance: for centuries large, expressive eyes have been an esteemed female attribute in India. Among the ways to call an Indian woman beautiful is to allude to her *meena kshi* (fish-shaped eyes) or to her *mrig nyani* (fawn eyes). Eyes fitting these descriptions seem common enough among Indian women to make one wonder if women with the trait haven't enjoyed a reproductive advantage over those without it. The problem is how to define the trait objectively, and to decide who has it and who doesn't. As a case of the reverse pattern—a genetic trait being reinforced culturally—scientists have proposed that myopia may have been selected for in trades like goldsmithing, which require close work and have traditionally passed from father to son.

The Pakistani squash-playing family, the Khans, which has produced champions on three separate lines over three generations, offers another possible case of culture reinforcing genes. The fact that both Hassim and Safiullah Khan, brothers-in-law with no genes in common (genes "identical by descent," that is), were both top players suggests that there is a cultural element in the concentration of squash talent in the Khan family. I recently asked one of its members, Gul Khan, whose American ranking has been as high as three, whether he thought genes or family pressure had been a greater factor in the Khans' domination of the game. He said, "Family pressure, definitely. It all started with my grand-father, and we took it over step by step. It was a good move for the family, and now it's the family thing. All the sons have to play. I started at four. My son Masir is four and a half, and I'll be starting him next year." Certain physical characteristics—the Khans are known for their catlike agility, their extraordinary hand-to-eye coordination, and their stamina (perhaps having grown up at high altitude, near the Khyber Pass, enhanced their lung capacity)—have undoubtedly contributed to their success, but these qualities benefited from cultural reinforcement at the family level—having a family tradition to live up to—and per-haps at the tribal level, too: the Khans belong to the Pathan, a tribe renowned for fierceness and physical prowess.

Psychological inheritance is really a subtype of cultural in-heritance, in which the trait is often transmitted unconsciously and can have tremendous, sometimes devastating importance for the individual, but is comparatively short-lived, rarely lasting in his family more than, say, four generations. Probably the most common mechanism in this mode of inheritance is the psychologi-cal process of identification, which involves not only conscious imi-tation but an unconscious projection of oneself into the model. A woman who never marries, for instance, may not even be aware that she has identified with her spinster aunt. The concept of identification overlaps closely with the notion of "relational loy-alty" proposed by the Hungarian family therapist Ivan Borzhe-menzy-Nagy. Children of concentration-camp survivors generating their own menace by starving themselves, to create a world com-parable in some ways to the one their parents had to face, and a child who has been constantly put down by his mother having a low opinion of himself and thus confirming the correctness of her view, are examples of such "loyalty." "We play back parts of our parents we didn't plan to," the family therapist John Pearce told me. "My father, for instance, used to bury himself in the newspaper when he came home; and now I find myself doing it, even though I fight it."

In general, people tend to reproduce what produced them, even experiences that were unsatisfactory—a process known as "repetition compulsion." A woman may be critical of her daugh-ter's appearance, for instance, because as a child she suffered the same criticism from her mother. Child-rearing behavior has a particularly strong tendency to be repeated in families, the psychotherapist Paul Wachtel recently explained, because parenthood is such a new experience for the young parents; having no other frame of reference, they tend to fall back on the way they were treated as children.

Another important process, the reverse of identification and loyalty, is rebellion, "the dedication to something opposite," as Wachtel described it. Generational cycles of rebellion, somewhat like Hegelian thesis-antithesis sequences in history—life-style swings from puritanism to libertinism, occupational swings from business to the arts, for instance—are common in families. Because it is the specific mechanism by which traditions are broken with and change is effected within families, the psychological process of rebellion has, of course, played a crucial role in the history of kinship.

5

The Aristocracies of Europe

HAVING NOW GOT SOME PERSPECTIVE ON THE MATTER, AND SEEN that the significance of lineage of any depth is purely cultural, we can resume our history of the genealogical practices of hereditary elites. As in Africa and Asia, the pedigrees of the rich and powerful had already begun to deepen in the West well before the Christian era. The scrupulous lists of "begats" in Genesis, Kings, and Chronicles are considered quite accurate by many Jewish historians, and the historian Edward Gibbon writes of a Roman senator of the fifth century A.D. named Rogatus who traced himself, more dubiously, all the way to Agamemnon. None of these genealogies, however, can be continued to the present; they fade out, for the Jews, with the dispersion following the destruction of Jerusalem, in 70 A.D.; and for the Romans, with the deposing of Romulus Augustulus—the traditional end of the Roman Empire, in 476 A.D.

The ancient Hebrews were as intensely preoccupied with descent as their Arab cousins. Their basic texts were, of course, the twenty-eight genealogical tables in the Bible. The descents between I Chronicles 8:37 and 9:44 alone are said to have provoked nine hundred camel-loads of commentary. Political and social status was largely a function of which sept, or subdivision of the tribal tree, one had been born into; of whether one was descended

from firstborn sons, or belonged to a collateral line—sometimes
through an ancestor's concubine, who was often a bondmaid of his
original wife—or to a later group that had been incorporated by
the tribe and given the status of illegitimate issue. Priestly genealogies were recorded with particular care. "Purity of descent was
indispensable and, when necessary, minutely investigated," Rabbi
Emil G. Hirsch has written. "A special office seems to have been
entrusted with these records, and a court of inquiry is mentioned
as having been instituted in Jerusalem. . . . A priest was bound
to demonstrate the purity of the pedigree of the priestly maiden
he desired to wed, even as far back as her great-great-grandfather
and great-great-grandmother." One thing that could confuse the
pedigree searchers was the institution of blood covenants, in which
two unrelated men became "brothers." In time the Pharisaic school
of thought, which ranked a man according to how much he knew,
prevailed over the Sadducean school, which emphasized purity of
descent, and an aristocracy of the mind replaced the aristocracy of
the blood in old Judea.

Each of the roughly fourteen million Jews alive today is almost certainly—if the family has belonged to the faith for any
length of time, the mathematical probability is overwhelming—
descended from at least one of the ninety-seven thousand survivors
of the war with Rome who, according to the historian Josephus,
left Palestine after 70 A.D. Specifically, they would be descended
from the tribes of Judah, Benjamin, or Simeon, because the other
nine tribes of Israel disappeared in the Diaspora after the Baby-
lonian captivity in 597 B.C.E. People with Sephardic or Ashkenazic
Jewish ancestors titled Ha-Kohen or Ha-Levi can be even more
confident about having biblical antecedents. The priestly order of
Kohanim began with Aaron, the brother of Moses, who led the
Jews out of Egypt in the thirteenth century B.C.E., and it was
carefully passed from father to son. The Levites were a hereditary
order of temple servants, much as the *sharifs* were the hereditary
keepers of the holy cities of the Hejaz, Mecca and Medina. But
neither of these genealogies survived the Roman conquest of Judea,
and having the name Cohen or Levy does not necessarily mean
that an ancestor belonged to one of the orders.

Most Jewish surnames are very recent, of about the same vintage as American Indian surnames, and they too were imposed by
governments with European naming traditions. A traditional He-

brew name consisted of the given name followed by the patronymic—Zevi ben Moshe, Avraham ben Zevi, for instance. The
Ashkenazim had a taboo against naming a child for a living forebear; they traditionally gave the first son his paternal grandfather's name (if the grandfather was dead) and the second son
the name of his maternal grandfather—a system that may be of
Greek origin and often resulted in the same two names alternat-
ing generations, in the manner of Scandinavian and Russian
given name–patronymic sequences.

By the late eighteenth century it had become difficult for
Jews in some parts of Europe to cross national borders without surnames, and from 1787 on, all sorts of surnames began to appear
on public registers, wherever Jews had been forced to adopt them.
Some were animal names—Ochs ("ox"); Hirsch ("stag," later
converted into Hertz, Hartwig, Harris, Cerf, Herzl, and Jellinek).
"Jews living in crowded, airless, and sunless ghettoes frequently
adopted names (like Rosenblum and Greenblatt) which alluded
to green woods and fields," Elsdon C. Smith has written. Many
adopted the place name of wherever they happened to be. Vienna,
for instance, is ringed with towns that are now Jewish surnames:
Bernstein (which means amber), Rubinstein, Eisenstadt, Gold-
berg, Rosenberg. The same is true in Italy: anybody with a geographic surname, like Milano or Turino, probably has Jewish
patriliny.

Ashkenazic Jews in the Pale of Settlement, which extended
from present-day Lithuania to the Ukraine, were not required to
submit copies of their synagogue registers to their local duma, or
city council, or to take surnames until 1844, and it is hard for the
descendants of people who emigrated from the Pale to trace themselves back much farther. It was often a liability for a Jew in that
part of the world to have identification, and many of the records
have been lost. Later on, many were destroyed to keep them from
falling into the hands of Nazis. A number of prominent rabbini-
cal families of Sephardim and Western European Ashkenazim go
back well into the Middle Ages: the De Solas have an ancestor in
ninth-century Navarre, in northern Spain, and the Schiffs began
in fourteenth-century Vienna. The present-day Trèves family of
France goes back to Rabbi Joseph Trèves of fourteenth-century
Marseilles, who was said to be a descendant of Judah Sir Léon

of Paris (1126–1224), alleged third great-grandson of the famous Talmudic commentator Rashi; and Rashi was traditionally a descendant, through Hillel the Great (100 B.C.), of the House of David. But "traditions about the House of David were probably a great comfort to an oppressed people during the Middle Ages, and that is probably the main reason these traditions were devised," Dan Rottenberg has written.

A number of noble Italian families—the Markgraves of Este and the Ruffas, for instance—have claimed to be descended, like the last of the Valerii in Henry James's story, from patricians of ancient Rome, but the descents are unverifiable. Only one Western lineage, one demonstrable descent—that of the Bagratid kings of Georgia— seems to bridge what the British genealogist Anthony Wagner has called "the dark chasm" between classical antiquity and the Middle Ages. In his book *Pedigrees and Progress*, Wagner explains how special conditions promoted long dynasties and deep pedigrees in that part of the world: how the rugged Caucasus Mountains kept the Bagratids from being overthrown by Romans to the West or by Parthians, Turks, Persians, or, later, the Tatars to the East, and yet "the great centres" were near enough for these rulers to be literate and organized record keepers. The Bagratids were descended from an Armenian noble family called the Bagratuni, who were the traditional coronants of the branch of the Arsacid kings that ruled Armenia from the first to the fifth century A.D. After the Bagratids attained prominence in Georgia, they intermarried with various Iranian, Pontic Greek, and Byzantine dynasties, which gave them genealogical connections to the Paleogi, the Comneni of Trebizond, to Herod of Judea, and, through the Ptolemies, to Cleopatra, an ancestor of the famous one, whose father, Mithridates VI Eupator (120–64 B.C.), was the king of Pontus and an implacable enemy of Pompey. Their control of Georgia was intermittent until its annexation by Russia in 1795, and princes of the line continued to use their titles until the Menshevik revolution in Georgia dispensed with such formalities. A seventy-three-generation pedigree, pieced together several years ago by Prince Cyril Toumanoff, himself a Bagratid, begins with Queen Elizabeth II, who connects to the dynasty through a marriage between the Lusignan House of Cyprus and the Crusader House of Savoy, and ends with Pharnabazus, King of Iberia (not

the Iberia made up of Spain and Portugal, but the one in eastern
Georgia), in 326 B.C. Wagner considers the descent "probable"—
broken or conjectural at only three points.

There are numerous living descendants of the Bagratids in
Georgia and abroad.* One, Prince Teymuraz Bagration, is the
director of the Tolstoy Foundation in New York. In the eighth
or ninth century the Bagratids, who had previously claimed descent from a god named Angl-Tork' but were now Christians, acquired a more respectable "replacement" pedigree connecting
them to David, King of Israel, which was completely spurious.

The first attempt to tie in with the House of David, of course,
was made in Luke 3; it had been prophesied that the Messiah
would come from the House of David, and the author of the gospel carefully shows how Christ fulfilled this genealogical requirement by tracing the pedigree of Joseph to King David. The descent goes back even further, all the way to "Adam, son of God,"
so that in effect Christ was God's son through both of his earthly
parents. Jewish genealogists, who do not accept Christ as the Messiah, consider Luke's pedigree of Joseph fabricated, but some of
the Bagratids in old St. Petersburg, on the strength of their mutual, but alas bogus, descent from David, claimed to be "heirs of
our Savior Jesus Christ," according to Fitzroy MacLean, and "at
least one elderly Princess Bagration would wear mourning on the
feast of the Assumption on the grounds that it had been a family
bereavement." Muslims accept the pedigree of Joseph. So do
Mormons. One Mormon, Thomas Milton Tinney, used it along
with genealogies in the Book of Mormon to trace his son back for
a hundred and fifty-six generations to Ahman, Supreme Member
of the Godhead and the father of Adam. Tinney's work, however,
is discounted by non-Mormon genealogists.

This side of the dark chasm, a number of equally unverifiable

---

* In an elegant piece of research, my great-uncle, Andrei Avinoff, who after the
Russian Revolution began a new life in Pittsburgh—where he became interested in genealogy, partly I suspect for nostalgic reasons, and partly so that the
future generations of his sister's offspring would know something about their
origins—traced his mother through five female lines and a governor of Simbirsk murdered during the Pugatchev rebellion of 1774 to a seventeenth-
century *stolnik* of Tsar Alexis (a court position abolished by Peter the Great)
named Prince Pankrat Davidov, who had a direct male descent from Alexander, ruler of Georgia (d. 1442). From there, through Alexander's wife
Thamar, he was home free, on firm male-line Bagratid territory, until 314.

early descents on the northern fringes of the Roman Empire, and beyond its frontiers, lead to the present. The O'Neills of Ulster may have the deepest extant pedigree in Western Europe; in a three-volume history of the clan, published in 1910, Thomas Matthews traces it to a king named Krimthan Niamar (74–98 A.D.), whose legendary forebears go back for another couple of millennia. Wagner mentions an extant Irish line from the High Kings to Niall of the Nine Hostages, who died in 405 (the word "clan," in fact, comes from the Gaelic *clann*, meaning "descendants"); a traceable Welsh princely line to Cunedda (ca. 430); a possible female descent from the Frankish line of the Merovingian kings (who begin with Clovis in 487 and end with the relegation to the cloister of Childeric III in 751); and a number of modern descents, through marriages to Crusaders, from various Byzantine houses, in whose records, however, there is a breach between the sixth and ninth centuries.

The Icelandic prose sagas and verse eddas, which were composed by bards and went from mouth to mouth until about 1100, trace some very early lines. They name the jarls, or tribal chieftains, who refused to submit to Harold the Fair-Haired, the first king of Norway, and sailed to Iceland in 875. Several dozen sagas go back to Odin, and claim descent through him from a son of Noah. The first recorded Norseman in Iceland was named Ingjolf Arnasson (some Irish priests had already settled there earlier in the century); by 930 enough had arrived for a Book of Settlements to be started. Today thousands of sagas of individual families are on file in the National Archives of Reykjavik, and the interest in genealogy, as one might expect on an island, is intense.

Around 1850 a good many Icelanders headed for America, taking their sagas with them. In Cheyenne, Wyoming, today, as a result, there is a woman named Charlene Horsley who knows exactly how she is descended from Snori, the first recorded Caucasian born in North America. Snori was the son of Gudrid, the widow of Leif Ericson's brother, and of her second husband, a man named Thorfinnur Karlsefni. In 1003, Ericson, pregnant Gudrid, and Karlsefni sailed from Greenland with a group of Vikings for a forested coast that Ericson had accidentally discovered three years earlier and called Vinland; but before they got there, winter came. They went ashore at a place they called Straumfjord, "Stream Fjord," which most scholars suspect was somewhere in Newfoundland, and there Snori was born. No trace of their shelter has been found, but in the spring they returned to Greenland, and the Karlsefni Saga, which relates their adventures, became part of Icelandic lore.

❧

In 732, Charles Martel, the grandfather of Charlemagne, repelled the Moors at Tours. The victory was important not only because it kept Europe from becoming Islamic, but because it marked the debut of what Wagner calls "mounted shock combat with the lance at rest." As a result of it, a new elite of elaborately armed warriors on horseback—knights—came into being. Stirrups, which had just been invented, enabled the knights to brace themselves as they battered adversaries with their lances and deflected blows with their shields. The Huns, the Goths, the Visigoths, the Magyars, and the other marauding barbarians who had overrun Europe after the collapse of the Roman Empire were powerless against these invincible horsemen. It was only around the end of the twelfth century that new weapons—crossbows and longbows, whose missiles could pierce chain mail—forced the knights to wear cumbersome suits of armor and put an end to their supremacy. "Unhorsed and flat on his back," writes Robert Lacey, "the heavily armoured knight was a ludicrous and pathetic figure—and the advent of gunpowder completed his obsolescence." But by then the knights had served the purposes of delivering Europe from the Dark Ages, and of giving rise, under whatever kings they served, to an attendant nobility.

The European system of feudalism, in which these knights were "enfeoffed," offered land for service. In return for protecting and furthering the interests of their "liege lords," the knights were granted "demesnes," or a king's most powerful subjects were made barons and *they* were granted demesnes in return for agreeing to provide him with a certain number of knights. The barons recruited knights by "subinfeudation"—by leasing land to them— and the knights in turn leased whatever they didn't need as pasture for their horses to peasants, serfs, and other vassals. The knighthoods were not at first hereditary; that development usually parallelled the appearance of surnames, to which the title and property could be "entailed." Elsdon C. Smith describes how surnames evolved in Europe.

After the Crusades . . . people began, perhaps unconsciously, to feel the need of a family name, or at least a name in addition to the simple one that had been possessed from birth. The nobles and upper classes, especially those who went on the Crusades, observed the prestige and practical value of an added name and were quick to take a surname, usually the name of the lands they owned. When the Crusaders returned from the wars, the upper classes who had stayed at home soon followed suit.

When the clerks who kept the records in the manors and on the feudal lands of the nobles and the great landowners noted the payment of fines and amercements by the vassals, they needed an additional description in order to distinguish one Robert or Leofric from another. . . . It would do no good for the lord's clerk to ask the peasant what additional name he possessed. He didn't have any other name and hadn't thought about the matter. Therefore, when the clerk noted the vassal's name in the manor records he added, on his own initiative, a brief description. It was likely that the vassal was not known among his neighbors by the description put down by the scribe. The very earliest bynames were not names by which those so described were known, except in isolated instances.

European surnames are of four basic types: place names, like Heath (English, "one who came from a wasteland with low shrubs"); patronyms, like Fitzroy (Norman, "bastard son of the king"; of Charles II in the case of the deeply religious captain of the *Beagle*); occupational names, like the tremendously successful Smith (or German Schmidt, Danish Smed, French Lefèvre, Czech Kovar, Bulgarian Kovac, Polish Kowalsky, Russian Kuznetsov, Finnish Seppane, Italian Farrari, and so on); and descriptive names, including nicknames. They first became hereditary in the patrician class of Venice during the ninth and tenth centuries; and in Bavaria around then limited sets of Christian names and even surnames, written down in *Libri Memorales* by monks who would repeat them in their prayers, had begun to run in some families. But patrilineally transmitted surnames were not generally adopted in Europe until around 1400. By then knighthood had already become a matter of "noble" birth, the word "noble" itself had come to mean a large hereditary landowner, irrespective of moral character, and several systems of devolution were in practice among the various nobilities.

In the twelfth century jousting tournaments became an important means of displaying the pomp of royalty and nobility and of demonstrating valued martial skills; and heraldry—a sort of genealogy in pictures, which had been developed by the Arabs—was brought back from the Crusades and adopted as a means of identifying armored adversaries. For example, at one early tourney the knight Geoffrey Anjou, in a primitive heraldic gesture, stuck in his helmet a sprig of blossoming broom, *Planta genista,* and his descendants, who provided England with its monarchs through the reign of Edward III, became known as the Plantagenets. As the protocols of jousting and heraldry developed together, the shields of combatants were "charged" with "lions rampant," "dragons passant," "stags' heads caboshed," and other fabulous beasts, and they were "quartered" to show that each grandparent had possessed a coat of arms in his or her own right. Four noble grandparents were required of anybody who planned to joust. One day in the mid–fifteenth century, the historian Barbara Tuchman has written, "a knight rode into the lists followed by a parade of pennants bearing no less than thirty-two coats-of-arms."

As the hereditary principle replaced the need for force as a guarantor of status, and armies of mercenaries replaced knights who had become tied to their holdings; as Europe stabilized and merchants grown rich from commerce, which had begun to flourish among its states and its numerous little principalities, were ennobled and, along with elevated professional civil servants and court ministers, formed a new *noblesse de la robe,* as opposed to the nobility of the sword; as the devastating destructiveness of projectiles propelled by gunpowder helped convert the nobleman's house from a "fortified stronghold," in Lacey's words, into a "visual display . . . designed to reinforce the lord's authority"; and as the concept of the "gentleman" evolved from the medieval code of chivalry—the pedigrees of the various nobilities deepened and

intermingled. The recorded history of Europe from the ninth to
the nineteenth centuries, as Lacey explains, is mainly the history
of noblemen. Their "rolls, chronicles, and record books are virtually our only evidence for hundreds of years of life [and] tell us
next to nothing about anybody else."

In the History and Genealogy Section of the New York Public Library I was shown one afternoon a large old book whose
pages, disintegrating at the edges, traced many of the deepest and
most illustrious lineages of Europe and the rest of the known
world, past and present. It was called *Royal Genealogies, or the
Genealogical Tables of Emperors and Princes*. The fruit of "seven
years of hard Labour," as its author, John Anderson, explained in
a preface, it was published in London in 1726. Later studies—
Prince William Karl von Isenberg's monumental *Stauntfeln zur
Geschichte der Europaischen Staaten* for the Continental nobilities; Burke's for the British aristocracy—have more accurate dates
and descents, but this book was of interest because in 1726 most
of the genealogical "houses" in Europe were still intact, and because, as I turned the pages, I gradually realized the scope of
Anderson's intent: he was trying to capture in one volume no less
than the entire stream of history as it was then known and understood—by listing the names and relationships of everybody who
had ever seemed to matter.

⚘

Marriage was the main method by which the noble and royal
houses extended and consolidated their power, and before long
everybody who belonged to one house had the blood of many
others; a network of cousins, who could ask each other for (but
would not always get) the allegiance due them as kinsmen,
spanned the Continent. To give an idea of how interconnected
everybody was, by 1973 all ten of the still reigning European
sovereigns were descended from Jan Willem Friso, Prince of
Orange, who died in 1711, and three of them—Queen Margrethe
of Denmark, King Olaf of Norway, and King Constantine of
Greece (who was deposed in 1973)—belonged to the same house,
that of Schleswig-Holstein-Suderburg-Glucksburg). To give an
idea of how cosmopolitan everybody's ancestry was, even in the
relatively insular Spanish aristocracy the late Duke of Alba bore
the Scottish surname Fitzjames, which he had acquired through

illegitimate descent from the House of Stuart; and on a recent trip to London I met a young Bavarian prince named Tobias Herzog von Julich Kleve-Berg, of the House of Cleves (the same one to which Anne of Cleves, one of Henry VIII's wives, had belonged). The house had been founded by the Ponce de León family of Seville.

Structurally, the European "house" is like the Chinese clan and the kinship groups of some central African tribes. Robin Fox describes the system as "spinal-cord segmentary." It has a senior lineage, or "nominative line," the "cord" on which the surname, the title, and the property ideally descend; and sublineages of cousins, waiting in the wings in case there are no eligible offspring. The succession to the throne after the death of Henry VIII offers a classic example of how the system works. First the throne went to Henry's sickly third surviving child, Edward, because in the order of royal succession throughout Europe, male issue take precedence. But Edward had no children, so the throne reverted to his elder sister, "Bloody" Mary, who also failed to reproduce, and on her death the throne passed to their sister Elizabeth, who had no children either. With Elizabeth's death the House of Tudor became extinct, and a successor had to be brought in from the nearest lineage: James V of Scotland, the son of Mary, Queen of Scots, whose mother, Margaret Tudor, had been Henry VIII's sister. James V, Elizabeth's first cousin once removed, was crowned at Westminster as James I. He united England and Scotland under the same aegis and started a new dynasty, the House of Stuart.

This type of succession, which can be described as preferential rather than exclusive male primogeniture, with females in the nominative line taking precedence over males in sublineages, has prevailed in the royal houses of Europe except where Salic law, which forbade titles to be held by or transmitted through females, was in effect, as in France at the time of the Hundred Years' War, when the King of England, Edward III, proclaimed his hereditary right to the throne of France through his mother, Isabella, the daughter of France's Philip IV. The advantage of having a title pass through both sexes is that it can stay longer in the nominative line; there is less zigzagging to sublineages, and less extinction than when an unbroken male descent from the original patentee has to be found each time the latest bearer of the title dies.

There has been a remarkable run of preferential male primogeniture in the pedigree of the present Duchess of Medinaceli, who lives most of the year in Seville and, besides her principal title, which dates from 1368, has accumulated fifty-nine others— more than anybody in the world; the runner-up is another of the Spanish aristocracy's great ladies, the Duchess of Alba, who has forty. On the death of her father, in 1959, the Duchess of Medinaceli, whose full name is Doña Victoria Eugenia Fernandez de Cordoba Y Fernandez de Henestrosa, but who is known to her family and friends simply as Mimi, received ten duchies, seventeen marquesates, sixteen counties, and four viscountcies, plus eight more titles that have not yet been officially conceded to her. These titles, added to the marquesate and three counties left her by her mother years earlier, brought her total titles to sixty, fourteen of which are *grandezas*, the highest subroyal rank in the Spanish nobility. The Duchess has "lent" (actually a rather involved procedure that requires petitioning the Ministry of Justice) nine of her titles to her four children, two to her sister, one to her first cousin, and one to her aunt; when these relatives die, the titles revert to her, unless she chooses to let them pass to their descendants, which she probably will. After they have been in the same line for three generations, they automatically become hereditary.

The reason the Duchess has all these titles is that, even with females being allowed to succeed, title-bearing lineages have been going extinct in her pedigree for around seven hundred years; the titles have been transferred through marriage or have shifted over to sublineages, and have ultimately all converged on the lineage on which the Duchy of Medinaceli has been descending. The lineage was initially known as the House of De la Cerda, a surname that arose from an epithet of Fernando, King of Castille (1255–75); he was known as *"El de la cerda,"* "he of the [one in particular] long chest hair." On his death his throne was usurped by his youngest brother, who became Sancho IV, but his epithet passed down to his son, who became Alfonso de la Cerda, and from then on it was hereditary. Alfonso's granddaughter Isabel married Bernardo de Foix, the first count of Medinaceli (Medinaceli, from *medina,* Arabic for "city," and *coelus,* Latin for "heaven," means "heavenly city"). Four generations later, the county became a duchy, and eighteen generations after that, Doña Victoria Eugenia was born.

In a back room on the second floor of the Duchess's magnificent Moorish palace in Seville, I recently visited a young paleographer named Antonio Sanchez Gonzales, who told me that he had been working on her pedigree for three years and hoped to finish it in another year or so. He unrolled the master chart, which showed how and when the fifty-nine title-bearing houses had merged into the Medinaceli line, and was about seven feet by three. The deepest lineage was that of the Counts of Ampurias, the oldest title in Spain, granted in 810. The complete pedigree, Gonzales predicted, would be about two hundred feet long and would have about ten thousand names.

In most of the countries of Europe, counterparts of the House of Medinaceli can still be found—people who can still, directly or indirectly, bank on their hereditary status, and remain, at the least, well-off private citizens—though few boast pedigrees of such stupendous antiquity. In Italy and Austria noble titles officially no longer exist, but they continue to be used. German aristocrats have retained the nobiliary "von" by incorporating it into the surname. Even behind the Iron Curtain, members of the defunct Polish nobility are still allowed to live in their castles, as caretakers, and enjoy almost the same local status their ancestors had. The aristocracies of Europe have proved, on the whole, remarkably durable and adaptable. Most of them still play a significant role in the social, political, and economic life of their countries. The late head of the Italian Communist Party, for instance, Enrico Berlinguer, was a nobleman.

The British aristocracy is probably the most entrenched of the European nobilities. The peerage, whose senior males sit in the House of Lords, is still a political entity in its own right. "Lords is the constitutional stopgap," the Earl of Gowrie, who a few years ago was the Conservative Whip at Lords and is now Mrs. Thatcher's Minister for the Arts, explained to me recently. "Though it was deprived of the veto in 1910–11, it still contributes significantly to our political process by initiating, improving, and stalling legislation; and because it is not an elected body and is therefore less subject to the pressure of unpopularity, it tends to be more liberal on such issues as homosexuality and hanging." The British aristocracy still occasionally produces men of brilliance, like Lord Gowrie, with his effortless command of English ("Lord Gowrie can be amusingly world-weary and has a casual, transatlantic knowingness that is not always unattractive," the *Times Literary Supplement* has said of his poetry); and Lord Carrington, who until he allowed himself to be made a scapegoat for the Falklands invasion, was one of the most highly regarded foreign secretaries in modern times. Some of its families, like the kindred that included Lytton Strachey and Bertrand Russell, have seemed genuinely aristocratic, and as Robin Fox writes, "The web of kinship and marriage around our 'great families'—the Cecils, Devonshires, Churchills, etc.—[still] spreads into most corners of political and public life."

The British aristocracy consists of the peerage—some seven thousand titled men, women, and children; the junior or "cadet" branches of titled families; the landed gentry, made up of more than three thousand families, many of whom, although titleless, are much older and more embedded in the rural life of the country than most of the peers; and perhaps also a vaguer category, the "gentleman," who as Mark Bence-Jones and Hugh Montgomery-Massingberd remark in their *British Aristocracy*, "occupies a certain place in society through birth, education, merit, wealth, or rank, and also on account of his values, his manners, his magnanimity, and his sense of honour." The British aristocracy is probably the most fluid of Europe's hereditary elites. Not every peerage has equal social value. There are "disreputable" Victorian ones granted for "contributing to the coffers of the Liberal Party," a woman from an old landed-gentry family explained. The families in the brewing business—Allsopp, Bass, and Guinness—were thus made Lords Hindlip, Burton, and Iveagh, respectively, and are referred to by some as the "Beerage." New blood is constantly being introduced. An ambitious commoner like the journalist David Frost, for instance, who married a daughter of the Duke of Norfolk, can get his blood into the aristocracy in the next generation.

Although the hereditary principle had evolved in Europe partly as a more orderly way than force of succeeding to high status, in England after the Middle Ages, being knighted or elevated to a higher rank of the peerage took on an even more overtly meritocratic aspect; it became primarily a form of recognition, the

greatest honor a subject could receive. Making the honor hereditary was only an extra reward, a slightly better guarantee that
one's name and deeds would live after one. But in spite of its comparatively open admissions policy, the British aristocracy has func-
tioned much like any other self-perpetuating elite; it has, in fact,
been one of the world's most effective elites in recent times. Once
a commoner has got in, he has tended to close the door behind
him. In 1873 seventy-five per cent of the land in Great Britain
was owned by seven thousand people, and early in this century
the elite was often referred to as "the upper ten thousand." Even
today the accident of birth plays a critical role in British society:
some three-fourths of the millionaires who die in Britain each year
were born noble, and a recent article in the London *Times* reported that one's chances of being in the British *Who's Who* are
at least one in five if one's father was in it, but drop to one in fifteen hundred if one's father was working-class; and that in the
upcoming term at Oxford forty-seven per cent of the new undergraduates were coming from public (the counterpart to American
private) schools, which educate only six per cent of Britain's
schoolchildren, still mainly those who belong to the aristocracy.

The status of the aristocracy is reinforced by a marvellously
intricate and intimidating protocol, much of which is of surprisingly recent invention. It is easy to forget that one is essentially
dealing with just another elite, made up of families trying to hold
on to their property and prerogatives for as long as they can. The
correct forms of address for the various ranks of the peerage are
particularly tricky. If, for instance, one were going to write a
letter to the Dowager Marchioness of Montgomeryshire, one
would begin the letter Dear Lady Montgomeryshire; but if one
were having a conversation with her, in person, she would be
Lady Jane (or whatever her first name was), unless, of course, one
were on such intimate terms with her that one could address her
by her Christian name alone. But if one were speaking about her
to a third party, it would be a terrific gaffe to call her anything
but Lady Montgomeryshire—even though it would be perfectly
fine in a conversation about the Duke of Middlesex to refer to him
as the Duke of Middlesex; the form of address changes for the
higher grades of the peerage. "This shibboleth is so often trans-
gressed by novelists and others who love the peerage better than
they know its ways, that it may seem a little hard to believe how

wrong it appears to be among the people who know," the un-identified author or authors of *Titles and Forms of Address: A Guide to Their Correct Use,* which is generally regarded as the last word on the subject, write disdainfully.

The remarkable persistence of Britain's elite has been explained in a number of ways: "the inability of the English to abolish anything," according to one wry observer; "the peculiar character of English society," as Sir Lewis Namier has written, "civilian and plutocratic, though imbued with feudal habits and traditions." Lord Gowrie warned that one should "never underestimate the English aristocracy. They're superb showmen, and they will put up with any humiliation as long as they can keep their land." He also felt that the "ferocious and ruthless system of primogeniture," in which virtually everything goes to the eldest son and "the winner takes all," has had a good deal to do with it, as did the late Nancy Mitford (herself a daughter of the second Baron Redesdale), who declares in one of her novels that "the rule of primogeniture has kept together the huge fortunes of English lords."

The most prevalent and characteristic system of devolution in England—the way titles and upper-class landholdings have commonly descended since the seventeenth century—can be described as exclusive male primogeniture as opposed to the preferential-male type that made Doña Victoria Eugenia heiress to sixty titles. Some scholars call the English sort of primogeniture "tail-male," to distinguish it from the Salic primogeniture found in parts of Germany and France, which also excludes women. The English rule is "Heirs male of the body lawfully begotten": there must be an unbroken male descent from the original titleholder, or the title can go extinct. The Scottish rule has a little more play: *heredibus masculina quibiscunque*—heirs male whoever, even through a female line. Some Scottish titles can even be held by women. Not all English titles, moreover, have an exclusively male mode of inheritance. The succession to the throne is preferential-male, and medieval baronies created by writ of summons—a rare type of barony derived from the medieval common-law pattern for all free tenures—have a *nonrestrictive* mode of inheritance. If there is no son, the barony can go to a daughter. If there are several daughters, it can descend through either males or females *on each of their lines simultaneously,* in which case it is described as being "in abeyance." When all but one line dies out, the title can then be "called out of abeyance." "Some of the medieval baronies at present in existence were in abeyance for three or four centuries or even longer," Bence-Jones and Montgomery-Massingberd write; "and would still be in abeyance but for the nineteenth-century passion for medieval romanticism, which caused people who were the heirs of female co-heirs of long-abeyant baronies to petition the sovereign for the titles to be called out of abeyance in their favor. The tracking-down of abeyant peerages became a popular if expensive pastime, providing a comfortable living for professional genealogists and for the now all but extinct breed of 'peerage lawyers.' "

But most English titles have been created by Letters Patent, and the most common type of patent states unequivocally that if no male descended entirely through males from the original patentee can be found, the title and its entailed property revert to the crown. Sometimes an eligible descendant may exist but has not yet surfaced, and the title is declared "dormant" instead of "extinct," as in the case of one line of the Campbells, whose heir apparent went to the West Indies in the 1860s and hasn't been heard of since. Another case of dormancy involves a man named Richard St. Leger, of Santa Ana, California, who hasn't yet cleared his right to be called Lord Doneraile, although both Burke's and Debrett's recognize it.

If a male heir does exist, however, the other children can be completely excluded. The daughters, of course, are marriageable, and they receive a sort of premortem inheritance in the form of dowries, so their fate is not as dire as that of the younger sons, who are often left out in the cold and have to seek their own way in the world. In England, the accident of birth has been doubly important: not only one's class but which child one turns out to be has mattered tremendously. The fairy tale "Puss in Boots" is about the younger son of a miller, who upon his father's death gets only a cat, but the cat is very resourceful and proves to be worth the mill many times over: he tricks a king into believing that his penniless master is a rich marquis, which enables his master to marry the king's daughter. During the Middle Ages younger sons of poor knights often became troubadors. In later centuries they became clergymen, missionaries, Mounties, soldiers, colonial administrators. Some went into the professions and strengthened the middle class. Others became "remittance men" (who were paid to stay away) or degenerates. A few, like Randolph Churchill, the second son of the Duke of Marlborough, had distinguished political careers, but on the whole "their prospects in life were . . . not very good, especially as they were invariably brought up to enjoy a standard of living which they would never be able to afford on their own," Christopher Simon Sykes writes in his book *Black Sheep*. Randolph's son Winston would never have been able to launch himself in politics if he had not been able to supplement his small inheritance by writing books. "The weak-willed among them," Sykes continues, "such as Lord William Paget, and John Knatchbull, whose inheritance in 1819 was only £300, got into severe debt, and ended up turning to crime." On the Continent, wherever partible inheritance was in practice, younger sons fared better. In France, if the firstborn son became a count, for instance, his brothers at least got to be viscounts and received a portion of the estate. In Germany and Russia, everybody was a prince.

The system has not always been wholly good for the eldest son, either. "The very knowledge of the certainty of the inheritance to come often deprived them of any motive to lead a useful life," Sykes explains. "Many of them were condemned to spend years, living a kind of shadow existence while they awaited the death of a father, during which time it was only too easy for them to become men of luxurious tastes and corrupted morals. 'It requires a most gigantic resolution to suffer pain,' wrote Thomas Lyttelton, who was in such a position in 1766, 'when passion quickens every sense, and every enticing object beckons to enjoyment. I was not born a stoic, nor am I made to be a martyr.' In the Autumn of 1688, Lord Robert Spencer drank himself to death fourteen years before the death of his father, while George, Earl of Euston's dissipation was such that his father disinherited him in 1743."

Exclusive male primogeniture made for a lot more fluctuation than English society has generally been credited with. It was not unusual for a yeoman farmer, say, to be legitimately descended from the king, through several generations of younger sons whose fortunes had steadily worsened (as in Thomas Hardy's novel *Tess of the d'Urbervilles*); or for two grandsons of a duke to be in quite disparate circumstances. One grandson might be the present duke, with "a hundred thousand acres, three palatial country homes, and a priceless art collection," as Bence-Jones and Montgomery-Massingberd explain, and the other "a plain Mr. who has no money at all and has to earn his living." On the Continent class lines were harder to cross: "In Germany the *Almanach de Gotha*, the Debrett of Europe's royals and higher nobility," Robert Lacey writes in *Aristocrats*, "grades titles into separate classes according to the refinement of their pedigree—IA, IB, 2nd and 3rd—and with these distinctions go elaborate rules. Families in Section IA of the *Gotha* look down on the top ranks of British aristocracy, the dukes, because British dukes are allowed to perpetuate their dynasties by marrying barmaids and actresses—and have not infrequently done so. A German duke wishing to marry a barmaid would be required by his house rules to make his marriage only a morganatic one—his spouse and offspring being barred from the family title and inheritance. . . ." The concern with "blood" (a concept with little or no basis in biological reality, as we have seen) and with being *de bonne famille* has been much greater on the Continent, while in England, as Anthony Wagner writes, "each class shades into an indeterminable penumbra," and "to pretend that social mobility has been much less in the past than in fact it was" he dismisses as a "conspiracy of the conservatives and the revolutionaries."

Why this coldhearted system of devolution has prevailed in the British Isles is an interesting question. Other systems have existed. In thirteenth-century Shropshire, for instance, it was customary for the land to pass to the youngest son, while the "chattels" (everything else) went to the widow and her other children. (This strategy of "ultimogeniture" has been practiced elsewhere— by the Japanese before the Meiji Restoration of 1869, for instance, and by some Kirghiz and some Eskimo tribes—but it is uncommon. It creates "regency" problems: the young heir's guardians can take advantage of the situation, and many of them have.) In Kent there was a system known as *gavelkind,* in which all the brothers inherited equally. The Irish and the Welsh had similar modes of partible inheritance, but sharing proved counterproductive for them. In Ireland it led to poverty and overpopulation, and was a contributing factor to the potato famine of 1845. In Wales, by the time Henry VIII imposed primogeniture, perhaps three quarters of the population were *bonheddig,* "men with pedigrees," members of the ancient Welsh aristocracy "whose princely descent was un-impeachable," Bence-Jones and Montgomery-Massingberd write, but their land "had, through repeated splittings-up between broth-ers, dwindled to peasants' holdings." Partible inheritance is evi-dently not well suited to islands or small jurisdictions; there is not enough land to support it. In a tail-male system, however, the estate is transmitted each generation in one piece to only one heir, whose siblings tend to scatter; the ecological adaptiveness of the system may account in part for why the British aristocracy has lasted so long.

A map of the inheritance customs in Western Europe, however, prepared by the anthropologist Joan Thirsk, shows another intrigu-ing pattern and suggests an equally plausible cultural explanation: primogeniture prevails in the north, not only in Britain but in Scandinavia, while the south—Italy and most of the Mediterranean coast—is partible-inheritance country. Perhaps primogeniture re-quired a willingness to forsake one's kin which was unthinkable in the Latin countries, with their stronger extended-family attach-ments.

The disadvantage of primogeniture is that it puts a lot more pressure on the heirs, who must produce a male in each new generation to keep the title in their line. In preindustrial conditions, the anthropologist Jack Goody has told me, the chances that a couple would not have a male child who himself would live to reproduce were only about forty per cent. Examples of impressive dynastic continuity in the peerage, accordingly, are rare. All the roughly five thousand feudal knighthoods whose fees and services were enumerated in the Domesday Book of 1086–87 are extinct, and none of the three hundred-some families recognized by the late genealogist Lewis C. Lloyd as authentic descendants of Normans who came over with William the Conqueror are descended through males except perhaps for the House of Bassett (Norman for "short"). Although the primary sex ratio in Caucasian families slightly favors males—something like a hundred and six males are born for every hundred females—males in every society have had a greater chance of dying throughout life, even when childbirth was a great killer of women. "In the high Middle Ages, the aver-age noble dynasty in England lasted no more than three genera-tions," Lacey writes, "largely falling prey to battlefield mortality, for the code of chivalry was also the cult of death"; while Goody told me that at one point the Church owned about a third of England because of bequests from maiden women and widows. "The smaller ratio of male survivorship was critical to the buildup of all these great cathedrals we have," he said.

Male survivorship has been particularly problematic in the upper classes, where it has often mattered most, because family size has been smaller. As he studied the pedigrees of eminent Victorians, Francis Galton noticed that their reproductive success tended to be significantly lower than that of the general population, which puzzled him, because they were in the economically "fittest" segment of the population, and it stood to reason that they should have been having the most children. After considerable research and thought he came up with an ingenious explanation for the trend: a great number of the recently ennobled peers or their sons had tended to marry heiresses. For there to be an heiress at all meant that no male had been produced and was *ipso facto* proof that there was comparative infertility in her family. Testing his hypothesis, Galton found that the number of children the heiresses tended to produce did indeed correspond closely to the size of the families in which they had been born, and both were comparatively small. He concluded that sexual selection—the coupling of high ability with infertility—was ruining English society, thinning out its best sons. "I look upon the peerage as a disastrous situation," he wrote, "owing to its destructive effects on our valuable races. The most highly-gifted men are ennobled; their elder sons are tempted to marry heiresses, and their younger sons not to marry at all, for these have not enough fortune to support both a family and an aristocratical position. So the side-shoots of the genealogical tree are hacked off, and the leading shoot is blighted, and the breed is lost forever."

The survivorship of titles transmitted exclusively through males is comparable to that of surnames or Y chromosomes; in all three cases, a run of more than a hundred years is notable. Montgomery-Massingberd told me that in his experience with genealogy, the eleven "watertight" father-son generations in the pedigree of George Washington, who was "in remainder" to a peerage—in line if several people had died—was exceptional. The demographers James E. Smith and Phillip R. Kunz have calculated that in the United States in 1960 there was only a twenty-per-cent chance that a man would have descendants with his last name thirteen generations later, and that as many as forty per cent of the families existing in 1700 have been exterminated by war, famine, epidemic, or natural disaster, or have died out from failure to reproduce. "In principle all surnames are destined to die," the geneticist Luigi Cavalli-Sforza told me. The rate of extinction is tied to many variables: the political and geological stability of the region, its population growth rate, its social structure, the frequency of the particular surname, even accidents of fate.

American family names are probably dying out faster than ever before because people are having fewer children. Almost every time two people marry, a surname is lost. There may still be other bearers of the surname, of course, but a surprising number of surnames are held by only one person. Of the 1,286,556 surnames on the Social Security rolls of 1974, 448,663 were single occurrences. Assuming that the rate of surname extinction on a global basis is exceeding the number of new surnames being created, which seems reasonable (the question as far as I know has never been investigated), then we all seem to be slowly progressing to the day when everybody will have the same surname (except that maybe by then it will be a sur*number*). Surnames can provide information on the origins, admixture, and migrations of people, especially of males. Isonymy—the frequency of the same surname in a population—is "a better way to provide for remote consanguinity than any other pedigree method," Cavalli-Sforza and Bodmer write. When a surname dies out it is not as final as the extinction of a species, but a cultural artifact is lost, and even though the surname's original meaning may be long forgotten, the language is poorer, and the pervasive, relentless homogenization which our species seems to be undergoing chalks up another victim.

To offset the depressing fact that surnames, titles, and Y chromosomes are dying out all the time and are all, in principle, destined for extinction, one has only to consider that everybody who is alive today, male or female, has an unbroken patrilineal descent (assuming biological paternity in each generation), not only to the person who first acquired the surname but to the first male human. The names on the lineage are almost all lost, but the descent has to exist, because each of our fathers had to have had a father, and so did *their* fathers, and so on. After describing how in the seventeenth century a certain Countess Alexandrine von Taxis hired genealogists to fabricate a descent from the Torriani, a clan of warriors who had despotically ruled Lombardy until 1311, Lacey remarks, "Everyone has notable ancestors in their pedigree—after all in the last resort one can always go back to Adam and Eve." In fact, each of us possesses not only one but innumerable descents from Adam and Eve. Yet the world's present population represents only a small percentage of the possible number of people who could be living now: those of Adam and Eve's sons and daughters who have repeatedly defied the odds of dying out. And some of the lines that have survived have preserved not only surnames but generations of nobility. The twenty-four-year-old Ludovica Rangoni Machiavelli, for instance, who was recently held for three months by kidnappers, is a direct nominative-line descendant of the Florentine statesman and political theorist of the sixteenth century, Niccolò Machiavelli.

One way to save a surname from extinction is to hyphenate it. The numerous "double-barrelled" names in England are usually the result of a "special remainder" being granted to a man who has had no sons, so that his daughter can receive his inheritance on condition that she persuade her husband to tack his name on to his own (or to give up his own completely). Hugh Montgomery-Massingberd, who possesses surely one of the most orotund double-barrelled names in the realm, explained that the Massingberds had been extinct in the senior male baronial line since 1722. Massingberd had been assumed four times by females, the last of whom had married his grandfather, a man named Montgomery. "My father was obliged to take his mother's name to inherit tenancy of the house," Montgomery-Massingberd told me.

Some English people, like the young explorer who recently circumnavigated the globe from pole to pole, Sir Ranulph Twistleton-Wykeham-Fiennes, have triple-barrelled names, and there are even a few quadruple-barrelled names, like that of the Earl of Mexboro's sister, Lady Anne Sarah Alethea Marjorie Hovell-Thurlow-Cumming-Bruce. Others, rather than be stuck with such unwieldy monickers, have parted with their original surnames.

But before the options of hyphenation and relinquishment can even be entertained, a genealogical search must be initiated to find out if there are any male cousins with an unbroken patrilineal descent from the original patentee: however remote, they take precedence. "Now if only we were French," Lady Mountdore, the mistress of Hampton Place in Nancy Mitford's *Love in a Cold*

Climate, laments; "they really do seem to arrange things so very much better. To begin with, Polly would inherit all this instead of those stupid people in Nova Scotia." The dilemma of exclusive male primogeniture is that the title and everything that goes with it can pass to a complete stranger, and because cases of wildly zig-zagging devolution are found in many families, there has been even less biological continuity in the British aristocracy than there has been in other groups. "The blood-line in aristocracy is bunk," Dudley Fishburn, the executive editor of the *Economist,* recently observed to me. To make his point, he told the story of his maternal ancestors, the Copes, who, until the last of them—old Sir Mordaunt Leckonby Cope—died in 1976, carried one of the oldest baronetcies in England.

"The eleventh Baronet was childless and the title passed to an Irish sixth cousin, descended from a younger brother of the first Baronet, whose existence had not even been dreamt of. But if after two generations, or perhaps two years of the twelfth Baronet's installation, you had dared to suggest that his branch had had nothing to do with the building of his big house at Hampshire, his family would have been mortified."

🌱

Perhaps it was unfair of Galton to pin the low male survivorship rate of the peers solely on the comparative infertility of their heiress wives. Some lines have been extinguished by genetic effects of inbreeding. Others' chances of survival have been prejudiced by the tendency of families that have been *hors de combat* for some generations to become progressively refined or "etiolated," as the younger son of a duke described it to me; or by the males' penchant for homosexuality. "So many of the Somersets were homosexuals that it's rather surprising I'm here at all," a young woman named Anne Somerset, whose father is the first cousin once removed and heir presumptive of the Duke of Beaufort, told me cheerily. The Somersets are one of England's princely, almost subroyal families. Anne possesses an all-male descent with only one illegitimacy, from John of Gaunt, which makes her one of the last of the Plantagenets.

Most experts, however, are disinclined to believe that the effect of homosexuality on male survivorship has been significant, as most senior male titleholders, whatever their sexual orientation, have managed, as one expert puts it, to "do their duty to the line." The comparative infertility of the peerage is perhaps best understood as an example of a universal pattern, the negative correlation between affluence and family size. The further one traces the history of kinship, the clearer this pattern becomes.

The survival of an aristocratic line depends not only on its ability to produce an heir consistently, but on its ability to preserve its holdings through time—against which all sorts of things conspire, not least the tendency of the generations with inherited position, whose resources are often dwindling, to look down on the idea of work. In *A Distant Mirror: The Calamitous Fourteenth Century*, Barbara Tuchman describes the "sinking process" in the French nobility:

> Through disappearance by failure to produce a male heir or by sinking over the edge into the lower classes, and through inflow of the ennobled, the personnel of the nobility was in flux, even though the status was fixed as an order of society. The disappearance rate of noble families has been estimated at 50 per cent a century, and the average duration of a dynasty at three to six generations over a period from 100 to 200 years. An example of the sinking process occurred in a family called Clusel with a small fief in the Loire Valley. In 1276 it was headed by a knight evidently of too small resources to maintain himself in arms, who was reduced to the nonnoble necessity of tilling his fields and operating his mill with his own hands. Of three grandsons appearing in local records, one was still a squire, one had become a parish priest, and the third a rent-collector for the lord of the county. After a passage of 85 years no member of the lineage was any longer referred to as a noble.

Social trends are increasingly against the preservation of inherited holdings. The French aristocracy, for instance, has suffered a dip in its fortunes under the Socialist government of President Mitterand, and in England the devastating death duty, which can deprive an heir of up to eighty-three per cent of his inheritance, and the capital gains and capital transfer taxes (the latter designed to foil evasion of the death duty by premortem inheritance), have made it particularly hard on the lesser aristocracy, the "squirearchy," whose small estates are being lost through taxation at the rate of about twenty a year, although about two thousand are still left. "It's wretched to see them giving up, when their families have been in that part of the world for donkey's years," Montgomery-Massingberd told me, "but they have no choice. The squirearchy has always had the best Christian values, not the rich toughies."

And yet, on the whole, the British aristocracy, particularly its upper echelons, has held up remarkably well. Only eight per cent of the peerage has had to open its homes to the public and "to collect pennies from day trippers," Lacey reports. The point about aristocracy is not that it is biologically bogus, but that it continues to have such a hold on people. In the book section at Harrods department store, in London, a saleswoman told me that she was unable to keep books about the royal family on the shelf. And the aristocracy seems to be having a revival at the moment: while I was in England recently Mrs. Thatcher made her former home secretary William Whitelaw a viscount, the first hereditary title conferred since 1965, which a British acquaintance of mine applauded: "There's a limit to what you can strive for in your lifetime, but there's something beyond your life that matters to everybody." Whitelaw was an inscrutable choice, though, as he has no male children to pass the title on to.

The sociologist Vilfredo Pareto maintained that history is "a graveyard of aristocracies," a constant circulation of elites. Voltaire in a similar vein observed that the pageant of history is nothing but the sound of slippered feet going down the stairs as hobnailed boots are ascending them; and Nicholas Murray Butler, in his famous remark about decadence cycles in families, spoke of "three generations from shirtsleeves to shirtsleeves." "It seems a basic rule of human social organization that in any society—monarchy, dictatorship, oligarchy, or democracy—there is always a small ruling class and a larger class of those who are ruled," Lacey writes. "It is usual to protest to the contrary but in reality, power is never exercised totally by one man alone, nor, at the other extreme, by all the members of the society equally. In democratic countries, although the ballot box allows us to exercise some periodic control over which elite group should govern our lives, our choice is always confined to that sub-group of ambitious and thrusting individuals whose gratification stems from the public attention and self-esteem that they derive from being members of the ruling class."

The United States, in fact, offers, besides the government elite, an embarrassment of elites to shoot for, with little overlap in the genealogical qualifications for membership in them: the Wall Street financial elite, the New York theater, art-world, and literary elites, the Hollywood elite, the Texas "cashocracy," the Jewish "our-crowd" elite, the Irish "lace-curtain" elite, the Cosa Nostra, the Utah Mormon elite—to name but a few. Even the ostensibly classless societies of the Soviet Union and China have their party elites and their privileged families.

In his discussion of the pervasiveness of elites, Lacey mentions Plato's observation, thousands of years ago, that "to create a society in which men are truly equal, to prevent fathers from working to build up their status and then handing it onwards to their sons— the family itself must be abolished." But no society has been able to do without the family, though some (including the Soviets, as we shall see) have tried. The aristocracies of Europe are, in the end, only one case of such hard-working, devoted family men—a particularly important case, it happens, because modern individualism arose partly in reaction to the hereditary monopoly of resources and power they had succeeded in cornering.

6

The Rise of
Modern Individualism

DURING THE PAST FEW CENTURIES THE WEST HAS EXPERIENCED A revolution of consciousness which has dramatically affected interpersonal relations, particularly among kin. People have become aware of themselves and have begun to attach importance to themselves as individuals in ways, or to degrees, that had been largely unknown, and which are still unknown in much of the world. "Our fathers did not have the word 'individualism,'" Alexis de Tocqueville wrote, "which we have coined for our own use, because in their time there was indeed no individual who did not belong to a group and who could be considered absolutely alone." (According to the historian of ideas Steven Lukes, the word first appeared in its French form, *individualisme*, and "grew out of the reaction to the French Revolution and to its alleged source, the Enlightenment.") Even today people in other societies have little or no sense of ego, or one so radically different that the type of self-centeredness which has arisen in the West is often quite incomprehensible to them. "What we call a being or an individual or an I is only a combination of . . . five aggregates . . . [which] are all impermanent, all constantly changing," Walpola Sri Rahula writes in his *What the Buddha Taught*, for instance, and ". . . the idea of self (*sakkaya-ditthi*) . . . is a false idea, a mental for-

mation which is nothing but one of . . . [the] fifty-two forma-
tions of the fourth aggregate."

Several types of individualism were already quite well developed in ancient Greece. The philosophy of Epicureanism was
a kind of hedonistic individualism. Its goals were limited, as the
classical historian W. Windelband writes, to "a search for the
means of attaining individual happiness." It emphasized self-
development and self-regulation, and offered a complete method
of living well. Political individualism—the idea of civil rights—
started to evolve in Athens, but it applied only to the *polites*, citizens, both of whose parents had to be Athens-born. In Rome too,
after the Punic Wars, with the growth of the army and of civil
administration, the state became increasingly involved in guar-
anteeing individual rights, and by the fall of the Empire (when
hedonistic individualism had reached one of its historic peaks) it
had largely replaced the citizen's kinship group as his primary
focus of loyalty.

By 300 A.D. the other great rival and enemy of traditional kinship—the Church—had already begun to undermine Europe's
indigenous traditions of kinship and marriage. Most devastating
was its taboo of marriage to close kin of any kind. Adapting the
Roman bilateral approach to reckoning descent, the Church banned
marriage within "forbidden degrees" of relatedness (late Rome,
the legal historian Charles Donahue recently told me, had a comparatively mild taboo against marrying *cognati*, literally "those one
was born with." You could marry first cousins, but you couldn't
marry brothers or sisters, ascendants or descendants, aunts or
uncles, though an exception was made for the Emperor Claudius,
who wanted to marry his niece). The avuncular and first-cousin
alliances through marriage which were so important to traditional
kinship could now be made only with special dispensation from
the Church, or without its knowledge. The reason why the
Church got into this is not completely clear. "In the beginning the
Church seems to have pushed exogamy because it might lead to
peace," Donahue says. "The more people it could get everybody
related to, the less feuding there would be." Fox, however, believes
that the Church, like the modern state, has relentlessly persecuted kinship because it represents a rival center of power.

Whatever the Church's original motive for tabooing consanguineous marriage, by the late twelfth century the sale of dispen-

sations, like the sale of indulgences, had become an important source of income. The forbidden degrees reached their outer limit in 1059 with the encyclical of Pope Nicholas II, which required that "if anyone has taken a spouse within the seventh degree [his sixth cousin, in other words], he will be forced canonically by his bishop to send her away; if he refuses, he will be excommunicated." It was through this rule—on the ground that they were distant cousins whose marriage could not be sanctioned by the Church— that Louis VII of France was persuaded to divorce Eleanor of Aquitaine in 1152, which cleared the way for her to marry Henry Plantagenet, the Duke of Normandy, later Henry II of England. The Church also banned adoption, plural marriage, concubinage (which persisted in the nobilities, however: most of the people who claim Charlemagne as an ancestor, for instance, are descended from his children by concubines), and the levirate—a man's obligation to marry his brother's widow. It also eroded the rights of collaterals and wider groups of kin by emphasizing the nuclear unit as all-important, so that the family in Europe came to be perceived and perhaps even constructed differently from families anywhere else in the world.

There seems to have been a good deal of native individualism in Western Europe, even before the circle of kinship began to be narrowed by the Church. The Franks, as we saw, had a mechanism for checking out of their kinship group, which was apparently used mainly by those who didn't want to be involved in a feud. The Germanic tribes had highly individualistic notions of land tenure which lapped over into the Norman peasant land system. The people who colonized the British Isles seem to have become even more independent. Except in a few districts they didn't go in for the joint land ownership that prevailed on the Continent. They married late or not at all; a high degree of celibacy and delayed marriage for both men and women have been features of English society for as long as there are records of it; so has great respect for the individual, including tolerance of his eccentricities. At the time of King Alfred the Anglo-Saxon kinship group was known as a *sib*. It was a cousin of the kindred of the ancient Teutons, which reckoned descent by "stocks" (a "stock," Fox explains, was all the descendants of a person or a married couple; a kindred of second-cousin range thus had four "stocks," one for each pair of great-grandparents). The *sib* was bilateral, like the more loosely structured bands of hunter-gatherers. Members of the same *sib* could not marry and the males were under obligation to each other; when blood money was due, the "sword side," or patrilateral kin of the man who had committed the offense, had to pay out more than the "distaff side." Compared to structures that were evolving on the Continent like the Balkan *zadruga*, which could have up to a hundred and fifty members in the same household, and the *frèrèche* of southern France, in which whole lineages lived communally, in fraternal groups, the *sib* was small and fractured; the full complement of possible members within, say, second-cousin range was seldom represented.

Early in the century the anthropologist Bertha Phillpots advanced a theory to explain why this should be, which has yet to be disproved: kinship tends to be weak among people who have had to travel a long distance to get to where they eventually settle. The *sibs* were already small by the time they reached England; not everybody got on the boats. Once there, primogeniture had a further dispersing effect. The oldest son or heir stayed in the fold, forming what is known as a "stem family" (the parents, the heir and his wife, and their children), while the other sons moved on, some to form nuclear families of their own, others to remain single. Thus the "neolocal" residential pattern prevalent in industrial societies was already established for the younger sons by primogeniture.

A further indication of the early prominence the English gave to the nuclear family is that by 1066 its members were already linguistically marked off from the other relatives who were included in larger family systems. This stunningly obvious fact (as it now seems) was pointed out to me by Goody: after the Norman Conquest, the words for people in the nuclear family—father, mother, son, daughter, brother, sister—remained Germanic, but Norman French was used for everybody outside—uncles, aunts, and cousins. In addition, the distinction between mother's side and father's, which is still critical in places like the Middle East and China, was eliminated; in anthropological terms, the kin terminology shifted from a "bifurcate—collateral" system to a "lineal" one. "See how Shakespeare uses the term 'cousin,'" Goody remarked. "It could be anybody."

Although it has been fashionable in some anthropological circles since the nineteen-twenties to regard the nuclear family as a creature of the Industrial Revolution, Goody considers this view "nonsense." A careful study of English parish records and other demographic sources made in 1972 by his colleague Peter Laslett revealed that the English have lived mainly in nuclear-family blocks since at least the late sixteenth century; that the mean household size did not in fact plunge dramatically, as it was assumed to have between the late eighteenth and mid-nineteenth centuries, when the country industrialized; and that the "classical family of Western nostalgia," as the family historian William Goode has trenchantly described it, may never have existed, at least in England and much of Western Europe.

This startling discovery led some to revise their assumptions about the nuclear family; it is now seen, in the description of the sociologists Brigitte and Peter Berger, for example, as "a *precondition*, rather than a *consequence*, of modernization." "Why did the Industrial Revolution take place in England, anyway?" Fox asked me recently. "England didn't have the greatest accumulation of capital. She wasn't richer in natural resources than other countries; so the revolution didn't spring out of commerce. If it had, Italy would have been a more probable choice. I think it happened there because of the highly individualistic and thus potentially capitalistic nature of Anglo-Saxon society."

🌳

Three "ages" in the history of Western civilization—the Renaissance, the Reformation, and the Enlightenment (to the extent that these ages existed, and are not just oversimplifications designed to package history more coherently for later generations)—are credited by most writers on the subject with having had a hand in the rise of modern individualism. The Renaissance, of course, produced an extraordinary flowering of artistic self-expression. By the thirteenth century, according to the Swiss historian Jacob Burckhardt, Italy had already begun to "swarm with individuality; the ban on human personality was dissolved"; and the sixteenth century, as J. Bronowski and Bruce Mazlish write in *The Western Intellectual Tradition*, "was a century in which individualism was a dominant characteristic. The ability and power of the individual—whether artist or statesman—was given great respect, and perhaps exaggerated importance." At the conclusion of their book the two historians make the following argument:

> In the 500 years since Leonardo, two ideas about man have been especially important. The first is the emphasis on the full development of the human personality. The individual is prized for himself. His creative powers are seen as the core of his being. The unfettered development of individual personality is praised as the ideal, from the Renaissance artists through the Elizabethans, and through Locke and Voltaire and Rousseau. This vision of the freely developing man, happy in the unfolding of his own gifts, is shared by men as different in their conceptions as Thomas Jefferson and Edmund Burke. It is the picture which Hegel had of the heroes of the age of Napoleon, and—though this will be a surprise to those who have not read him—which Karl Marx had of the artisans and workers whom he idealized. . . . The self-fulfillment of the individual has itself become part of a larger, more embracing idea, the self-fulfillment of man . . . which inspired much of the scientific and technical progress in the centuries that followed.

The second idea was the idea of freedom; and even in the Middle Ages, with the signing of the Magna Carta in England, and with the creation of a representative assembly called the *vieche* in Novgorod, then one of the most important city-states in Eastern Europe, there were important developments in political individualism. But these developments, like the Greek *demokratia,* enhanced the civil rights only of the upper class—the English barons and the Novgorodian boyars.

A final effect of the Renaissance was that it put Europe back into intellectual touch with the individualistic traditions of the classical world, and gave people in the fifteenth and sixteenth centuries new models to consider as the old feudal order came apart and Europe started to emerge from what the sociologist David Riesman has described as the "collectivist, tradition-directed" society of the Middle Ages.

The Protestant Reformation provided a religious foundation for the heightened sense of individual capability which had begun to flower during the Renaissance, and provided those who left the Catholic Church not only with new approaches to Christianity but with a new orientation toward their society and themselves. With Martin Luther's defiance of the Diet of Worms, one of the great moments in the history of Western individualism, the man who dares to follow his own conscience and to stand up against the corrupt "system"—a figure still celebrated in countless novels and movies—became one of our most popular heroes. The next three centuries were spanned by what Riesman has called the "inner-directed" phase of intensive individualization. From now on, the individual was not as much responsible to others— whether they were in his family, community, or class—as he was to himself and to the personal commitment he had made to God to make the most of his abilities, to eschew vices like (this list is the Bergers') "idleness, thoughtlessness, intemperance, vanity, and self-indulgence in all forms," and to develop such qualities as "hard work, diligence, discipline, attention to detail, frugality, and the systematic (not sporadic) cultivation of willpower." With Benjamin Franklin's words, "Help yourself, and God will help you," "*any* individual," the Bergers write, "regardless of the accident of birth, is now liberated to advance himself."

🌲

Although "Luther himself hated the economic individualism of his age and fiercely attacked it in his pamphlets," Bronowski and Mazlish write, ". . . the result of Luther's divorce of man's inner life from civil activity was to free economics from ethical and religious constraints and to foster economic as well as religious individualism." Specifically, the Reformation went hand in hand with what has come to be called the "Protestant work ethic," which helped provide the spiritual basis for capitalism.

In the reclaimed salt marshes of the northern Netherlands, between 1600 and 1690, a new breed of businessman, with the blessing of the "Great Governor" (as John Calvin had recast the Christian godhead the century before) and no local aristocracy to hold it back, fell to realizing its calling—making as much money through commerce as it possibly could—and became the envy of Europe. (It should be emphasized that Calvin was as opposed to religious and political individualism as Luther was to economic individualism, and that the significant contributions he made to them were unintentional. To Calvin, material success was the religious duty of the lucky few who had been included by divine predestination among the Elect; nobody really had a choice in these matters.)

As this new class took hold in cities and towns across Europe, a new type of family—"the small and intensely private family that is frugal and ambitious, circumspect and child-centered," in the psychiatrist Robert Coles's description—slowly evolved. It was not structurally different from the nuclear family in which some Europeans were already grouped, but it had novel attitudes about child rearing: instead of being inducted into adulthood as quickly as possible, as they had been during the Middle Ages, children in the new bourgeois family were given a world of their own to play and develop in, a period of grace before joining the company of adults. They were dressed in their own distinctive clothes and given their own work to do—schoolwork. Boys were the first "specialized children." In his fascinating study, *Centuries of Childhood,* the French historian Philippe Ariès amasses a great deal of evidence for his controversial thesis that childhood, as we now understand it, was "invented" by the rising bourgeoisie. One part of the process which must have contributed greatly to the individualization not only of children but of everybody in the family was the reorganization of the bourgeois house. "It is easy to imagine the promiscuity which reigns in these rooms where nobody could be alone," Ariès writes of the medieval house, "which one had to cross to reach any of the communicating rooms, where several couples and several groups of boys or girls slept together (not to speak of the servants, of whom at least some must have slept beside their masters, setting up beds, which were still collapsible, in the room or just beside the door), in which people forgathered to have their meals, to receive their friends or clients, and sometimes to give alms to beggars." But in the eighteenth century the modern house came into being: separate bedrooms, each with its own door, and outfitted with the new water closet and hygienic equipment, opened on a hallway that channelled through traffic, and there were special rooms—parlors and dining rooms—for gathering at mealtime and entertaining visitors. For the first time, people had their own space.

Other developments reinforced the process of individualization. People began to have their own plates, instead of descending together on a communal platter. Through the eighteenth century it was not unusual for a traveller putting up at an inn to have to sleep in the same bed with a complete stranger; gradually this came to be seen as an intolerable impingement on the paying guest's privacy. By the end of that century, too, as the cost of making silvered glass decreased, mirrors were no longer a luxury that only the rich could afford, and they began to appear in the homes of ordinary people and to enhance their self-consciousness. As infant mortality decreased, the psychologist Howard Gadlin recently told me, children began to be named soon after birth—it had been common to delay naming until the child's survival seemed fairly certain—and to be given their own names, instead of that of a dead older sibling.

Perhaps the most important preindustrial technological contribution to the process was the privatization of time, which was made possible by the mass production of clocks and watches. David Landes, who has written a history of timekeeping, recently told me that domestic clocks appeared in the houses of courtiers, noblemen, and rich bourgeois in the fifteenth century; by the seventeenth century they began to look alike, to have a "semi-batch pattern," suggesting that quantities of them were being made by the same people; by the end of the seventeenth century, with the invention of the coiled mainspring, which enabled clocks to be made smaller and more portable, they were widespread in the commercially oriented societies of Holland and England—even in the country, where "people were picking up the values of city dwellers." As for pocket watches, the rich had them by the beginning of the sixteenth century, and by the end of the seventeenth century the English were "most ready to use them as an instrument, not just as an ornament." By the end of the eighteenth century workers were pooling their money to buy watches, were buying them on time, or were holding lotteries whose prize was the price of a watch. The invention of the balanced spring made for a quantum leap in accuracy, and when time could be kept by anybody with a loss of only two or three minutes a day, it became a precious possession. People could order their day as they wanted it, within the limits of their work requirements; they achieved temporal autonomy, and they started to become resentful of being kept waiting, of having *their* time taken from them. Time became something the driven individualist had to capitalize on. Important people who had condescended to give you a few minutes of their time began to glance nervously at their wristwatches, signalling that the interview was over. To Jean Jacques Rousseau, whose father Isaac was a watchmaker, watches symbolized what was wrong with eighteenth-century Europe. "He even sold his watch, that fundamental instrument, practically and symbolically, of modern mechanical civilization," Bronowski and Mazlish write. Toward the end of his life, he commented on himself in the third person: " 'It was one of the happiest moments of his life when, renouncing all plans for the future in order to live from day to day, he got rid of his watch. "Thank heavens!" he exclaimed in a transport of joy, "I shall no longer need to know what time it is!" ' Time had created all the institutions of corrupt society; Rousseau, in becoming an 'anarchronist,' had sponged it all away. Society could now be reconstructed, on a 'natural' footing."

More than Luther or Calvin, or perhaps any one person, John Locke (1632–1704) deserves to be considered, and traditionally has been considered, the father of modern individualism; it is in Locke that the entire complex historical process until then, and the revolutionary developments that were already changing the face of Europe, seem to crystallize. Locke was a vigorous opponent of absolutism and hereditary privilege, and his most tangible contribution to Western individualism was political. It had already been clear since the Peasants' Revolt of 1381—when manors had been torched, landlords and lawyers murdered, and perhaps a hundred thousand men, revolting against the attempt of the aristocracy to restore the old servile tenures, had marched on London and taken the Tower—that not everybody went along with the hereditary principle. A famous bit of egalitarian doggerel that circulated around this time asked:

> When Adam delved and Eve span,
> Who was then a gentleman?

In Locke's own turbulent century Charles I had been beheaded in 1649 by Puritan Roundheads repudiating the divine right of kings, and the House of Lords had been abolished. Although the Puritan Revolution failed in itself—eleven years later the House of Stuart was restored—it "developed and extended [the beliefs in religious, political, and economic individualism] from their origins in the Reformation and handed [them] on to modern times in dramatic and unforgettable terms," as Bronowski and Mazlish write. In the Glorious Revolution of 1688 the British aristocracy, legislated out of existence by the Commonwealth as "useless and dangerous," made a remarkable comeback: the great noble Whig families took matters in their own hands and overthrew James II. The Glorious Revolution was a glorious victory for Parliament; from then on the sovereign no longer ruled by divine right, but by the grace of the people, and England became a constitutional monarchy.

Locke wrote his *Two Treatises on Government* in 1690 on behalf of the Whigs while he was living in Holland. His main purpose was to refute "the False Principles and Foundation of Sir Robert Filmer," whose *Patriarcha: or the Natural Power of Kings* had appeared in 1680. In it Filmer reiterated the traditional arguments for royal absolutism: that the king's right to rule is God-given, inherited by direct patrilineal descent from Adam; that his kingdom is like a family, and he has as complete authority over his subjects as a father has over his dependents.

Special relationships with divinities and paternalistic similes such as Filmer propounded are standard at the chiefdom and kingdom stages of social evolution. Many of the elaborately faked pedigrees—why the Bagratids, for instance, traced themselves first from the pagan god Angl-Tork', and later from the House of David; why the late emperor Haile Selassie proclaimed himself a direct descendant of Solomon and Bathsheba; why, as the Russian intellectual historian James Billington has written, "hagiography was applied wholesale to the description of tsars, and imperial ancestries were traced to miracle-working saints as well as emperors of antiquity"—are explained by this need for divine or superhuman sanction. In chiefdoms, absolute monarchies, and totalitarian dictatorships, the idiom of politics is kinship. Private law becomes public law, *patria potestas* is taken from the male head of the primary kinship group, whose authority has weakened, and is transferred to the chief or king.

Locke felt that the equation of sovereignty with fatherhood

was dangerously fallacious, that government and kinship were completely different things and should not be confused in people's minds. Even the parents' authority was restricted, because man possessed himself only in a sort of stewardship, and children were artifacts of God, held in trust by their parents, who had the obligation to preserve, nourish, and educate them, as the anthropologist Thomas de Zengotita, who has studied the impact of Locke's social thought and the intellectual climate of his time, explained to me. Locke's conception of the State of Nature was diametrically opposed to that of Thomas Hobbes, who argued that men by nature are nasty, brutish, self-seeking animals at constant war with their fellows, and that in order to transcend their natural anarchy, they must submit to the absolute authority of a sovereign. Locke saw the State of Nature as a "State of Perfect Freedom" for men "to order their Actions and dispose of their Possessions as they think fit . . . without asking leave, or depending upon the will of any man." The insistence that private property was the natural right of every man was a direct blow at hereditary privilege, and at the same time, Locke went after heredity from a different direction in his philosophy of empiricism, declaring that each person was at birth a blank slate, a *tabula rasa,* and what he became was the sum of his experiences (which, as we have seen, is true of cultural and psychological inheritance, if not of genetic inheritance); although the nature-nurture controversy was centuries from erupting, he was already a staunch environmentalist. In his personal life, he was very much the detached individualist. He had no family, no church, no community. He never stayed in one place for very long and valued his freedom from engagement.

The impact of Locke's ideas on Western history is incalculable. The theorists of the American Revolution drew heavily on his politics. The famous phrase in the Declaration of Independence, "life, liberty and the pursuit of happiness," echoes both his declaration that no one has the right to harm another in his "life, liberty or possessions" and his ethical position that happiness and pleasure are universal goals, which everybody is entitled to pursue.

The French Revolution was more directly influenced by the egalitarian rhetoric of Rousseau, but Rousseau himself was heavily indebted to Locke. The slogan *Liberté, Egalité, Fraternité* retained the idiom of kinship but projected a more democratic image by substituting paternalism with fraternalism. Locke continued to influence affairs for another century and a half or so, wherever states were ready to outgrow the hereditary principle.

The unparallelled progress of mathematics, physics, and the natural sciences—particularly medicine—during Locke's lifetime had a profound influence on him and, de Zengotita claims, played an important role in the making of the modern "detached" consciousness. "It was in the seventeenth century that the fear of touching the dead was overcome," he told me. "A few Renaissance humanists like Leonardo had dissected cadavers, but they had been greatly criticized. Now doctors began to perform autopsies and to look at the body as if it were a piece of machinery. William Harvey, who was studying how blood circulates and had been impressed by a spectacular water pump that had been installed near his house on the Thames, discovered that the heart was a pump. There was an almost unbounded faith in the power of reason, and a euphoric belief in the possibility of human omniscience. Locke, who had studied medicine and, though he never took a doctor's degree, became the personal physician of Lord Shaftesbury, the leader of the Whig faction, was well aware of these developments. Like Newton, he believed that God was the great mechanic, the maker of the cosmic clock, and that the intricate workings of the natural world had been created for man to take apart and rearrange to suit his needs. He referred to the 'almost worthless raw material' that 'Nature and Earth furnish,' and wrote that 'the intrinsic value of things depends on their usefulness to the life of man.' All this represented a huge transformation of attitude. For thousands of years people had been in awe of nature. Now they were out to 'harness' it, and this generated the detached, self-centered, manipulative outlook of Westerners today."

A luminous figure who came on the scene a little later, championing the ideas of Newton and Locke; a great propagandist of individual potential—his famous metaphor spoke of the need to cultivate one's own garden—was born into the French bourgeoisie and given the name François-Marie Arouet. His father was a well-to-do notary, and when his son came of age he offered to get him a position leading to advancement in the civil service. But the son would have no truck with nepotism. "He saw the family as a provincial trap that prevented people from becoming free, cosmo-

politan citizens of the world," de Zengotita explained. "He wanted
to be a completely self-invented person, so he changed his name
to Voltaire."

❦

The individualism that was already a conspicuous feature of
European society by the time of the Enlightenment came about,
as I have tried to show, as the result of many mutually reinforcing
developments. At the same time that people were becoming more
differentiated as individuals, their kinship groups were diminishing, perhaps in importance as well as in size. Three products of
scientific experimentation in the late eighteenth century—the spin-
ning jenny, the steam engine, and the steam railroad—had shat-
tering repercussions for traditional kinship. They brought on
what is usually labelled the Industrial Revolution, and essentially
dissolved agricultural society as it had been known for millennia.
The Industrial Revolution subverted the traditional gerontocratic
nature of kinship by recruiting the young and giving them independent earning power, so that they were no longer controlled by
their elders (although this had already begun to happen before
the Industrial Revolution, the Bergers point out, with the rise of
wage labor at the very beginnings of modern capitalism). The
Pied Piper of Hamelin may have in fact been an allegorical figure for the process of generational severance in the Rhine Valley,
where factory jobs had already begun to lure the young from
farm families centuries before industrialization. The newly recruited generations became neolocal, like young sons cut loose by
primogeniture; the family (where it was not already nuclear) became nuclear; as van den Berghe writes in his book *Human Family Systems: An Evolutionary Approach*, "It is bad enough having
to move from Kansas City to Buffalo when the company promotes
you, or to follow the harvest of industrial crops as an agricultural
laborer; it would be unthinkable to take a whole tribe of relatives
with you." Fulfilling the demands of a large kinship group was
clearly incompatible with the individual's new need to be mobile
in order to make the most of his skills and his opportunities, so
the group reduced itself to the bare minimum and came to resemble, paradoxically, the kinship systems of the most ecologically
precarious hunter-gatherers like Eskimos, who do not have a
stable, dependable source of livelihood either. The modern Amer-

ican family is in fact classified by anthropologists as "Eskimo-type." "A loose system of bilateral descent and neolocal residence with shifting combinations of nuclear families is a flexible system suitable to both the simplest and most complex of societies," van den Berghe writes, "the reasons being basically the same: to make the best of available resources, given the level of technology, or, in other words, to maximize individual benefits." "The most effective individual in this society is someone whose ties are severable," de Zengotita told me. His own family, he said, followed the typical American middle-class pattern. "My brothers and sisters have radiated all over the country and started families of their own. My parents still live in the house in Duxbury, Massachusetts, where we grew up. We used to touch base only on holidays or whenever things went wrong, but now that we've had kids, we go there in a different spirit. I've never even met my father's brother."

Besides shedding most of its members outside the nuclear family, the kinship group gave up many of its functions with industrialization. It was no longer "society" for the individual—his main political, military, or religious affiliation. As more and more people went off to work—a process which by the end of the nineteenth century had become the rule rather than the exception—their households changed: they went from being units of production to being units of consumption. "Only in more advanced industrial societies is the divergence between family and economic production almost complete," van den Berghe writes. "The phenomenon is barely a century old in a few countries; much less in a few more; still largely unknown in most."

Children were no longer educated at home past the age of five or six, and after they had finished school they operated increasingly in settings that were not controlled by their kin—the university, the factory, the office (although family businesses were common in the early phases of industrialization, and in developing countries they still are). The relationships that developed in these settings often mimicked kinship, however. In Japan, for instance, where factory jobs are often held for life, the worker-boss relationship has been consciously modelled after the father-son relationship. The academic world is strongly paternalistic and gerontocratic: the graduate student must join the school of thought of his mentor and often produce work that will be published under his mentor's name; his progress depends largely on his ability to cast himself as a helpful and willing protégé, because his mentor controls not only his funding but his ability to secure a "tenure-track" appointment, for which competition is increasingly intense. A great professor can elicit from his students admiration and respect that are tantamount to filial piety; to honor him on his retirement, students of the limnologist G. E. Hutchinson, for instance, drew up a "phylogenetic tree" of his "intellectual descendants," which was "restricted to those possessing doctoral degrees," the legend explains. "Main branches and capitalized names represent Hutchinson's own doctoral students. Secondary branches and twigs with lower-case names indicate second- and third-generation students. Terminal leaves indicate completed degrees, their absence means Ph.D. expected in 1971. The attendant fauna represent people who have done post-doctoral work with Hutchinson."

For many who belong to the postindustrial, "informatic" age, the most important human organization after the family is the office. For some single people, especially, their career is their life, and the office is their family, providing them with many of the same types of relationships, services, and experiences that are found in traditional kinship groups. The office offers: health insurance and a pension (instead of a medicine man and care by the younger generations); camaraderie; father figures in the form of supportive bosses; gerontocratic hierarchies; figurative nepotism (protégés are promoted and advanced as if they were kin); the same sort of intrigues, power struggles, and double dealing; similar obligations. Many businesses, of course, are controlled by an infrastructure of actual kin—the people who started them, and relatives by blood or marriage, who later become involved. But the analogy between kinship and work place is imperfect: "You can join an office, leave it, or be kicked out of it," the business reporter John Brooks recently explained; and as a man who works in a New York office recently observed, "The glue isn't blood, it's ambition." A close relationship formed at work often dissolves when the colleague is transferred; people get along because they are "in the trenches" together and they have to.

Inevitably, as parents lost control over the adult lives of their children; as marriage for "love" (a recent luxury, according to some scholars) replaced arranged ones; as industrial society grew increasingly "hot," in Lévi-Strauss's term—changing so rapidly that history was no longer measured in secular "ages" but in decades—the generations within families, having grown up in different mini-eras, had increasingly little in common with each other besides their genes. The "generation gap" is also a comparatively recent phenomenon (the term itself, in fact, didn't come into common use much before 1970). It is a sign that traditional values are obsolete or in transition. One such gap occurred in the United States two decades ago, between the generation that came to maturity during the nineteen-sixties and their parents, who had grown up in the nineteen-thirties—a completely different mini-era.

As medical advances dramatically increased the life expectancy of people in industrial countries (in the United States, from 47.3 years in 1900 to 73.6 years in 1980), a new and increasingly important category of "senior citizens," whose needs were taken care of by extrafamilial agencies and whose collective experience was no longer valued, arose in the population. After the Second World War retirement communities began to appear, particularly in Florida, where people past the mandatory retirement age, whose children were already caught up in nuclear families of their own, could live out the rest of their years. The first communities were simple—trailer parks, bungalow colonies—but as the trend continued, they became more elaborate. In recent years entire towns have been built from scratch exclusively for senior citizens, and according to a recent estimate, about nine hundred and twenty-four thousand of the country's twenty-seven million Americans sixty-two years old and older live now in two thousand three hundred and sixty-three nongovernmental retirement communities, and six hundred thousand are in federally provided housing—a small but significant minority. The journalist Frances Fitzgerald has compared the segregation of the elderly and the creation of a separate category of "senior citizens" with the "invention of childhood," at the other end of the age spectrum, centuries earlier, by the rising bourgeoisie. Many people have deplored the phenomenon as one of the most inhuman aspects of our society. Some nomadic societies, like the Bakhtiari, of southern Iran, leave their elders behind to die when they are no longer able to keep up and have become a drain on the group; but the elders are valued and honored up to the moment of their abandonment, sometimes on one side of a river that is too wide and fast for them to cross.

In addition to making it possible for the elderly to live by themselves, affluence has reduced kinship literally, by lowering fertility. This is one of the great paradoxes of human behavior: the better off people are, the fewer children they tend to have, even though they are in a better position to have children and, if they belong to Western society, the risks involved have been largely eliminated. The negative correlation between affluence and fertility was already clear in the Roman Empire: "Wealth rotted out the best in the Roman character," John Shaw Billings writes. "Family life went on the rocks of unbridled sexuality, and the birth rate fell precipitately." Galton found low fertility in the peerage and attributed it to infertility of the heiresses the peers had married. The rest of English society, however, was having a population explosion characteristic of the early stages of industrialization and comparable to the one triggered by the Agricultural Revolution.

It was only after the fruits of industrialization, mingling with the fruits of colonial exploitation, and the tapping of vast reservoirs of latent energy in the form of fossil fuel brought unprecedented prosperity in England and a few other countries, and various mechanical and chemical methods of birth control were made widely available by mass production, that the growing middle class in these countries had a reasonable hope of attaining a high standard of living by curtailing reproduction, and began to have fewer children. The mean household size in England did not begin to fall sharply until 1891; and it has been falling continuously ever since. The United States has exhibited the same pattern: the increasing "self-consciousness" of the individual has overridden the drive of his "constituent genes" to be perpetuated in the bodies of children, as van den Berghe puts it; the individual has come to "value increasingly things that are made possible through advanced technology and a high material standard of living but from which 'excessive' reproduction detracts, and . . . [to subordinate] reproduction to other, more valued goals."

In 1959 the sociologist David M. Potter perceived that "plenty" was not only lowering fertility but weakening generational bonds: "By making it economically possible for newly married couples to maintain separate households of their own, it has almost destroyed the extended family as an institution in America and has ordained that the child shall be reared in a 'nuclear' family, so-called, where his only intimate associates are his parents and his siblings, with even the latter far fewer than in families of the past."

At present American couples, according to one census, are having an average of only 2.2 children—barely replacing themselves, in other words. Some groups are not even doing that: the birth rate of American Jews, for instance, is 1.6 children per couple. While the population growth rate—the ratio between births and deaths—in the United States was only .6 per cent in 1977, Brazil, which did not have any heavy industry to speak of until the nineteen-fifties, had a rate of 2.8 per cent. Van den Berghe reports different figures: in 1790 the mean family size in the United States was 5.7; in 1981 it was 2.7; "nearly all of that decline," he writes, "is attributable not to a shift from extended to nuclear family, but rather to a reduction of fertility." Carolyn Peters, a researcher with the Fertility Branch of the United States Department of the Census, recently traced for me a precipitous drop in the number of children that American women, married or not, in the childbearing years of fifteen to forty-four, have been having in the last three decades: from 1955 to 1959 they had an average of 3.7 children; at the beginning of the nineteen-seventies they had 2.5; in 1976, 1.7; and in 1980 the average went up slightly, to 1.8. "To replace the population, each woman would need to have 2.1 children," she explained, "so at the moment we are not replacing ourselves. The population growth rate is below replacement level, and if there is no change in the rate over a long period, and no significant immigration, eventually we will reach zero growth." By contrast, during the mid-nineteen-seventies women in Afghanistan were having an average of 7.7 children; in Algeria, 7.4; and in Bangladesh, 7.2.

The decline in fertility is not only tied to postindustrial affluence, however. Urbanization has dramatically diminished family size, too, and as van den Berghe points out, with eighty to ninety per cent of the population living in cities, it is their reproductive behavior that largely determines the demography of the entire country.

> Trying to raise six children in New York City is quite a different proposition [from having six children on a farm in Kansas]. Family space, for

one thing, is reduced from the 160-acre farm to the 1200-square-foot apartment. The cost of living is so high that the incentive for the wife to earn wages increases proportionately, and, of course, if she works outside, she can't very well be pregnant and raise infant children all the time. For most urban families, having two children or having six children is the difference between a comfortable middle-class standing, often sustained by a double income, or what most Americans have come to consider intolerable poverty. Not unexpectedly, many people opt for fewer children.

The cultural anthropologist Marvin Harris has a different economic theory about reduced fertility. People have children, he suggests, according to the return they expect from the investment, and because "the cost to parents of rearing a middle-class child to college age in the United States now [in 1977] stands at $80,000, only a minuscule portion of which is returned in money, goods, or services," they are not prolific, unlike poor parents, whose strategy is to have a lot of children in the hope that one of them will make something of himself, rescue them from poverty, and take care of them in old age. Children in the managerial classes of industrial societies lose their usefulness and become commodities or "expensive pets," in a mordant description Fox told me he once read somewhere.

The low fertility rate is also intimately connected to the recent change in the status and the self-perception of women, more of whom are wanting or having to work—the greatest revolution in our society in recent times, which has probably had a more reductive and disruptive effect on kinship than any other development. Having her best years taken up with producing and taking care of children usually means that the mother gives up the chance of a career for herself, a sacrifice that fewer women are willing or able to make. (Harris dramatizes the dilemma for modern women of choosing between motherhood and individual self-fulfillment by asking the question, What is more rewarding, to raise a child who will grow up to be a surgeon, or to be a surgeon oneself and have no children?) But for many women it is not a matter of choice. The growing phenomenon of women postponing or forgoing motherhood and opting for careers instead (which will be discussed in more detail in the next chapter) is not only a function of the growing need of women to be "somebody in their own right"—a natural evolutionary step in the history of Western individualism. For many women it is simply a matter of necessity. "Women have to work now because nobody else is going to take care of them," the anthropologist Lionel Tiger argued recently. "They can no longer assume there will be a husband to support them while they look after things on the domestic front, and the time when being in a kinship group provided them with a secure situation is long gone. The whole thing has been stupidly politicized by feminist theorists when it's simply a matter of survival. Women have no option but to work. They are on their own now as never before." Not to mention that increasingly fewer working fathers are able to support their families with their salary alone.

That more women must work now is partly a function of the breakdown of the sexual division of labor in traditional family life, of the instability of marriage, and of the demographics of the postwar "baby boom." Historically, women have tended to mate with the cohort of males in the age group just above them, but there were not enough males in that cohort for the female children of the baby boom, so they have had to raid the males in their own cohort, as well as to "cradle snatch" younger males; Fox cited an estimate that there were 1.8 million excess women "at risk of marriage" in the country, with about half a million in New York City alone. Tiger's contention that the feminism of women today is simply a rationalization of their condition—that they have no men (and joining a polygynous household is not an option, as it would be for unattached women in other societies)—is of course not popular with the feminists themselves, but Fox, who agrees with him, pointed out that there was a similar surge of feminism in the nineteen-twenties, when another baby boom had produced an excess of females. Peters told me that American women in 1981, whether married or not, still expected to have 2.2 children; yet a 1983 poll by the *New York Times* found that women "generally regard work and independence as elements of life that are as satisfying as husbands, homes, and children." Peters suggested that worry about overpopulation—having gone through schools that were overcrowded with baby-boom peers and having then had difficulty getting a job—may have affected some women's plans for motherhood. Any biological population must shrink when its numbers have exceeded the capacity of its environment to sustain it—as the human population threatens to do, and has already done in some parts of the world. The historical correctives for excessive human population growth have been war, epidemic, and starvation. With every effort being made to keep such cataclysms from breaking out, the only other option is for the women to make a conscious decision to have fewer children. Lowered fertility has the most direct bearing on kinship. Kinship can't exist, of course, if the kin aren't there.

🌱

The modern individualistic consciousness and the attendant decline of traditional kinship seem to have come about as the result of a multidetermined, multiply self-reinforcing process in which virtually the whole Western tradition has been involved. I have so far implicated, in this attempt to reconstruct how they may have arisen, the societies of ancient Greece, Rome, and the Anglo-Saxons; the Church, the Renaissance, the Reformation, the rise of bourgeois capitalism and democracy, the Enlightenment, and the scientific and industrial revolutions, as a result of which grandparents were left to fend for themselves, people began to have fewer children, and the family shrank. Another important component in the process has been the growth of the modern state, which has promoted individualism and persecuted kinship as relentlessly as the Church.

The essentially antagonistic relationship between the state and the kinship group was already established in the Middle Ages. In his study of society in the Mâcon country of France from the thirteenth through the nineteenth centuries, the historian Georges Duby traces how the old Frankish state, which had granted considerable independence to freemen (allowed them, for instance, to prefer the company of friends and neighbors over that of relatives), dissolved, and was followed by a period in which kin were obliged to group themselves more closely, large, clanlike frèrèches were formed, and "knights sought refuge in lineal solidarity." "In fact," Duby concludes, "the family is the first refuge in which the threatened individual takes shelter when the authority of the State weakens. But as soon as political institutions afford him adequate guarantees, he shakes off the constraint of the family and the ties of blood are loosened. The history of lineage is a succession of contractions and relaxations whose rhythms follow the modifications of the political order."

The antagonism continues to this day. To start with a remote but graphic example: during the last decade the Asmat of New Guinea's Casuarina coast, who for as long as anybody can remember have lived in extended families of up to two hundred people, have been forced by the Indonesian government to live in nuclear families. The writer Tobias Schneebaum recently spent four years among the Asmat, during which he saw much of their traditional life disintegrate as a result of having to adopt this new residential pattern. "When they still lived in two-hundred-foot-long compounds made up of houses with connecting porches, the men were separated from the women during the day," he told me recently. "The women went fishing, the men hunted, and at night they had the whole day's work to talk about. Now they spend the day together, fishing or pounding sago palm fronds, whose starchy pith provides them with ninety per cent of their diet, and at night they have nothing to talk about, and little to do besides have sex. They used to have a wonderful cooperative day-care system in their compounds: one or two women would stay and baby-sit all the children, while the others went fishing; now that has gone. Their strong traditions of ancestor worship—the men's skulls are saved for six or seven generations and passed down to either male or female descendants—are already disappearing. Clothing—a recent introduction—is spreading ringworm and other diseases, because they still have no sense of personal property and everybody wears the same clothes. The children used to go fishing in the morning. Now they don't have time to catch their breakfast, because they have to go to school, and they sit in class hungry and inattentive."

One modern state—the Soviet Union—has gone so far as to try to do away with the family altogether. In his 1884 classic, *The Origin of the Family, Private Property, and the State,* Friedrich Engels argued that the patriarchal family was the root of social injustice and sexual inequality: men "owned" women, he argued, as instruments for the production of legitimate offspring to whom their property could be passed. His views on the exploitative character of traditional kinship were endorsed by Karl Marx, who saw the victims of brutal working conditions in factories owned by rich bourgeois capitalist families, and who predicted in *Das Kapital* that the workers would unite to form a "community of free individuals." (The early rhetoric of communism has a surprising emphasis on individual rights and self-realization.) One of the early goals of Soviet policy, during the nineteen-twenties, was accordingly to phase out the family by making divorce a simple matter of unilateral renunciation by either spouse, by curtailing the family's socialization functions and "rescuing the child," as the sociologists Mark G. Field and David E. Anderson explain, "from the conservative atmosphere of the patriarchal family to a setting that could be entirely controlled by the regime." The family, it was hoped, would "wither away" under communism, and Engels' and Marx's "free individualism" would reign. Children were to be placed from the age of two months in "crèches," so their mothers would be freed to go back to work. Vladimir Lenin hailed the crèche as the "germ cell of communist society." But within a decade it was clear that "many children in the first Soviet urban generations," Field and Anderson go on, "simply lacked the kind of socializing experiences to fit them intellectually or emotionally to the new society the regime was attempting to build."

During the mid-nineteen-thirties Soviet policy accordingly became more supportive of the family. Divorce became "a complicated adversary procedure" and much of the responsibility for starting future citizens, at least during their earily childhood, down the "road to life" was restored to the parents. Today the Soviet state even subsidizes the purchase of wedding rings. Not only has the family survived in an antagonistic environment, but after more than sixty years of the Soviet experiment, a familiar pattern of hereditary elitism has established itself: "Intergenerational transmission of differential advantage," in the phrase of the sociologist Robert A. Feldmesser, far from being eradicated, has created a new meritocracy, drawn from the power elite and the higher ranks of the intelligentsia. There are families like the Mikoyans, whose grandchildren enjoy hereditary prestige rivalling that of high nobles during the old regime. "The parents typically did not inherit their position, power, or status," Field and Anderson explain. "They had to work and struggle, often against considerable odds. But some of them seem unable to resist the temptation to provide their children with the 'good life' they themselves never enjoyed. The children are brought up with pocket money, cars, vacations, and unearned leisure, in luxurious surroundings apart from the rest of Soviet society, leading lives often sheltered from the scrutiny of the common herd."

A similar situation has arisen in the People's Republic of China, where children of the "cadres," of government and party officials, "flaunt a life of privilege in an ostensibly classless society," as the *New York Times* reported recently. "Such young people are called *huahua gengzi,* a disparaging Chinese term meaning playboys. They attend special kindergartens, grow up in spacious homes, ride in cars assigned to their parents and shop at special stores closed to the public. On weekends, they hang out in restaurants that ordinary youths have trouble entering." In October 1980, a grandson of Marshal Zhu De, the revered commander of the Communist armies that conquered China, was executed for rape in the city of Tianjin, while another of his grandsons "was spared the death penalty for serious economic crimes only because some Chinese felt it would insult the great marshal's memory to execute two of his progeny." Communism and kinship are natural enemies. On balance, Communist regimes warily tolerate the family as an institution with which they must compete for the allegiance of their citizens, and while they have tended to do everything in their power to weaken the bonds among kin (in China, by attempting to break up the clans, to replace the farm family with the production brigade, and to severely limit family size), they haven't hesitated to use kinship for the purpose of terror or intimidation.

None of the other attempts to do away with the family have been any more successful. One of the earliest was by a man named John Humphrey Noyes, who started a communistic religious utopia in western New York State in the eighteen-thirties. The Oneida Community, as his utopia became known, practiced "free love" (Noyes's term, in fact), abolished personal property (even the children, van den Berghe recounts, after a big doll-burning ceremony, weren't allowed to own toys), forbade family groups, required children to be raised communally and to treat all the adults as their parents, and imposed a ban on having children from 1848 to 1868. In 1881 it dissolved into conventional family groups which incorporated themselves into a highly successful joint stock company that still exists.

The Israeli kibbutzim, some of which predate the creation

of Israel and have been in continuous existence for more than half a century, were founded on utopian hopes of eliminating class distinctions, private property, inheritance, and the sexual division of labor—much as in Engels' and Marx's formula. They have been, on the whole, remarkably successful except in their early attempt to suppress kinship. In the early days of the experiment, marriage was not supposed to be formally sanctioned, but now most of the kibbutzniks get married and stay married, van den Berghe reports (drawing on studies by Lionel Tiger and Joseph Shepher), and some kibbutzim go so far as to finance and organize the wedding party. In recent years the segregated "children's houses" in which, during the first decades of the experiment, eight to a dozen children were raised communally, have been replaced by conventional single-family housing, with parents and their children living together under the same roof. "Over the years pressure mounted overwhelmingly from women to have more and more contact with their children," van den Berghe explains, "at first after work in the evening, but increasingly during the 'hour of love' in the middle of the day. This . . . restricted mothers to jobs within easy running distance of the children's house. The *metaplots* (women in charge of the children's houses) increasingly complained of meddling mothers interfering with their routines. It was also found that even though mothers made the best *metaplots,* no woman could be entrusted with a group containing one of her own children, for fear of favoritism. This imposed an additional constraint on the system."

It is in modern states of the democratic type, particularly the United States, that individualism of every sort—political, religious, economic—enjoys fullest expression. From the very beginning the American government has been concerned with protecting individual freedoms. Amplifying the famous Lockean "unalienable rights" asserted in the Declaration of Independence, the first ten amendments of the American Constitution, which comprise the Bill of Rights, spell out the individual's basic civil liberties—freedom of worship, of speech, of the press, of assembly; assure the right to a speedy public trial by an impartial jury; and protect from "unreasonable searches," from double jeopardy, from having to testify against oneself, from "cruel and unusual punishments," and from being "deprived of life, liberty, or property, without due process of law." Later amendments abolish slavery, assert the citizen's right to vote regardless of race or color, and grant the vote to women; and the boundaries of the individual's legally protected sovereign territory are continually expanding. We are poised uncertainly on the threshold of an equal rights amendment that would end discrimination on the basis of sex; homosexuals are endeavoring to have "sexual orientation" added to the race and color injunctions of the Fifteenth Amendment; there are right-to-life as well as right-to-die activists; some of the rights accorded to humans have been extended to other animals; and in 1972, in an effort to stop a thirty-five-million-dollar complex of motels, restaurants, and recreational facilities from being built by Walt Disney Enterprises in California's Mineral King Valley, the Sierra Club even argued, eloquently but unsuccessfully, that natural objects like trees, mountains, rivers, and lakes should have the same legal rights as corporations.

Recently there have been efforts to secure rights for individuals who haven't even been born yet. The advocates of "fetal rights" are not only people who oppose abortion on religious grounds. In April 1983 a physician in Baltimore went to court in an effort to stop a pregnant woman from taking drugs ("substantial amounts of Qaalude, Valium, cocaine, and morphine") which he said threatened the life of her unborn child, and four months later, in a suit against two doctors and a nurse who had been charged with negligence in treating a woman's ruptured uterus, which caused her baby to be stillborn, a Missouri court ruled that a viable fetus is a person deserving the protection of the Fourteenth Amendment.

The essence of our society (as opposed to, say, the ancestor veneration that is at the core of traditional Chinese society) was caught in the phrase, "the American spirit of rugged individualism," which Herbert Hoover uttered during a 1928 campaign speech. Terms like "self-made man," "self-reliance," "self-starter"— even the word "competitive," when used in an athletic or a commercial context—all describe this admirable, character-building, prototypically American individualism. The next great American value is "family." No political candidate would think of being against "family"; yet the rights of the family have not been a concern of the federal government, and in fact, when the interests of an individual and his family have been in conflict, the courts have generally tended to side with the individual, and have asserted prevailing cultural values when the legality or morality of a deviant family system has been questioned. Such matters as fetal rights, along with the rules governing marriage, incest, sexual perversion, divorce, child custody, visitation, and unacknowledged paternity, are left for each state to determine. This whole area, which is known as family law, is in great flux. Connecticut and now Missouri, for instance, allow an action to be brought on behalf of an unborn fetus. New York and New Jersey do not. Texas recently had to deal with the problem of when a sex change becomes effective, after somebody who had just had one applied for a marriage license. In Belle Terre, Long Island, grandparents can't live with their children or grandchildren. The whole village is zoned exclusively for nuclear families. The ordinance, which was designed to keep the homes of Belle Terre from becoming rooming houses or communes for students from the nearby state university at Stony Brook, was contested in the United States Supreme Court, which upheld the community's right to determine its own zoning, even if the zoning struck an inadvertent blow at the extended family. In a later case in Ohio, however—*Moore v. City of East Cleveland*—involving a grandmother who was living with her son and two grandsons (who were first cousins), the Cuyahoga County Court of Appeals ruled that the city's single-family housing ordinance was unconstitutional.

✢

The ferocious persecution of the early Mormons for their practice of "plural marriage" is a puzzling chapter in the annals of American family law; Fox describes it as "tyranny in the name of democracy." One wonders why a nation that had itself arisen from the need to flee religious persecution, the early patriarchs of whose religion had many wives, should be so threatened by polygamy. The practice was adopted by the Mormons in 1843, when Joseph Smith, their prophet, announced he had received a "revelation" from the Lord that having more than one wife was acceptable. Many plural marriages were solemnized in 1846, the year of the Mormons' exodus to Utah, and in 1856, the year of the famine, but never more than five to ten per cent of the men were polygamous; it was a goal to which every Mormon man aspired, but few attained, and few of those who did attain it were "given" more than two wives. Only men who were spiritually, socially, and economically qualified were "commanded" by the Lord or requested by the church's priesthood to add another wife to their household. The additional wife was frequently a homeless immigrant, a spinster, or the widow of a deceased relative or of a victim of the Mormon massacres in Illinois and Missouri during the eighteen-thirties and -forties. In 1856 there were two thousand more women than men in the Territory of Utah; polygamy not only gave them a chance to have children but built up the church's membership. Procreation was considered a sacred duty, and success in reproduction an index of righteousness. In the words of Orson Pratt, one of the church's early apostles, the righteous would be blessed like Abraham with "seed as numerous as the sand upon the seashore." The most prolific and thus the most righteous man in the territory was appropriately its governor, Brigham Young. During one week in the spring of 1854, nine of Young's wives gave birth. "I think there is only about one-fifth of the population of the globe, that believes in the one-wife system," Pratt wrote, and these were "some of the nations of Europe and America, which do not know anything of the blessings of Abraham; and even those who have only one wife, cannot get rid of their covetousness, and get their little hearts large enough to share their property with a numerous family; they are so narrow and contracted in their feelings, that they take every possible care not to have their families large; they do not know what is in the future, nor what blessings they are depriving themselves of, because of the traditions of their fathers; they do not know that a man's posterity, in the eternal worlds, are to constitute his glory, his kingdom, and dominion."

Visitors to Utah discovered that the polygamous families of the Mormons were not the harems a sensational press had made them out to be. They found instead neat, flourishing farms, converted in a short time from desert by an intensely communal, cooperative pioneer spirit in which individualism had been submerged. The Victorian traveller and ethnographer Sir Richard Burton, who passed through the territory in 1860, was highly impressed. In his book *The City of the Saints* he cited the conventional "physiological" Mormon defense of polygamy—that it abolished prostitution, concubinage, celibacy, and infanticide. "The old maid is, as she ought to be, an unknown entity," he wrote. The Mormons he talked with insisted that "all sensuality in the married state is strictly forbidden beyond the requisite for ensuring progeny," which made polygamy, he pointed out slyly, for the males at least, "a positive necessity." "Contrary to the common belief," he reported, the women were not "thin, badly dressed, depressed, and degraded," but "exceedingly pretty and attractive, especially Miss ———," and he felt that the Mormon wife, supreme in her domesticity and motherhood, contrasted favorably with "a certain type of British and American woman" who was "petted and spoiled . . . set upon an uncomfortable and unnatural eminence, aggravated by a highly nervous temperament, small cerebellum, constitutional frigidity, and extreme delicacy of fibre." Mrs. Belinda Marden Pratt, one of the six wives of Parley P. Pratt (a brother of Orson), who had collectively given him twenty-five children, told Burton, "All these mothers and children are endeared to me by kindred ties, by mutual affection, by acquaintance and association; and the mother in particular, by patience, long-suffering, and sisterly kindness." Burton was receptive to the Mormon experiment because (according to his biographer Thomas Wright) he had come to believe from his study of societies in the Middle East, Africa, and the Orient that "man is by nature polygamic, whereas woman, as a rule, is monogamic, and polyandrous only when tired of her lover. The man loves the woman, but the love of the woman is for the love of the man."

Another visiting Englishman, a member of Parliament named Sir Charles Dilke, found polygamy "a powerful engine of democracy," because it prevented the concentration of wealth in one class through inheritance. "A rich man in New York leaves his two or three sons large property, and founds a family," he wrote. "A rich Mormon leaves his twenty or thirty sons each a minute fraction of his money, and each son must trudge out into the world and toil for himself."

But the system didn't make everybody happy. A woman named Jennie Froiseth, for instance, wrote in 1881 that after fifteen years of marriage with a man to whom she had borne seven children, he was counselled to take a second wife, a woman who had been a servant in the family several years earlier, whom Jennie had discharged for "her effort to attract the attention of my husband" and "for an unkind action toward my little girl, whom she appeared to dislike extremely." "There is neither law, justice, nor mercy for women in this territory," she wrote. "Satan himself could not devise any worse torture than women experience in the infernal system known as 'Celestial Marriage.' "

The public outrage against plural marriage was frenzied from the beginning. Joseph Smith was tarred and feathered and eventually killed not so much for daring to call himself a prophet of God, it would appear, as for practicing and advocating polygamy. There was something very threatening to the "hypocritically monogamous Calvinist bourgeois" mentality of the time, Fox suggests, about a man openly having more than one woman. In their 1858 debates Abraham Lincoln and Stephen Douglas both agreed that slavery and polygamy were "the twin relics of barbarism," and in 1862 Congress pleased the great majority of its constituency by passing the Morrill Act, which prohibited polygamy and cohabitation in the Territory of Utah. The Morrill Act had no teeth, however, and in 1878 lawyers for the Mormon Church decided to challenge it by seeing if the courts would uphold the First Amendment rights of Brigham Young's secretary, George Reynolds, who had several wives. Reynolds lost the first round and was convicted in the territorial court of violating the Morrill Act. An appellate court overturned the conviction on a technical point and remanded the case for retrial, at which Reynolds was convicted again. The conviction was upheld by the United States Supreme Court. "Polygamy has always been odious among the northern and western nations of Europe, and until the establishment of the Mormon Church, was almost exclusively a feature of the life of Asiatic and African nations," according to the decision, which Robin Fox described to me as "absolute bunk." In fact, he pointed out, until Christian monogamy was imposed by Gregory the Great circa 600 A.D., "both kinds of plural marriage [polygyny and polyandry] flourished among the Celtic and Germanic tribes—both are reported among the Britons by Caesar. . . . Among the Anglo-Saxons, the 'hold-fast wife' and the 'hand-fast wife' shared uxorial duties and favors. The nobility and royalty were openly polygynous and [so was] the Frankish dynasty—the Merovingians." Even after its establishment, Fox argues, "kings rarely took monogamy seriously *in practice,* however much they may have paid lip service to the institution for the sake of the Church"—the classic example being Henry VIII, who finally broke with the Church over his right to more than one wife (though in succession); and in modern society, although monogamy is the legal form of marriage, a sort of staggered polygamy, for both sexes, is increasingly what seems to be actually in effect. In a bit of invective Burton would have applauded, Fox dismisses Christian monogamy as "a charade, a short-term intrusion by celibate misogynists into an ongoing plural-mating system."

The persecution of Mormon polygamy by the American government is better understood in the context of the global effort, which both the Catholic and the Protestant arms of the Church had been making for several centuries, to convert non-European populations to Christian monotheism and monogamy and to dissuade them from their idolatrous worship of clan totems and their other heathen practices (in the process introducing the Western individual self-consciousness). At roughly the same time Reynolds was on trial, the famous Victorian missionary David Livingstone was in the wilds of South Africa trying to convert a tribe called the Bakuena. Only the chief, Sechele, and the daughters of three of his subchiefs, whom he had married to "cement the allegiance of his tribe," were receptive, however. After three years of "consistent profession," Livingstone relates in his book, *Missionary Travels and Researches in South Africa*, Sechele at last asked Livingstone to baptize him, which Livingstone agreed to do with some reluctance, knowing how politically and personally traumatic it would be for the chief to "put up all his wives but one"; some of them had become Livingstone's best scholars. In preparation Sechele

> went home, gave each of his superfluous wives new clothing, and all his own goods, which they had been accustomed to keep in their huts for him, and sent them to their parents with an intimation that he had no fault to find with them but that in parting with them he wished to follow the will of God. On the day on which he and his children were baptized, great numbers came to see the ceremony. Some thought, from a stupid calumny circulated by enemies to Christianity in the south, that the converts would be made to drink an infusion of "dead men's brains," and were astonished to find that water only was used at baptism. Seeing

several of the old men actually in tears during the
service, I asked them afterward the cause of their
weeping; they were crying to see their father, as
the Scotch remark over a case of suicide, *"so far
left to himself."*

After Reynolds lost his case (he ended up serving a year and
a half in prison), twelve years of "polyg hunts" by deputy mar-
shals followed, and by 1890 every Mormon man of distinction was
in hiding, exile, or prison. That year the church's fourth president,
Wilford Woodruff, announced that he had received a "revelation"
that Mormons should "refrain from contracting any marriage forbidden by the law of the land." Die-hard polygamists fled to
Wyoming, Oregon, Idaho, New Mexico, Mexico, and Alberta. Utah
was admitted to the Union in 1896, only after promising in its state
constitution that polygamy would be "forever banned."

Having more than one spouse at once is still a third-degree
felony in Utah, although as many as forty thousand of its residents—fundamentalists who do not recognize the divine origin of
the Woodruff Manifesto—may be members of multiple-parent
households. Nobody had been prosecuted for polygamy in decades
until December 1, 1982, when a two-year veteran of the Murray
City police force (Murray City is a suburb of Salt Lake City)
named Roy Potter was fired after a complaint was lodged that he
was living with two women. The ground for his dismissal was
that he had violated his oath to uphold the Utah constitution.
Potter's case was taken *pro bono* by a lawyer named Dennis Haslam, who appealed to the Civil Service Commission on the ground
that Potter was exercising a right guaranteed by the First Amendment. The commission ruled that he had engaged in serious mis-
conduct which had affected the morale of the Murray Hill police
force, but said that if he got rid of one of his wives, he would be
reinstated. For Potter, who has four children by his first wife and
one by his second, and has since taken a third wife, and who believes, as the early Mormons did, that the practice of plural marriage is a theological necessity, without which he could not achieve
salvation or exaltation, the offer was "not even a Hobson's choice,"
as Haslam told me recently. Haslam had filed suit in federal district court to have the antipolygamy and antibigamy laws in the

Utah constitution declared void on the ground that they violated
Potter's First Amendment rights; and against the Murray City
police force for violating Potter's civil rights and for back pay.

❦

One of the most explosive areas in American family law is
that of child rights. The rights to marry, to procreate and enjoy the
custody of one's children, and to divorce have been established,
but what if the parents are not acting in the child's best interest?
What if the association is harmful? How binding is their authority? The issues of *patria potestas* versus child rights and of the
state's obligation to step in to protect a child versus the sanctity
of the family have recently met headlong in the case of Walter
Polovchak, who in 1980 immigrated to Chicago with his family
from a small town in the western Ukraine. After several months
Walter's father and his wife, at sea in Chicago, decided to return.
But their children, Natalie, almost eighteen, and Walter, then
twelve, were learning English and adjusting happily to their new
life. They wanted to stay. Natalie had her own passport and there
was nothing her parents could do about her decision, but Walter
was still in their legal custody, and they didn't want to give him
up. He applied for and was granted federal asylum by the Immigration and Naturalization Service, and was later processed as a
"minor in need of supervision"—a term usually applied to run-
aways—and declared a ward of the state by the Juvenile Division
of the Cook County Circuit Court. His parents, baffled and bitter,
returned to the Ukraine without him. Since they left, Walter has
lived in a succession of foster homes; as a ward of the state, he is
not allowed to live with his sister in the home of their cousins, the
Polowczaks.

In December 1981, the Illinois Court of Appeals, acting on
an appeal filed by the American Civil Liberties Union, which is
representing the parents, reversed the juvenile-court ruling on the
ground that Walter was still in the legal custody of his parents,
but said that the issue of asylum would have to be decided separately in a federal court. Henry Holzer, a professor of constitutional law who is one of Walter's lawyers, has explained to me
that if Walter were to be sent back, he would probably be prosecuted for "treason" because he had given interviews in which he
spoke out against the Soviet system, and that he would be sent at

the least to a "reorientation camp" if not to prison. To Holzer, the child-rights case was as solid as the asylum case, because the parents, by wanting to take Walter back to the Soviet Union, were not acting in his best interest. "As far as our children are concerned," Holzer told me, "we have no rights, only obligations."

Another area in which the conflicting interests of parents and children can require mediation by the state is adoption. The pathos of being adopted is that one must go through life completely cut off from one's flesh and blood, with the basic question of one's origin unanswered. In recent years the courts, which have traditionally protected the parents'—or, most usually, the mother's—right to privacy and have obstructed the child's quest to learn who he or she is, have been increasingly disposed to rule that the child's right to know is more important and to give him or her access to sealed birth records. Their change of attitude reflects the changing values of our society, in which the stigma of illegitimacy is no longer so great. But there may also be medical information the child needs to know—perhaps a hereditary disorder in his pedigree. In the recent case of a twenty-six-year-old man from Coal Valley, Illinois, named Jerry Blandford, a critical liver ailment prompted his adoptive mother to obtain family medical records that might be of help in his treatment; it turned out that Blandford had delivered groceries to his real mother for several years without either of them knowing they were related. As the cloud of secrecy surrounding adoption is gradually lifting, more women are looking for the children they had given up and are finding them, either through an "adoption underground," which for a fee searches for the information in sealed adoption records, or through a favorable court ruling. A recently enacted New York state law allows natural parents and their offspring access to certain records and to be reunited if all parties, including the child's adoptive parents, agree. One mother, who had found her daughter after a thirteen-year search, said recently, "We can't have the years back, but I can know my daughter and begin to have a relationship with her rather than continue to have a black blot in my heart"; another woman, a thirty-five-year-old executive recruiter from New Jersey who had given birth to a daughter at the age of eighteen, surrendered her for adoption, and begun searching for her in 1980 after a divorce caused her to "start re-evaluating my life," said, after finding her daughter in Georgia, "It's given me peace of mind just to know she's alive and well and healthy. It has allowed me to grow up in a lot of ways. Part of me was frozen at age eighteen."

🌱

It shouldn't be surprising that little remains of traditional kinship, with the family head's *patria potestas* undisputed, in a continuously evolving democracy. Alexis de Tocqueville recognized the pattern as early as 1835. He wrote in *Democracy in America*:

> It has been universally remarked that in our time the several members of the family stand upon an entirely new footing towards each other; that the distance which formerly separated a father from his sons has been lessened; and that paternal authority, if not destroyed, is at least impaired. . . .
>
> When men live more for the remembrance of what has been than for the care of what is, and when they are more given to attend to what their ancestors thought than to think themselves, the father is the natural and necessary tie between the past and the present, the link by which the ends of these two chains are connected. In aristocracies, then, the father is not only the civil head of the family, but the organ of its traditions, the expounder of its customs, the arbiter of its manners. He is listened to with deference, he is addressed with respect, and the love that is felt for him is always tempered with fear.
>
> When the condition of society becomes democratic and men adopt as their general principle that it is good and lawful to judge of all things for oneself, using former points of belief not as a rule of faith, but simply as a means of information, the power which the opinions of a father exercise over those of his sons diminishes as well as his legal power.

By the second half of the nineteenth century adverse effects of the accelerating individualism had begun to be felt. People who were alienated, or an alienated sensibility, began to appear in literature—in the poetry of Charles Baudelaire and Arthur Rimbaud, in the fiction of Fyodor Dostoevsky. Early in this century, in the disturbing work of Franz Kafka, "reality" itself—whatever commonly agreed-upon outer world one's society teaches one to believe in—seems to come apart. The alienation in these works is an urban phenomenon, as it generally is in life: the city dweller is more likely to be severed from his kin (perhaps he has even deliberately divested himself of them), and he has definitely lost the ancestral contact with nature, which in most large cities has been reduced to little more than the sky, the weather, a few particularly hardy species of introduced trees, and an impoverished, largely furtive and nocturnal fauna.

During the nineteen-seventies several types of individualism that were not admirable—competitive individualism, narcissistic individualism, and a more all-inclusive self-centeredness which the Bergers call "hyperindividualism"—became so conspicuous in American society that the trend watcher Tom Wolfe was moved to call those years "the Me Decade." The clinical manifestations of excessive self-centeredness were identified. "Paranoia is a recent cultural disorder," a 1974 article in *Harper's* magazine claimed. "It follows the adoption of rationalism as the quasi-official religion of Western man and the collapse of certain communitarian bonds (the extended family, belief in God, the harmony of the spheres) which once made sense of the universe in all its parts. Paranoia substitutes a rigorous (though false) order for chaos, and at the same time dispels the sense of individual insignificance by making the paranoid the focus of all he sees going on around him—a natural response to the confusion of modern life."

The psychotherapist Paul Wachtel recently suggested to me that competitive individualism is "an offshoot of capitalism. It didn't appear until around the mid-nineteenth century, when individual initiative began to make a difference. Before then people were more or less in the same boat. It became strongest in the United States because there was no rigid class structure and because there were so many successive waves of immigration. Each wave started the race at the beginning again. A positive value was placed on being competitive. It became almost a moral virtue."

Another factor in the growth of competitive individualism has been population growth. There are simply more people in competition for jobs, resources, land—for everything. Expectations have risen, as has the number of people who are qualified for positions in the managerial class. During the nineteen-seventies, for instance, huge numbers of young adults in the "baby-boom" generation earned doctorates, but the number of openings in the academic world failed to rise accordingly. Fox told me that an instructorship in a not particularly distinguished department of anthropology recently attracted fifteen hundred applicants.

A lot of research has been conducted recently to determine the physiological and psychological characteristics of competitive individualists. For one thing, they seem to be able to quickly raise their level of a hormonelike neurotransmitter called serotonin. The connection between the ability to raise one's serotonin quickly and "dominance acquisition" was first discovered in male vervet monkeys by the neuropsychiatrist Michael T. McGuire: when the dominant male is removed from a vervet monkey troop, he will be replaced by the male whose serotonin level has risen highest. In another experiment, at the University of Iowa, seventy-two male students were studied for relationships between whole-blood serotonin levels and competitiveness, and a very definite relationship was found. "Serotonin has to do with male-male interaction, stand-offs and pushing," McGuire explains. "Its levels are higher in males, and individual variability is most pronounced in multimale societies with tight resource control. One would expect clear distinctions in situations in which there is no exit and authority has to be unambiguous, like a submarine. Chairmen of academic departments and Nobel Prize winners have much higher serotonin than their subordinates."

No cross-cultural studies have been made comparing the serotonin levels of males in Western individualistic societies with those of males in Third-World, kinship-oriented societies, but McGuire told me that "clear distinctions" would be anticipated. The problem with such a study would be assessing the importance of other variables, particularly the position of each male within his society.

Another concept, however, the Type A personality, which came to public attention during the nineteen-seventies, is firmly linked to postindustrial competitive individualism. The Type A person is impatient, aggressive, and achievement-oriented. "He has to be there first," McGuire explained. "He is the one who digs

out before everybody else when the light changes." Type A people
are quick to anger and have a basic distrust of human nature and
motives. Type A behavior seems to be adaptive in our society, and
it seems to contribute to career success. Type A students get better
grades than Type B students with the same IQ, who are distinguished by a comparative lack of time urgency and competitiveness.
Evidence of all three modes of inheritance has been found in the acquisition of the behavior pattern: certain children seem to be genetically predisposed to anger, competitiveness, and the need to be in
control, but mothers of such children also tend to push such children more, and fathers are more apt to reinforce the predisposition
by using physical punishment. According to a recent article in the
New York Times, the cardiologist Meyer Friedman "believes Type
A behavior sometimes grows out of childhood feelings that parental love is dependent on what one does (getting high grades,
winning, etc.) rather than upon what one is. . . . Type A people suffer from a basic insecurity stemming from their failure to
receive unconditional love." Other students of the pattern maintain that it is culturally reinforced. The psychologist Ingrid Wal-
dren believes "the pervasive 'Horatio Alger' myth feeds the Type A
behavior of Americans," while the psychologist Margaret Chesney
said in the same article, "Our schools encourage competition between individuals and encourage individuals to compete with
themselves to achieve all they can possibly achieve. For some this
attitude leads to a spiral in which they can seldom feel satisfied
with their achievements. Our culture, too, has such a strong focus
on individual achievement, on being 'the best.' "

In contrast to their lower serotonin levels, employed women
display "close to" the same Type A features that employed men
do; suburban middle-class schoolchildren are far more Type A
than rural schoolchildren are; and in many parts of the Third
World the pattern is unknown. It seems to be part of the price of
success, part of the burden of individualism—a particularly American trait—like periodontal disease, whose prevalence in the United
States is partly a function of stress.

Recent changes in the spectator sports seem to reflect the rise
of competitive individualism: the old values of teamwork and
sportsmanlike conduct have been subordinated to sheer winning;
in team sports like baseball and football individual performance is
emphasized by "most valuable player" awards, and the teams them-

selves have become fragile, transitory coalitions—each player has his own contract, and is often waiting to become a "free agent," so that he can sell his talent to another team for more money. But the most dramatic development has been the recent surge in the popularity of tennis—a one-on-one rather than a team sport— which has been turned in America, at least, from a gentleman's game into a gladiatorial spectacle, with players insulting referees, hurling their rackets violently to the ground, and howling expletives, to the delight of their fans. But a tennis match is still a kind of dance: the opponents are locked in a battle of wills, subtly reading and responding to each other's body movements, like dancers, and probing for spatial or psychological openings. Later in the Me Decade even that contact seemed to become too much: solitary sport—jogging—became the rage, and with the introduction of Walkman radio and cassette players, the jogger clapped on his headphones and perhaps (withdrawing eye contact) sunglasses, and his detachment was complete. The transition from one-on-one to solitary sport perhaps parallels the change in dancing style which has taken place since the advent of rock-and-roll: first partners stopped holding each other, then they stopped dancing with each other and began to dance with nobody in particular, with themselves. Some "punk rockers" even go in for bloody collisions.

Jogging became popular because it was "good for you"; it was a manifestation of what has been called the "narcissistic individualism" of the nineteen-seventies. Having failed to reform society during the nineteen-sixties, the postwar "baby boomers," Landon Y. Jones suggests, turned to "reforming themselves." Jogging was part of a multifaceted program of self-improvement which also included attention to diet and spiritual development. Many of the pursuits that have been ascribed to narcissism are, in fact, positive correctives to "the dilemmas posed by the consumer society," Wachtel pointed out to me—a diet too rich in proteins and carbohydrates; lack of exercise; emptiness resulting from the pursuit of purely material forms of gratification and self-definition. (Some people, furthermore, have found camaraderie in jogging. According to a recent *Times* article, the sport is "a sure-fire way of meeting terrific people" and "the springboard for an ever-increasing number of romances, both casual and serious.") Wachtel believes that "narcissistic individualism has been partly confused with the pursuit of self-worth in individualistic ways.

What is narcissistic is the withdrawal from public life and participation in larger communities."

The trend that Wolfe and the writer Christopher Lasch have called narcissism was perhaps in part an indication that Americans, atomized as no people had ever been before, were beginning to look after themselves, were "taking care of number one," in a currently popular expression, because no other support system could be counted on to do it any more; and perhaps, too, that the society was swinging back to a more inner-directed phase. At the same time, as I will argue two chapters from now, there were other indications that the idea of personal freedom had been carried to dangerous and unhealthy extremes, and that the mystique of free-floating individualism was beginning to pall.

7

New Patterns of American Kinship

IN THE UNITED STATES AND IN POSTINDUSTRIAL SOCIETIES AS A whole, the nuclear family is still the preferred model and still the dominant family type in practice, but far from everybody conforms to it. Many people have been unwilling or unable to have children or to stay in a relationship as partner or parent, and have settled into other living arrangements. There is no single pattern at the moment, but "a plurality of norms and arrangements," as Jack Goody explained to me. The stepfamily and the single-parent family have become commonplace, and the number of single adults who are turning to figurative types of kinship has been growing steadily.

The extended family, prevalent in much of the world, has never been very popular in America. It is more common in the country and among poor blacks, for whom it can serve as a marvellously effective support system, as we shall see. Recent immigrants, especially those from Latin America, Asia, the Middle East, and the Mediterranean countries, sometimes bring theirs with them or reunite in extended-family groups once they are here; hard times can force a married couple to move back in with a spouse's parents, or a family can be reextended when an elderly parent or grandparent is taken in; but the number of households with "related subfamilies," as the Bureau of the Census describes the form, has fallen sharply, from 2,402,000 in 1950 to 1,236,000 in 1981, to currently less than two per cent of the total number of households in the country.

On the other hand, there has been a growing tendency, first noticed in the nineteen-eighties, for young Americans—millions of them, demographers have estimated—to delay leaving their parents' home or to return after finishing college, partly because of the intimidating competitiveness of the job market and the high cost of housing—as kinship contracts with affluence, so it regroups when the individual family members are unable to launch themselves on their own—and partly because of "subtle changes that have occurred since the early nineteen-seventies in the relations between many parents and children," the *New York Times* reported recently. The article quotes the researcher Michael Carliner: "We have fundamental social changes going on. Children are not as alienated from their parents as they were for a while. They're not rebelling as much as they did. They're getting married later, and it's acceptable to live longer at home." The high divorce rate is probably also causing more young people to return home, sometimes with children.

Some mothers, suffering from a condition that has been called the "empty-nest syndrome," are delighted to have their children back with them a little longer. Others, though, who had been looking forward to the time when they no longer had to cook and housekeep for and worry about their children, are less enchanted to have them still around. "Haven't we done enough for him?" a woman whose twenty-four-year-old son was still living at her home in Westchester County, New York, and showed no interest in moving on complained to me.

1. *The Nuclear Family*

Although there has recently been a lot of discussion in books and articles and on television about "the death of the family"—by which the nuclear family is meant (some anthropologists have spoken of "nuclear family decay")—more than half of the households in the United States are still composed of married couples with or without children. Life-term monogamy still has a large, loyal following. The most recent count by the Census Bureau, made in 1983, determined that of the 83,918,000 households in the country, 49,908,000 were headed by married couples, and the actual number of couples was somewhat larger, because those who were living together but were not married, and single householders with "unrelated subfamilies"—such as a single person who has married servants living in the house—were counted in the category of "nonfamily households." (The Census Bureau's definition of "family" is very comprehensive. It requires no more than two people who are related by blood, marriage, or adoption, one of whom is a householder. A person living with a sister, an adopted son, a cousin, or a brother-in-law—each of these is a family.) The proportion of married-couple households to the total number of households fell sharply, however, from 70.5 per cent in 1970 to 59.9 per cent in 1981, which suggests that more people were choosing or were involuntarily finding themselves in other arrangements—raising children by themselves, or living alone—than were getting married or remarried.

Many are worried by this trend. In 1982 *Time* magazine, for instance, wrote in its Behavior section: "In the age of ego, marriage is often less an emotional bonding than a breakable alliance between self-seeking individuals. The proportion of married couples in the population decreased by an average of .4% a year in the late sixties; by the late seventies the rate of decline rose to an average of 1.05% a year. 'If the nuclear family continued to be dismembered at the same accelerating rate,' says [the sociologist Amitai E.] Etzioni, 'by the year 2008 there would not be a single American family left.' But he expects 'some major social force to change the present course, if only because no complex society has ever survived without the nuclear family.'" And indeed, the most recent statistics, which will be discussed in the next chapter, show a rise in the proportion of newly formed married-couple households—which may be an indication that marriage and commitment are enjoying a renaissance from their all-time low point in the previous decade.

A startling finding by the Women's Bureau of the Department of Labor, that the four-person configuration, with the father at work, the mother at home, and their two children at school—a classic American profile, one would have thought—now fits only five per cent of the households in the country, lends credence to the hypothesis that the nuclear family, if it is not dying out, is certainly a beleaguered institution. And yet millions of people—

most of our population, the census reveals—are not only products of nuclear families but have gone on to start new ones as adults. Marriage still has "narrative appeal," in the words of the writer Phyllis Rose; people enter into it, she says with a touch of irony, because of "the clear-cut beginnings and endings it offers, the richly complicated middle"; while the largest and most comprehensive study of the American couple, for which more than twelve thousand questionnaires were distributed in 1975 to couples of all types in Seattle, San Francisco, and New York—and half of them were sent follow-up questionnaires eighteen months later to see if they were still together—concluded, in the words of Pepper Schwartz, one of its conductors, that "it is the fondest wish of most people to be a couple." "Every couple is a strong advocate of the nuclear family until they get divorced," a man whose marriage had recently ended remarked to me.

The presence of children is, of course, a strong incentive for couples to stay together. Just under half of the married couples counted in 1983 had children under eighteen, while seventy-five per cent of the children under eighteen counted in 1982 lived with two parents, though in many cases only one was their biological parent (down from 83.1 per cent in 1970, however). "The key reason why the nuclear family retains its importance in industrial societies is that, so far, no satisfactory substitute has been found to raise children, especially during the first five or six years," van den Berghe writes.

The socioeconomic correlation between kinship and hardship is also a factor: the working and lower-middle classes tend to have a "strong family sense" and greater commitment to and maybe even contentment in their marriages. Lula Aaron, for instance, a fifty-four-year-old mother of five and grandmother of seven from Queens, New York, who had been married for thirty-eight years to a freight handler and security guard, recently described herself as a "domestic engineer" to reporters who had come to interview her after she hit a record ten-million-dollar jackpot in the New York State Lottery.

In the past twenty years or so a number of sociologists have rallied around the nuclear family, and a full-scale controversy has erupted over its vintage and about whether it is, as G. P. Murdock declared it to be in 1949, "a universal human grouping"—the way humans have always lived, and are meant to live. Philippe Ariès argued in 1960 that the self-conscious parent-offspring unit, the whole idea of "the family," is a comparatively recent development: "For a long time it was believed that the family constituted the ancient basis of our society, and that, starting in the eighteenth century, the progress of liberal individualism had shaken and weakened it. The history of the family in the nineteenth and twentieth centuries was supposed to be that of decadence: the frequency of divorce and the weakening of maternal and paternal authority were seen as so many signs of its decline. The study of modern demographic phenomena led me to a completely contrary conclusion," he wrote. "It seems to me (and qualified observers have come to share my conclusions) that on the contrary the family occupied a tremendous place in our industrial societies, and that it had perhaps never before exercised so much influence over the human condition. The legal weakening proved only that the idea (and the reality) did not follow the same curve as the institution. Is not this disparity between living ideas and legal structures one of the characteristics of our civilization? The idea of the family appeared to be one of the great forces of our time. I then went on to wonder, not whether it was on the decline, but whether it had ever been as strong before, and even whether it had been in existence for a long time."

In 1972 Peter Laslett reported that the nuclear family predated the Industrial Revolution by centuries, and in 1975 the sociobiologist E. O. Wilson, citing articles written by V. Reynolds and Lila Leibowitz seven years earlier, wrote that "The building block of nearly all societies is the nuclear family. . . . The populace of an American industrial city, no less than a band of hunter-gatherers in the Australian desert, is organized around this unit. In both cases the family moves between regional communities, maintaining complex ties with primary kin by means of visits (or telephone calls and letters) and the exchange of gifts."

Opposing views were presented by Robert Linton, who wrote as early as 1936 that the nuclear family plays "an insignificant role in the lives of many societies," and in 1968 by Robin Fox, with his proposal that the mother-child unit is in fact the universal building block of human society, that the continued presence of the father is not strictly necessary for survival, and that in many families around the world he in fact plays no further role.

Murdock himself, as Laslett points out, was "not claiming

that the nuclear family . . . is the universal form of coresident domestic group, as we call it here [in England]. His position is that within all such groups, whether simple, extended, or multiple . . . the conjugal unit of spouses and children retains an independent identity." In fact, three hundred and one, or 54.8 per cent, of the cultures in Murdock's atlas are characterized by the extended family system, and Fox recently told me that more comprehensive ethnographic surveys, made since the atlas appeared, suggest that about eighty-four per cent of the world's cultures practice and/or permit polygamy. The outcome of this controversy, which is nowhere in sight because neither side concedes any validity to its opponent's position—is of burning interest to anybody today who is confused, as well he or she might be, about what sort of family system he or she is actually involved in.

2. *Serial Monogamy and the Stepfamily*

The latest divorce proportion projection by the Census Bureau, based on the 1977 divorce rate, estimates that roughly half the marriages performed today in the United States will end in divorce—up six per cent from the 1974 projection and eleven per cent from the 1969 projection. Between 1957 and 1978 the divorce rate rose by two hundred and fifty per cent. In 1981 a record 1.21 million divorces were performed; in 1982 the number dropped to 1.18 million, and the divorce rate went down to 5.1 divorces per thousand people—the first decline in two decades. California led the nation, with eleven per cent of the divorces, and Vermont had the least.

The sociologist Paul Bohannan recently put the matter of divorce into perspective for me. "The divorce rate has been going up in the country since the 1600s," he said. "Sometimes it levels off for a while, then it goes back up like a bull market. The United States was the first country with legal divorce. The Puritans brought it to New England. The first cases were in 1630–40. In 1804 Timothy Dwight, the president of Yale, complained about the one-per-cent divorce rate, but anthropologists have turned up stable societies with a hundred-per-cent divorce rate, like the Kanuri of Nigeria. We have a high divorce rate only among record-keeping people, and the impact of divorce is particularly severe for us because the neolocal household exploded. In other societies the household survives. But I am convinced that we too are getting to the point where we will understand that the family supersedes divorce, that we have been dwelling for centuries on the wrong variable; and once the stigma of divorce is removed, we will get back to good parenting. Already, although the misery of the divorce experience hasn't changed in the last twenty years, the support group has got much better, and the industry that surrounds divorce has changed beyond recognition."

Out of the fifty per cent of marriages that are projected to fail, if present trends continue, about five-sixths of the divorced men and two-thirds of the divorced women will marry again, and about two-thirds of the people who get divorced will remarry within three years. Hope will triumph over experience, as Samuel Johnson said of second marriage. Clearly, if half the marriages are failing, and more than half the couples that are splitting up are making new matches, a pattern of serial monogamy, now almost as common as marriage for life, has pervaded American family life. Many theories have been proposed to account for this phenomenon. Perhaps the first point is that serial monogamy is not unknown in preindustrial societies. The Semang of the Malay forests, for instance, limit themselves to one spouse at a time, but marry repeatedly. Traditional, simultaneous polygamy persists in rural Ghana, but in the cities, the importer Kari-Kari Ofori-Atta recently told me, it has largely given way, under Western influence, to monogamy with a very fast divorce rate, to a sort of successive polygamy that is still acceptably within the bounds of Protestant marital practice. "Every year or so the men change their wives," he told me. "The divorce is handled as the marriage was, between the families. The man gives his wife back to her parents with a bottle of whiskey or, if he is rich, a cow or a goat, and her parents go to his parents and say, 'I don't think your boy is working out.'" The Brazilian "elusive reprobate" mentioned in Chapter Two, who had nine children by three women, each of whom lived in a different city and two of whom he was married to at the same time, was both a bigamist and a serial monogamist.

The United States doesn't have a polygamous heritage, however, and the pattern of serial monogamy which has recently established itself here has largely been the result of the many pressures to which married couples are increasingly subject in our time (another pattern of serial monogamy, resulting from widow-

hood, has been part of American family life from the beginning).
"The industrial nuclear family system puts an enormous burden
on the pair bond," van den Berghe writes. "The married couple in
America consists, in a very real sense, of two persons against the
world. There's little effective outside support. The success or failure of the family, unsupported by outside pressures and interests
with a stake in keeping it going, hinges on whether the spouses
can bear to stay together. Not surprisingly in a species where the
formation and maintenance of a pair-bond is a complex and by no
means automatic or irreversible process, many couples . . . do not
stay together." (Not to mention the directly negative influence
that in-laws can have: if either set of parents is against the
match, they can undermine its chances for survival by exploiting
whatever hold, psychological or otherwise, they still have over
their child, which may be considerable.)

The proportion of couples who have found their marriage to
be a sort of half-life or, in Priestley's famous description, "a long,
dull meal with dessert at the beginning," has probably not changed
(it has probably always been high) as much as the willingness
and ability of unhappy partners to extricate themselves. The recent sexual and economic liberation of women, in particular, has
made many of them less dependent on men and has given them
the new luxury of being able to get out of relationships that have
become routine and boring—an option that men, to a greater extent, had already been able to exercise. (Early in the century
H. G. Wells, for instance, suggested that the ideal was to be married twice, once when young, and again in middle age, when one
had become a different person.) As a result of the changed status
of women, the sexual division of labor which the traditional marriage partnership had come to take for granted was challenged,
and the structure and function of the institution were called into
question. (Some women, of course, already had reservations about
marriage well before the nineteen-seventies; Mae West said, "Of
course I'm ready for the institution of marriage, but who says I'm
ready for an institution?") It is no longer viewed as a necessarily
permanent alliance, with the wife in the supporting role, and it
is seldom entered into any more with the same confidence and
sense of commitment (witness the frequency of "prenuptial agreements").

The writer Landon Y. Jones, however, has attributed the im-

permanence of marriage in the postwar "baby-boom" generation
not to the women's movement, but to the generation's sheer numbers:

> Marriage was the next institution (after school)
> entered by the baby boom on its journey to ma-
> turity. And, like every institution before it, mar-
> riage was not easily able to assimilate this giant
> generation. In the space of a decade, the baby
> boom changed all our rules about courtship and
> marriage. In doing so, it came precariously close
> to balkanizing our basic unit of cultural trans-
> mission: the family. The baby boomers married
> less often, married later, and had fewer children,
> divorced more often, left more children in single-
> parent homes, and have done more to under-
> mine kinship than any previous generation. We
> have had to create an entire new vocabulary to de-
> scribe the new transitory relationships that are re-
> placing the family—cohabitants, mates, "blended"
> or "reconstituted" families, and so on. In short, the
> boom generation was doing all it could to break
> the hold of the family over the individual.

But whatever forces, from without or within, have brought
their marriages down, all but the most bitterly disillusioned, it
would seem, do not give up on the institution, but try again with
somebody else, even though the risk of failure for second marriages is even slightly higher. Simply living with somebody is apparently not a popular arrangement: although the number of unmarried couples doubled from 1970 to 1976, it represented less
than one per cent of the total number of households.

According to the Census Bureau, the average American marriage today lasts twenty-three years—seven years less than it lasted
between 1948 and 1960—and in 1980, the median duration of
marriages that ended in divorce was 6.8 years (a comprehensive
earlier figure is not available). Marriage is not only ending sooner
but being postponed: men marry today at an average age of 25.2,
women at 22.5—later than they have been doing since 1890—and
at the same time they are remarrying about five years earlier than

they were in 1950 (women in 1979 at the age of 31.9, and men at the age of 35.3). Fox sees this chopping off of the length of marriage from both ends as a "return to sanity." "What was the average length of marriage a hundred years ago?" he asked me recently. "Not much more than twenty years—the same sort of length we are heading toward now, except that most of the marriages today are ending in divorce instead of death. Twenty years are all you need to bring up children. In the old days, children went out into the world when they were fifteen. The unnaturally long duration of marriage in this century, like our nearly doubled life expectancy, is the result of medical progress. We are being asked to stay married three times longer. It's a strainful, weird, and absolutely unprecedented situation. But divorce is returning us to normality. It's reminding us that one of us should be dead."

According to one source, the life expectancy of marriage in England in 1850 was seventeen years in the working class and twenty-two years in the middle class and the aristocracy; in the United States then it was, for the population at large, twenty-two years.

The advantages to a man of having several wives are the same as they are for a baboon or for any other animal with a polygynous reproductive strategy: more offspring and a better chance that his genes will survive and proliferate through them. The advantages of serial monogamy to a woman are less clear. Economically, if she is a divorcée with children, she is usually better off marrying again: the average divorced mother's income has been estimated to decline by seventy-three per cent in the first year after her divorce. But there may be a net disadvantage to a woman in the pattern, because the pool of males for her to choose from is usually smaller; a divorced woman past thirty with several children in tow usually can't be as selective as a divorced man past fifty, say, with good earning power. On the other hand, it may be *healthier* for her to get involved again. Studies have shown that people tend to recover more quickly from physical setbacks when they are not alone—even having a pet makes a difference—and that people who are married tend to live longer than those who are single. Having several prolonged involvements over a lifetime may enhance personal growth (Wells's argument) or may make inner compromises less necessary. But both of the last two arguments are equally applicable to men. Perhaps the most important effect of postindustrial serial monogamy for women is that for the first time (except in a few societies in India and Tibet which practice polyandry or group marriage) it makes polygamy equally available to them.

The rise of serial monogamy probably also reflects a more general decline in the capacity for intimacy. Not only mating relationships but close associations of every type have become harder to form and more transitory (we shall discuss this in greater detail later).

Serial monogamy gives rise to a comparatively complex and often troubled structure that goes by several names: the "reconstituted," "blended" (as it is usually called on the West Coast), "recombined," or "joint" family, which is like the traditional stepfamily experienced by children after the death of one parent and the remarriage of the other, except that both "exes" are still around, so that there are usually at least two more sets of steprelations, living elsewhere, for everybody to contend with, as well as, nearly always, additional emotional complications. Writing about family life in seventeenth-century North America, the sociologists Donald M. Scott and Bernard Wishy explain that it was

> not at all rare for people who lasted into their sixties to have a succession of two or three spouses. With little restraint on fertility, this often yielded families with an extremely dense and complex mix of natural and stepparents and full and half siblings, not to mention the vast network of kin outside this core. A man who married at age twenty-five, for example, might lose his wife when he was thirty-five, after she had borne him four or five children. He might then marry a young widow with one or two children who would then provide him with several more. He might then die and she herself might remarry and have children in that marriage. One such "chain of marriage and remarriage" in Virginia from about 1655 to 1693, made up of six marriages among seven people, yielded at least twenty-five children. A visit to this household in 1680 would have found the presence of children

(ranging from infancy to the early twenties)
from four of the marriages. Some of them did not
have any parents in common.

With its capacity for generating even more steprelatives, the
modern stepfamily, created by divorce instead of by death, is sometimes seen as a potentially positive alternative to the sterility and
isolation of the nuclear family. "With so many siblings, the modern stepchild has never had it so good," Paul Bohannan told me
recently. "He's living in the kind of extended family we wished
we had in the nineteenth century." Fox talks of how divorce is
"breaking up the nuclear family, which is an aberrant product of
capitalism and affluence, a consequence of the mobility of labor,
and creating the new possibility for an extended family," and
Tiger has written, "When anthropology first started out, the difficult trick in studying any culture was to discover just what the
kinship system was—who was married to whom, and why, and
what connections counted for inheritance, status, and authority.
We found that marriage was the instrument for creating the extended family, which provided for most human needs in the tribal
societies. If an anthropologist from the Trobriand Islands came here
now, he or she could well conclude that by stimulating further marriages, divorce has come to be an important organizing principle in
our society, since kinship alliances among divorced people are so
extensive and complex."

With more than thirty-five million Americans now living in
them, including six million children, or one in every ten, stepfamilies are one of the nation's fastest-growing social phenomena,
and if they continue to form at their present rate of around thirteen hundred a day, by 1990 they and the also rising number of
single-parent families will outnumber the nuclear families. Stepfamilies have been appearing with increasing frequency on tele
vision—on a short-lived but much-praised series on ABC during
1982 called "The Family Tree," for instance, and in a 1983 situation comedy on NBC called "It's Not Easy."

The frictions and rivalries that can develop between steprelatives are quite similar to those that can arise in polygamous
families; the folkloric "wicked stepmother" is, in fact, thought to
have derived from the domineering figure of the senior wife in
the polygamous household. "The word for co-wifehood in Man-

dinka, the language of Senegambia and Guinea, is *sinamaa,* which
also means jealousy or factionalism," the African linguist Sandra
Sanneh has written.

> Ask anyone raised in a polygamous household
> and he/she will readily admit a closer relation-
> ship with siblings of the same mother and con-
> stant feuds and tensions with those of the other
> mothers. These quarrels extend frequently to the
> mothers themselves, who naturally favor their
> own offspring. One such person I know still car-
> ries the scar from a beating for something he did
> not do which was given him by his brother's
> mother, who disliked him because he did better
> at school than her son. The role of the father is
> of course to settle all such disputes and deal
> justly with all; no easy task, as Solomon himself
> well knew. In the event of the father's death the
> question of inheritance sometimes gives rise to
> very bitter quarrels.

Similarly, in the stepfamily the most common conflicts are between recently merged bloodlines. Stepparents are responsible
for about eighty per cent of the cases of child abuse in the United
States.

The psychotherapist Vera Muller-Paisner, who is both a step-
daughter and a stepmother, has written with great understanding
about the form. Its most important structural difference from
other families, she says, is that the relationship between the parents and their children predates the marriage. Instead of being
brought about by somebody's death, "the modern death suffered
is the death of an idealized marriage, for each adult," and the
common theme is still "one of loss. . . . All too often the family
colludes in trying to live happily ever after again, in order to
avoid further pain and disappointment. Problems are denied in
the hope of not repeating prior history. Eventually the family system explodes, commonly through a symptom developed by a
family member such as illness or inappropriate behavior." For the
first few years, reorganizing the adults and children into a work-
able, cohesive family unit is "chaotic at best. Everyone copes in

individual ways under stress. Some withdraw from the situation, some become aggressive and demanding or sick." But it is important for everybody to understand that the problems are "indigenous to the stepfamily situation rather than to its members. Changing homes, sharing rooms, developing parental and sibling relationships between different blood lines are not everyday occurrences."

The feminist writer Letty Cottin Pogrebin has described some specific problems that can arise:

> There is anger when money needed by the new family goes to one spouse's children from the old family. There is hurt at the recurring evidence of a past history shared with the first family and forever closed from the new spouse. Some children feel ashamed of the parents' divorce or hide the fact that they shuttle between two households in a shared custody arrangement. Others are made uncomfortable by the affection shown by partners in the new marriage, or by the stepparent's eagerness to be liked, or worst of all, by the arrival of a baby—living proof that the newly constituted family is a fact.
>
> A father feels guilty about spending every day with his stepchildren while his own kids, in the custody of their mother, hunger for more time with him. A young childless woman suddenly has four adolescents in her life because she married their father. A long-time wife suddenly has no husband, or has a new husband who doesn't care about her kids. Stepparents and biological parents disagree on discipline, spending money, or nutrition.

The most striking pattern is that "the stepfamily configuration seems to increase the power of the child . . . compared to other parents, remarried parents seem more desirous of their child's approval, more alert to the child's emotional state, and more sensitive in their parent-child relations . . . [while] the child is in this odd position of control, wielding the power to hurt by being hurt, to divide his or her parent's loyalties, to punish the adults who have 'destroyed' the child's *real* family."

From talking recently with a man I know, it emerged that he belonged to both an unofficial stepfamily and a "binuclear" family at the same time, and that he was involved in four modes of parenting. He had been married twice, the first time with no children, the second producing a boy and a girl. For the past three years he had been exclusively involved with a divorced woman who had two daughters. He was happier with this woman than he had been with either of his wives, he told me, but after two marriages that hadn't worked out, he was "less interested" in getting married again. "When the contract is no longer permanent and you've fulfilled the purpose for which it was designed—having children and bringing them up responsibly—you stop and think about the advantages and disadvantages of marrying again," he said. The woman and he weren't living together, but that was largely an economic decision. "We can't afford to give up our separate apartments," he explained. (They both lived in New York City, in cheap, rent-controlled units which they had moved into years earlier.) "Our rents together come to half of what a new lease on a three- or four-bedroom apartment would go for now.

"Luckily our children don't seem to have any serious emotional problems, but there are some curious semantic difficulties that have psychological weight. My kids, for instance, don't have a word for Marilyn. They still say 'my father's girlfriend.' The whole organism we are all part of is so new that there isn't a word for somebody in her position. I mean what do you call her—or me, for that matter? Coparent? Partner? Copartner? We were talking about it the other day. I sort of go for the French word *copain*. It doesn't have the melodramatic quality of 'lover' and it's more dignified than 'old lady' or 'old man.' But maybe a new word should be invented. How about *copar*?

"Another semantic problem is getting everybody to agree on what the family is and who is in it. The children have the binuclear concept." (The term "binuclear family" was proposed by Constance Ahron of the University of Wisconsin to identify a divorced couple with joint custody of their children, who feel equally at home in either parent's household.) "Marilyn's daughters reimprinted on me soon, but as a friend, not as a father. Their father remarried and his new wife is expecting, so they feel better because Daddy's got somebody and Mommy's got somebody. But for my kids the transition hasn't been as smooth. It's difficult for them to accept Marilyn's intimacy with me because their mother hasn't had any 'significant other,' so there's an imbalance. Marilyn, on the other hand, feels that 'we,' the six of us—me, her, her two, my two—are the family, even if we don't meet the Census Bureau's criterion of living under the same roof, because we could and we may still. Her ex-husband is not family any more, as far as she is concerned, even though her girls' definition is different— he *is* family—and she is *adamant* that *my* ex is not in any family that she and I are in. We've had arguments about that. I say my ex was in a family unit that included me, and as far as I'm concerned, she's still family, she's still the mother of our children. And what about her parents, whom I always liked but rarely get to see any more? Aren't they still my children's grandparents? Don't they still get to take their grandchildren to the circus for the afternoon as they used to when they come up once a year from Florida?" I asked how the four adults had scheduled the visits by their children. "Each of us has our children half the time during the course of a fortnight," he explained. "We have worked it out so that basically we have our kids separately with some overlap, so that most of the nights we have our children Marilyn and I are not with each other, although during some parts of the year she is with me and the children. We have done it this way because we want some time alone." All told, he calculated that he was involved in four modes of parenting: "1) the six of us together; 2) I'm with my kids, she's with hers; 3) I'm with hers and mine; and 4) I'm with her kids without her or my kids"; and two other "modes of existence": "5) Marilyn and I alone together; 6) she and I alone in our separate apartments. Talking about it, I realize how crazy and emotionally difficult it must seem, but it eventually gets to be normal and fairly organized. It's a lot calmer than the latter stages of either of my marriages. We can pretty much tell you where each of us will be six months from now."

3. *The Single-Parent Family*

The number of single-parent families, like the number of stepfamilies, has also been rising rapidly. Some scholars call the single-parent family the "attenuated nuclear family," but that is misleading, because some of these families have never had a second parent in the household. The 1983 census counted 6,445,000 single-parent households in the country. In 1970, 6.3 percent of America's families had just one parent; by 1982 the proportion had risen to 10.5 per cent. Even in Westchester County, New York, a bastion of the nuclear family, one would think, the proportion of single-parent families went up from 13.1 per cent in 1970 to 18.6 per cent in 1980. In 1982, 13.7 million children under eighteen—twenty-two per cent of all the children in the country (up from twelve per cent in 1970)—were living with just one parent, and "if today's trends continue," Pogrebin writes, "nearly one out of two children born from now on will spend a significant portion of his or her life in a one-parent family."

The increase in this category is due mostly to the rise in the divorce rate, and to a lesser extent to a decline in the remarriage rate, particularly among women between twenty-five and forty-four; only twenty per cent of the single parents in 1982 had never been married, and nine per cent were widowed. The other seventy-one per cent were heads of "broken homes"—nuclear families that had fissioned either into binuclear families or into what are called "disjoined" families, in which the resident parent has custody of the children and the other parent has visiting rights; or women with children (and, in a few cases, men with children) who had been abandoned. (As the household census is conducted by mail, and each householder answers the question "Who is living here?" on his own recognizance, there is a chance that the children in some binuclear households may have been counted twice.) The great majority of the single-parent families—5,717,000 in 1983—contained only the mother, although the 737,000 father-headed families counted that year were double those in 1970. How many of the single parents were serial monogamists in transit to their next marriage, and how many were going to remain single from then on, there was of course no way of knowing.

One wonders what the single-parent family, as an increasingly common "breakdown product" of the nuclear family, represents: is it a symptom of social deterioration, or is some sort of new adaptation taking place? Could kinship be streamlining itself even further, to allow even more mobility and freedom of self-expression, beyond the nuclear family, to the minimal, most elementary association of all, the real mammalian "nuclear family," as Fox would argue: the mother-child unit? Will single parent-hood be the norm in the future, as the nuclear family has been for the past few centuries? In the family courts, where such new problems as grandparental visiting rights and the husband's right to custody of his children are coming up with increasing fre-quency, the nuclear family is no longer always a pertinent model. (Forty-two states now protect the child's access to his grandparents in the event that his parents divorce or one of them dies; a recent decision in New York upheld the visiting rights of two grand-parents even though their son, the child's father, had allowed the new husband of his ex-wife to adopt the boy and no longer en-joyed visiting rights himself.)

But it is hard to imagine single parenthood completely re-placing the traditional mother-father-child triad, when few of the people bringing up children alone claim to be happy or to be doing it by choice; given the opportunity to merge into a new nu-clear family (to form a stepfamily, in other words), most of them would do so gladly. Among the least able to cope with the situa-tion are the small but growing number of single fathers with cus-tody of their children (a phenomenon that has been linked to the high divorce rate, to the blurring of sex roles, and to the greater participation of women in the labor force). Only forty-seven per cent of the 1,136 single fathers who belonged to an organization called Parents Without Partners said in a 1983 survey that they felt comfortable about being single again. Seventy-seven per cent reported that they had trouble balancing the demands of having to work with raising the children: 9.6 per cent had quit or been dis-missed because being a single parent interfered with their work.

One type of person who is becoming a single parent by choice rather than as a function of divorce is the well-educated unmarried career woman, getting older but still in her childbear-ing years, who decides, rather than miss out on motherhood en-tirely, to have a child out of wedlock. The number of families headed by never-married mothers has soared since 1970—from 234,000 to 1,092,000—an increase of three hundred and fourteen per cent (there is no information about how many of these preg-nancies were intentional, however), and from 1970 to 1979 the rate of first births to women, married or single, aged thirty to thirty-four went up sixty-six per cent, from 7.3 first births per thousand women to 12.1—a significant increase, considering that women in general are having fewer children. In 1981, fifty-three per cent of all births to white women in Washington, D.C., were to women over the age of thirty. "It is evident that large numbers of women have postponed marriage and motherhood to an unprecedented extent since the post-depression years of the 1930s," the demographer Stephanie J. Ventura has written. "The proportion of women aged twenty-five to twenty-nine years who are still childless has jumped sharply. . . . The desire of many women to complete their education and become established in a career appears to be an important factor."

Another factor is understanding that the risk to an older mother of having a child with a birth defect is much less than previously imagined. One of the most widely feared conditions, Down's syndrome, is caused by failure of a pair of chromosomes to separate during the formation of the sperm or the egg cells prior to their fusion, with the result that the child is born with an extra twenty-first chromosome, and with the slanted eyes, large tongue, poor muscle tone, and mental retardation characteristic of mongolism. This "meiotic disjunction" afflicts about one in every fifteen hundred children born to women aged twenty to thirty. The odds rise to roughly one in seven hundred and fifty for women aged thirty to thirty-five, to one in six hundred for women between thirty-five and forty, to one in three hundred for women forty to forty-five, and to one in sixty for women older than that. The chances that the baby will not be a victim of Down's syndrome, in other words, are excellent, and the availability of amniocentesis and other medical procedures that can detect the presence of most genetic disorders in the fetus, and of abortion, has given women the option of terminating the pregnancy, so there is little any more to stop an unmarried older woman who wants a child from deciding to have one.

The most common method for a woman in this situation who doesn't have in mind a specific father for her child is artificial insemination. Thus a nurse from Brooklyn named Jessica Curtis was recently able to have a daughter at the age of thirty-six. All she was told about the donor of the sperm was that he was a six-foot-tall, blond, blue-eyed medical student. Asked why she wanted another child when she already had a fourteen-year-old son from one of her two previous marriages, she recently explained to the

New York Times, "What I really wanted in life was life like the Waltons, with grandparents, ten kids, a dog, a cat, and a farm. But I also found that when you already have a kid it was very difficult to meet someone and establish a relationship. I tried with lovers for a year. They were willing, but I didn't get pregnant." Miss Curtis claimed that having the child by an unknown father had made for fewer problems. "With Armida . . . I'm not angry at anyone, and there is no father saying he sees her too much or not enough. And there are absolutely no custody problems." Another *Times* article, a few months later, headlined "Sperm-Bank Baby Joy to His Mother," and subheaded "Unmarried Psychologist Says Year Has Been Wonderful," told about a woman who gave birth to a daughter she named Doron after being inseminated shortly before her fortieth birthday with sperm donated by a Nobel Prize–winning scientist to the Repository of Germinal Choice in Escondido, California. "I had toyed with the alternative of inviting a man I care for to co-parent with me, but the parenting responsibilities and obligations would have involved some kind of compromises," the woman said.

But not all unwed mothers, as a poll of the members of Single Parents by Choice, an organization for which Miss Curtis is a spokeswoman, revealed, are such enthusiastic and self-reliant backers of Fox's law of the dispensable male. Almost all the members who were interviewed said, in fact, that they had not given up hope of being married some day. "I would have much preferred marriage, if it had been in the cards," said a preschool teacher named Risa Novikoff, who was raising eighteen-month-old twins on her own. "If some man were to come into my life, I'd be more than ready." The group is frank about the disadvantages of single motherhood: "financial worries about putting the child through college; the violation of still-present but lessening social taboos; the lack of a partner to share the child's accomplishments; the lack of spontaneity in the mother's life, and the feeling of being cooped up in an apartment with the child, which can sometimes lead to thoughts of child abuse."

A few months after an article about these women appeared in the *Times,* there was another article, headlined "Jersey Mother Held in Drowning of Two of Four Missing Children." It told the story of a single woman who was receiving welfare and was pregnant with a fifth child—a "good mother" but subject to "bursts of temper," according to *her* mother—when she apparently snapped under the strain of her situation. Pogrebin explains how badly the cards are stacked against the mother-headed family:

> Since men make seventy per cent of the nation's income, and since sex segregation in the work force relegates women to second-class jobs, and since many of these jobs still pay women as though they were supplementary wage earners, the discriminatory job market indirectly penal-izes the children of women who are primary wage earners. Women maintaining families have nearly twice as high a rate of unemployment as men. From 1960 to 1981, the number of people in poor families headed by women rose fifty-four per cent. The fact is, a child born into a male-headed family has only one chance in forty of being poor; but in a female-headed family, the odds become one in six. If present trends con-tinue, by the year 2000 "the poverty population would be composed solely of women and their children." That's bad for children. What's bad for women is this Catch-22: If a single mother works, she is said to "neglect" her kids; if she goes on welfare, she's "lazy." As a working woman, she is an inadequate *mother;* as a woman on welfare, she's an unsuccessful *person.* These no-win self-images added to the economic pun-ishment of low wages or welfare serve as a warn-ing to women who dare to try to survive *unde-pendent on a man.*

The highest proportion of single-parent families is found among American blacks, more than half of whose children are cur-rently being born out of wedlock, and 47.9 per cent of whose families with children under eighteen counted in 1983 had only the mother present—a huge increase from the twenty-one per cent of "nonwhite" families (ninety-two per cent of which were black) that were mother-headed in 1960, and the eight per cent in 1950. Among those who are alarmed by the growing number of black families in this category is Benjamin H. Hooks, the executive director of the National Association for the Advancement of Colored People, who said in a recent statement that "finding ways to end the precipitous slide of the black family is one of the most important items on the civil rights agenda today. We can talk all we want about school integration; we can file suits to have more black role models in the classrooms and in administrative positions to have a cross-fertilization of ethnic cultures and background. But if the child returns home to a family devoid of the basic tenets necessary for his discipline, growth and development, the integrated school environment must fail."

The rise in the number of mother-headed households among blacks has been linked to the decline in the employment rate among black men over the age of sixteen, which fell from seventy-four per cent to fifty-five per cent between 1960 and 1983; and to a growing feeling of futility and inadequacy among black men "hung up on prejudice and discrimination," as the embittered wife of one man described her listless, unemployed husband. ("The black man is castrated in our society," a social worker explained to me. "All the cards are stacked against him. This has inevitably affected his marriage.") The proportion of chronic illnesses ranging from cancer to diabetes among black men has risen more quickly in the past two decades than the proportion among white men has; in 1975 black men were admitted to psychiatric facilities at a rate twice that of white men; and the rate of imprisonment of black men is four to five times as great as that of white men, the journalist Ronald Smothers reported recently all of which supports the contention of the sociologist Walter Allen that "black men are under siege," and has contributed to the rise in black mother-headed families.

The rise in this category has also been linked to the comparatively high amount of sexual activity and pregnancy among black teenage girls (which was responsible for more than one in every four of the black children born in 1979); to the supportiveness and the strong religious views of the black community, which encourages its single women to have rather than to abort their babies; and to the welfare system. ("It presents her [the single black woman], at age sixteen, a chance for independence in an apartment of her own; free housing, medicine, legal assistance, and a combination of payments and food stamps worth several hundred dollars a month. There is only one crucial condition. She must have an illegitimate child," the conservative economist George Gilder has argued.) Fox offers two other theories for the upsurge of teenage pregnancy not only among black women but among American women generally: because the demographics of the "baby-boom" generation are "out of whack" and many women are condemned by them to be single, some are going ahead and having children without waiting to find a husband; and because the teens have been the prime childbearing years for women throughout history, perhaps the phenomenon merely represents a revolt against the "perverse restriction" placed on them comparatively recently, and only in this part of the world.

Others see the single black mother, with her long tradition of financial independence, as a vanguard of the society. "Black women have been in the work force in larger numbers for much longer than white women," the *New York Times* reported recently.

> After World War II, millions of blacks left Southern farms, the women often recruited to work as maids for Northern whites, the men to work in factories. Mechanization began to eliminate sharecropping, the economic system that replaced slavery in the South. The consequences were widespread. Black families and communities that had functioned as economic and social units for decades on the farm were cut adrift and scattered. An extended family structure surviving from African traditions and its attendant values largely succumbed to the impersonal isolation of the cities. Even among the middle class, which for white women has customarily meant staying home to care for the family, black women's income has usually been needed to keep the family at a middle-income level. As a result, black women, earlier than other women, have made the next step of having and supporting children independently.

Still others offer a cultural perspective. "A parental pair who provide joint caretaking for their children was not a tradition in most areas of Africa from which black people were brought to America for enslavement," a woman named Candice S. Cason pointed out in a letter prompted by the *Times* article. "The extended family was the norm in the majority of those societies. Once in America, the [nuclear family] was presented to slaves by their European-American masters as a desirable model, and concurrently denied them as they were subject to sale or trade independent of their families at the will of slave masters. [It] was officially allowed to develop [only] following the Emancipation Proclamation."

The community in suburban New York to which my wife and I and our two sons recently moved is proud of being one of the nation's oldest integrated neighborhoods and lends credence to the sort of cultural approach of Ms. Cason. Our neighbors are for the most part well-to-do and conservative blacks. Many drive late-model Cadillacs and have been living continuously since the nineteen-fifties in gracious turn-of-the-century mansions that are admirably suited to the extended families that have arisen as their children began to have children. One household, for instance, has a divorced woman who is a chemist, her unmarried daughter (a nurse), and her daughter's child, who is looked after by her unemployed son (by another man) while both women are at work. The father of the child lives nearby and visits frequently, often with a child he has since had by another woman. Another household has a man (a lawyer) and his wife, their grandson (whose father, their son, lives nearby and visits frequently; the mother is in Virginia, in the Army), and their grandson's half-brother (same mother, different father). A third household contains only a man and his wife, whose grown-up children live nearby and visit frequently with their children and stepchildren. "We've been married forty-four years, if you call that normal," he said to me recently. His wife takes care of one of their grand-daughters while the mother, their daughter, works.

None of these arrangements is directly the result of poverty; clearly, in the first two, a different family system, with many affinities to the Caribbean and Latin-American extended family, is at work, and from what I can see, it is a smooth, viable system, with good points. The children are largely brought up by their grandparents, as in many societies in which the single mother has an extended family to fall back on. (There is even a saying in Puerto Rico—I recently heard about a pregnant young Puerto Rican woman who evoked it in her refusal to have an abortion—"the first one is for Grandmother"; and the Samoans, as mentioned earlier, traditionally give their firstborn to be raised by the grandparents. A Jamaican variant of this generation-skipping system has the mother coming to the United States to work, often in a hospital, and not always with a Green Card, and sending money home to her children, whom she has left with her mother, and whom she visits once a year.) This is good for the grandparents; it gives them a continuing role. The grandchildren benefit from their wisdom and experience, hearing their stories and learning the "old values." (It was from the old women on his mother's side of the family, as we shall see later, that the writer Alex Haley heard about an eighteenth-century ancestor named Kunta Kinte who had been kidnapped into slavery from his home in Africa along a river, the "Kamby Bolongo." These fragments of family history set him off, as an adult, on a twelve-year quest for his "roots.") The single black woman is usually not in a vacuum, as white women often are when they decide to have a child out of wedlock or when their marriage breaks up; she often has a network of kin to help her take care of her children and is freed to try to develop a career and to overcome the disadvantages that go with being dark-skinned in this country. Often the father is in the vicinity, or even living with her (unless she was married to him, she would be counted as single by the census). For some black women, who as a group are one of the most upwardly mobile segments of our society, single parenthood may even be adaptive.

The social workers Elmer P. and Joanne Mitchell Martin have described the black mother-headed family as a "sub-extended family"—part of a larger group of mutually supportive kin. From 1969 to 1977 the Martins studied thirty black extended families made up of more than a thousand people, who lived in rural Mississippi and Florida and in two urban areas, Cleveland and Kansas City. Some of the families had nearly a hundred members. The black extended family, they concluded, is "a multi-generational kinship system which is welded together by a sense of obligation to relatives." It is organized around a "family base household" and has a "dominant family figure," a "Momma," as she is often called (the same term is used for respected female elders in Zaire), who is typically a woman between sixty and eighty-five years of age and a great-grandparent. It "extends across geographical boundaries to connect families to an extended family network" and "has a built-in mutual aid system for the welfare of its members and the maintenance of the family as a whole." It "has been responsible for providing many black Americans with basic economic and emotional security."

The Martins' findings support the conclusion of a 1968 study by the sociologist Andrew Billingsley, that "the Negro family is an absorbing, adaptive, and amazingly resilient mechanism for the socialization of its children and the civilization of its society"—a far more positive portrait than the one presented in 1965 by the (then) urban specialist Daniel Patrick Moynihan, whose controversial but influential report, *The Black Family: A Case for National Action,* found that family characterized by a "tangle of pathologies." In fact, the Martins argue, many blacks, with their pariah status, could not have survived in American society without the psychological and material support of relatives. For one of the families they studied in rural Kansas, the "Romans," this claim seems incontestible: the family had seventy-two members with a collective annual income of only a hundred and thirty-five thousand dollars. The Martins contend that the extended family has played as important a role for blacks as it has for the immigrants who have depended on it since colonial times: "Just as the extended family helped blacks survive an oppressive peonage system, so it helped European immigrants survive the cruelties of an industrial system." But a number of things now threaten it: affluence (in the now-familiar pattern)—after the Second World War more blacks were able to form nuclear families, though ironically "only at a time when nuclear-family life was beginning to deteriorate in the white community"; and migration to the cities, where it is seldom possible to accommodate all the members under one roof, and where the erosion of "extended-family values" is hastened—"they become just one set of values among many competing sets"—so that some of the members adopt urban values of individualism, secularism, and materialism. The form "should not be viewed as a matriarchal structure," the Martins argue. "The simple fact is that most of the aged females had outlived their

husbands . . . when alive, their husbands were either absolute
dominant family figures or shared that role with their wives." But
it is also true that the husband is often not present in black families, and when he is, the family is more apt to have "nuclear-
family values"; that many of the "sub-extended families" never
had a husband; and that a central function of the black extended
family is to be a support system for the single mothers it embraces.

Much of the evidence the Martins present in their fine study
suggests to me, at least, that the structure *is* matriarchal, if only
by default: the money that the various members of the extended
family earn is commonly turned over to the "Momma" for distribution; the role of dominant family figure commonly passes to the
"Momma's" eldest daughter; "when a marriage occurs between a
man and a woman who are both members of extended families,
the marriage tends to be closer to the female's family than the
male's." The fact that "children born out of wedlock in the extended family seldom grow up feeling stigmatized and are seldom,
if ever, referred to as 'illegitimate' further suggests that a certain
acceptance of the father's absence is built into the structure." (In
Billingsley's earlier study, which identifies twelve types of American
families, the presence of the father and of the nuclear-family type is
clearly correlated with socioeconomic circumstances.) I have encountered resistance from middle-class American blacks when as a
white man I have suggested that one of their characteristic family
types is African in origin—as if it were something to be ashamed of;
and I have encountered the feeling that, however "idyllic" the extended family may be in Africa, it is "dysfunctional" here. The
Martins conclude by outlining the "continued usefulness" of the
extended family: its "values of caring, sharing, and helping are more
humanistic and people-oriented than the dominant society's view
of 'claw your way to the top' competition and 'dog-eat-dog' individualism."

A final point about the rise of the single-parent family is that
it has new implications for the survivorship of surnames, which
as far as I know have never been investigated; with more surnames being transmitted matrilineally by single mothers, rather
than dying out on the mothers' lines because they married and
their children received their husbands' surnames, the mothers' surnames have another generation of life extended to them. One

would expect the survivorship of surnames in general to be positively affected by this newly opening avenue of descent.

4. The Single Person

Another category in the population that is dramatically on the rise is that of people living alone. In 1983, 19,250,000 of the country's households contained only one person—almost double the number in 1970, and a proportional increase of about six per cent, to twenty-three per cent. Some of the people in this group have already been identified: the new proliferation of widowed, financially self-sufficient "senior citizens"; the grown-up children of the baby boom who are leaving their parents' homes and striking out on their own (though increasingly, not immediately upon finishing college or attaining their majority); the women who are postponing marriage and childbearing in order to complete their education and get started in a career (the proportion of never-married women between the ages of twenty-five and twenty-nine, for instance, has risen from 10.5 per cent in 1970 to 24.8 in 1983). There are people who are failing to connect and people who are failing to reconnect—both the marriage rate and the remarriage rate are down (the 1979 remarriage rate for women aged twenty-five to forty-four was down thirty per cent from the rate of ten years earlier, and the rate for men was down slightly less). "There's a lot of evidence that divorce is an overwhelming stress for most people, even if they are getting divorced for the right reasons," the marriage and divorce counselor Robert Seagraves said in a recent interview with the *Times*. "There's tremendous internal and external reorganization required after a divorce. And the effects are not just short-term. We see a lot of people years later who are having trouble reconnecting with the opposite sex. Men, for instance, often have problems with impotence four or five years later because they're scared to death to be reconnected."

There are people who are simply indisposed to or precluded from heterosexual involvements, perhaps for psychological, hormonal, or temperamental reasons, and who become homosexuals, "confirmed" bachelors or spinsters, or priests or nuns—although celibacy is probably less common now than it was during the more sexually repressed past. There are artists who believe themselves to be merely vessels or witnesses to their times, placed on earth to fulfill a destiny higher than themselves, with which time-consuming and emotionally demanding involvements would interfere. A few highly principled individuals have realized how unfair it would be for somebody totally dedicated to a career to have children and have consequently put out of their mind the thought of parenthood, as Katharine Hepburn did while still in her twenties. Most movie stars, however, have married again and again; taken as a group, they have in fact been among our most exuberant serial monogamists. Assuming that they are to some extent acting out the fantasies of their public, this is an interesting phenomenon in light of the controversy about whether we are truly a long-term monogamous species. "I give it three years," the psychologist Joyce Brothers predicted in a "special analysis" of the late Richard Burton's fifth marriage, in which she also mentioned a survey which found "that seventy-five per cent of all movie actors are from broken homes." Perhaps Hepburn had seen too many children of "Hollywood marriages" suffer both from being in the shadow of adulated, self-centered parents and as neglected stepchildren to want to bring any more into the world.

Most single adults, however, have probably not chosen their status, but find themselves single for a variety of reasons they may not even understand. One recent evening I ran into a young black man I had known for a long time, sitting on a bar stool in a deep depression. His wife had left him several months earlier, he told me. He had wanted her to stay home and take care of their daughter, who had just turned one year old. In fact, he didn't like the idea of her working at all; he had envisioned himself as the good provider and the strong but gentle *pater familias,* the "tower of strength" his father had been, but his wife was intent on getting back to her nursing career. She was perfectly capable of supporting herself—in fact she was making more money than he was, as the dry-cleaning business he had started was still just getting off the ground—so he had no leverage over her, nothing to reward her with for her subordination; and, unable to agree on the terms of their life together, they had split up. In the familial Caribbean-black pattern, his wife had turned their daughter over to her mother.

Just as "family satisfaction" can have an effect on a woman's fertility—a twenty-four-year longitudinal study of women in

Pennsylvania, for instance, showed a strong positive correlation between number of siblings and number of children among the women who at age sixteen had expressed satisfaction with their parental family—family *dis*satisfaction may be intense enough to keep the product of a miserable childhood single as an adult. One woman of exceptional beauty, intelligence, and warmth, whom many men would have been glad to marry, but who as she neared the end of her childbearing years was still single, recently explained to me that for years as a child she was a helpless witness to her parents' stormy marriage, until they finally divorced, and that she had vowed to herself not to repeat the experience. The knowledge that she was attractive to men, and would probably never lack male companionship, she also felt, had kept her from rushing into marriage; and yet she said it would be a mistake to conclude that she was happy single. From time to time she visited her younger brother in the suburbs, a devoted family man with a wife and four children. His world seemed unbearably sterile and conventional, and she couldn't wait to get back to her apartment in the city, where there was such a variety of people and things to do, and yet she envied him for having a family. Most of the single women she knew "would kill to have a decent man," yet she had noticed that women on the whole tolerate and even enjoy living alone better than men do, an observation with which many would agree. "If men have not remarried by six years after divorce," the psychologist E. Mavis Hetherington recently concluded after studying a large number of men in that situation, "their rates of car accidents, alcoholism, drug abuse, depression and anxiety increase. Men have a harder time living alone than women do"; and their remarriage rate is accordingly, as already mentioned, slightly higher; they are quicker to act "on the rebound." (An interesting but probably unanswerable question is whether men have *always* been less able to live alone, or only recently, when they lost their "internal pilot system" as our society became "other-directed.")

Perhaps women are better able to live alone because more of them are doing it. The basic ratio of about half again as many female to male "live-alones" has declined somewhat as their numbers have gone up collectively, but it still approaches two to one. In 1983, 11,799,000 women were living alone, compared to 7,451,000 men; in 1970 the breakdown was 7,319,000 to 3,532,000.

Many of these women, to be sure, are widows who have survived their husbands, but others are women in their thirties and forties who in the past decade have gained the courage and the means to hold out for exactly what they wanted, and have become remarkably independent. "It is a single life I live, in many senses," Alice Koller recently wrote in the "Hers" column of the *New York Times*. "Single in being unmarried, single in being separate from others of like kind. But also single in being unified, integrated into an unbroken whole. The first of these was not a deliberate choice but rather a state I drifted into as a consequence of my unshakable desire to live in the country. The last of these is an intentional and unending pursuit, my journey of defiance against the final triumph of the disintegration that awaits me."

Another recent article, in the *Times's* Home Section, reported that an increasing number of women in their thirties and forties, who had established careers and were living by themselves in New York City, had begun to accept that their status may not be temporary and had begun to "feather out their solitary nests in a style that would have been unthinkable for most women of earlier generations"—providing themselves with china, silver, linen, and other traditional items of the bridal trousseau; hiring interior decorators to give their apartment a finished look of settled domesticity which they had previously stopped short of doing "for fear of giving the wrong message" to male suitors.

Similarly, changes in their self-image have made some men wary about marriage. Until roughly the early nineteen-fifties, the feminist writer Barbara Ehrenreich argues in a recent book called *The Hearts of Men: American Dreams and the Flight from Commitment*, men were more willing to consign themselves to oppressive marital patterns, with a "grasping" wife typically "spur[ring] them on to ever-higher paychecks" (according to a reviewer's paraphrasing), because "their very masculinity was at stake . . . to be male was—by sociological wisdom and almost universal consensus—to accept the obligations of marriage and paying the bills, and . . . to do anything else was to be branded a loser or, horror of horrors, a latent homosexual." But successive waves of "male revolt" caused that consensus to unravel. The first wave, of "gray-flannel dissidents," prided themselves "on a detached awareness of their own dull conformity" (the reviewer again) while still "play[ing] by the rules." A few years later *Playboy* magazine "legitimized an ethos of masculinity without marriage," though it still encouraged "hard work through a vision of hedonistic consumerism." Then, during the nineteen-sixties, hippies and male liberationists emerged and, "bolstered by the optimistic insights of humanistic and 'growth' psychology . . . questioned not only conventional family structures, but the credibility of maleness itself. Masculinity began to be perceived as an oppressive carapace or 'role' masking real, more 'androgynous' humanity."

In another recent book, *The Peter Pan Syndrome*, the writer David Hellerstein also traces to the present this male reluctance to enter into deep, binding relationships with the opposite sex and describes a new (he claims) type of man who can't be counted on as lover, colleague, or friend; since the book is a best-seller, a good many people must feel that Hellerstein has identified something that is really happening. "Over the last few decades the upper limits of adolescence in America have stretched so far that they've practically disappeared," he writes in a short version of his thesis which appeared in *Esquire*. "Single men from their late twenties on through their thirties are struggling with issues of freedom and commitment, of pleasure and responsibility: issues that in previous generations would have been resolved by the age of twenty. It's not that these men are immature but that the world has changed: the solutions of previous generations don't work anymore." This *puer aeternus* or Peter Pan type is primarily a product of upper-middle-class suburbs and good colleges, and is often stuck at the sixth stage in the psychoanalyst Erik Erikson's eight-stage scheme of personality development: he has not developed the capacity for true intimacy—"that is [Erikson writes], the capacity to commit himself to concrete affiliations and partnerships and to develop the ethical strength to abide by such commitments, even though they may call for significant sacrifices and compromises"; and he is unable to move on to the seventh stage, which focuses on generativity (beginning to create or establish the next generation). "It's okay to change jobs every few years," Hellerstein explains; "in some circles it's even encouraged. It's not crucial to marry anymore either. You can have serially monogamous relationships or you can date casually year after year or you can live alone. Probably millions of us will never have children; that's acceptable too. And there's a huge pool of single people in our society: the never-married, the divorced, the between-relationships, and so on.

If you *are* a Peter Pan you'll never be lacking for Wendys." But it would be wrong to conclude that most single men are any less lonely than the majority of single women are, although few are as open about their loneliness as Barry Butkus, a thirty-five-year-old bachelor from North Easton, Massachusetts, who after trying everything from dating services to marriage brokers, recently planted a sign in his front yard which said, "I need a wife." "All I'm looking for is a woman with a good heart," he said. "Single life is the pits."

The main reason why more people are living alone is not that the sexes are shying away from each other, however, but that our society makes it possible for them to live singly: there are enough housing and enough well-paying jobs for a portion of the population—about 8 per cent—to have a solitary existence, which is hardly possible in other parts of the world (twenty-six per cent of Mexico City's families, for instance, each averaging 5.5 people, live together in one room, and seventy-nine per cent of Calcutta's 10.2 million people belong to one-room families). Once again we find evidence of the negative correlation between kinship and plenty, and between status and fertility. In the United States, there is such plenty that it is possible to have *zero* kinship. The people who live by themselves are drawn for the most part from the wealthier and better-educated ranks of the society. "It is remarkable and probably significant for understanding the intellectual life of the U.S.A. that one of its elite centers of communication, the *New York Review of Books,* is issue after issue chockablock with Personal Ads [of single people trying to connect with each other]," Lionel Tiger has pointed out.

Most single people live in cities because the best opportunities for careers, for alternatives to life-term monogamy, and for meeting other single people are there. Real estate in cities is at such a premium that it is most profitable for the developer to pile up small dwelling units on top of each other and to rent them out or sell them to single people. The intense competition for these units, particularly in New York City, further encourages city dwellers to remain solitary, to think twice (as the divorced man interviewed a few pages back did) before giving up the cheap, rent-controlled unit they have lived in for years for the sake of a relationship that past experience has taught may not work out. Fox maintains that the rise of single people in our society is an "epiphenomenon of modern technology," of the advent of apartments and restaurants, of laundromats and frozen dinners, and particularly of the refrigerator. "If you look at the bachelors of the century before, like Sherlock Holmes and Watson, they always had a housekeeper. The modern single person couldn't survive if he or she had to shop more than once a week." Other important technological developments that have given people the option of remaining single, rather than paying for the consequences of their sexual activity, are, of course, contraceptives and abortion. (With its vehement stand against abortion, the Catholic Church, the traditional enemy of kinship, is now promoting it.)

The most disturbing pattern of all may be that many people are no longer even getting to the marriage or the nuclear-family stages; many of the atoms aren't even binding. Were he alive, Francis Galton would probably be alarmed about the growing number of "never-married live-alones"—as demographers term the people who have completely removed themselves from the arena of biological kinship, whose connection with the world will end with them—because they are often our brightest talents, and their genes are being lost (although throughout human history "superior genes," if such things exist, have continuously been migrating up the social ladder and getting eliminated, eminent people have frequently been siphoned off from the reproductive cycle, and there is still no evidence of the "marching morons" effect that proponents of eugenics have feared would come to pass).

Why is this "exotic situation, almost an astonishment," as Lionel Tiger has described it, happening? "Recall we are gregarious animals for whom solitary confinement is a truly extreme punishment. When we impose it on ourselves, what do we call it then?" Besides the various economic and psychological explanations that have already been offered, this novel and unnatural "singles" phenomenon may also be due to a more generalized decline in the capacity for intimacy, to the simple inability of many people, because of the competitive and narcissistic individualism that have been encouraged in them, to make space for somebody else in their lives. Perhaps the increasingly widespread patterns of serial monogamy and single parenthood, too, are reflections of this pervasive self-centeredness. Not only marriages, but friendships, have been serial, and the capacity for making them and holding on to them has diminished. The problems of our times include how to get rid of old friends one has "outgrown." I recently saw a magazine article on the subject. The most successful people in our society, de Zengotita told me recently, are those who are able to "compartmentalize" their lives. He was talking about "switching modes" over short time frames—changing from the Machiavellian wheeler-dealer at work, for instance, to the gentle lover and devoted family man when one got home. "There are so many identities you can slip on nowadays. Life has become a sort of Bloomingdale's of the spirit. You turn into your own puppet master, and you're not completely any of these things," he explained—an ability that is hardly conducive to achieving long-term intimacy with another person.

But as all of one's relationships become progressively more short-lived and serial, it also becomes advantageous to "compartmentalize" over long time frames, to ruthlessly separate the past from the present, to stop "putting energy" into a relationship that no longer "delivers" and to move on to the next one. The more adept one becomes at "breaking clean" with people, the more they seem like expendable commodities, to be manipulated and dropped as soon as one has got what one wants out of them.

The greatest concentration of single people in the world, the world capital of rampant individualism, is New York City. In 1980, 1,902,262 New Yorkers, or thirty-four per cent of the city's entire population fifteen years old or older, had never married, and 349,373 of the 706,015 households in Manhattan had only one person in them. Manhattan actually had even more "singles" than that, because many of those counted had roommates who were also single but who didn't appear on the census rolls; and some "never-marrieds," as well as some of the divorced and the widowed who had not remarried, were living with their parents or with other kin. New York's conservatively estimated two million singles are probably its most characteristic subculture. An unusually large number of unmarried officials represent them at City Hall. Numerous businesses cater to their needs. Psychiatrists and newspaper columnists counsel the lonely, special bars provide places for them to meet, there is even a "video meeting service" whose subscribers can look each other over on videotape and decide if they want to meet in the flesh. More than a thousand New Yorkers have dialled home computers into a matchmaking service called Marc the Martian's Mixed-Up Matching and Message Machine, and several marriages have resulted; and a seminar was recently held at Bloomingdale's on how to "accidentally" meet members of the opposite sex at the department store. The instructor, a bearded, bespectacled sociologist named Martin Gallatin, who also taught tactics for meeting "mates" in museums, laundromats, food stores, and buses, charged twenty-five dollars per person. Bloomingdale's, he said, was a particularly good meeting place: besides having all sorts of gadgets and displays to aid conversation, "the sixty thousand people in the store on a busy day mean a lot of prospects, and the demographics are right."

With such an enormous pool of potential mates in New York City, and most of them eager to connect with somebody, the question is, What is keeping them apart?

The Return to Kinship

THERE ARE TWO INESCAPABLE AND CONTRADICTORY SIDES TO THE human condition. On the one hand, each of us is ultimately a prisoner of his singularity. Complete fusion with another person is impossible; there are parts of us, like the world of our dreams, which nobody else can ever know. D. H. Lawrence, who wrote with great beauty and understanding about men and women in love, maintained that "the central law of all organic life is that each organism is intrinsically isolated and single in itself. The moment its isolation breaks down, and there comes an actual mingling and confusion, death sets in." Because of our singularity, all kinship systems and genealogical networks are, in a sense, elaborate scaffoldings we erect to draw attention from the fact that we have come into the world alone and will die alone.

But the scaffoldings are not entirely illusory, because the kin are there, whatever we choose to make of them. Donne's famous observation that "no man is an island, entire of itself; every man is a piece of the continent, a part of the main," is quite accurate. Each of us has an unlimited number of kin—all the people who have ever lived, in fact (the surprising extent of our multiple interrelatedness will be seen in the next chapter).

The moral obligations of our common humanity, which Donne goes on to discuss ("any man's death diminishes me, because I am involved in mankind"), form the basis of jurisprudence. "Lives don't exist in a vacuum," the Riverside (California) County Counsel, Barbara Milliken, who represented the state in its successful attempt to prevent the twenty-six-year-old quadriplegic Elizabeth Bouvia from starving herself to death, argued recently. (A few months after the court ruling, Bouvia was befriended by a psychiatric technician who gave her the courage to try to "get better," and she decided that she wanted to live.)

The matrix of kinship is no more escapable than our ultimate singularity. Each of us, whether as adults we remain single or start families of our own, spends perhaps fifteen years as a child, during which our parents are the stars of our lives, and our experiences with them color all the relationships we have from then on, no matter how many miles we put between them and us afterward. The death of a parent, no matter how distant or difficult the relationship may have become, is usually one of the loneliest, emptiest moments in one's life.

The quest for personal freedom is mitigated by the fact that all thought and action take place within genetic, cultural, and psychological frameworks that are largely or totally transmitted by one's family. The numerous cases of adopted children and their real mothers trying to find each other, and the failed attempts of at least one government and two utopian communities to do away with the family altogether, both attest to the indestructible nature of primary kinship bonds. Evidence of their continuing strength is everywhere: an article in the *Times* about a television show in Korea that had been running for up to twelve hours a day, reuniting families separated during the Korean War, who had been out of touch for thirty years (so far three thousand live ceremonies of verification and reunions had taken place, twenty thousand families had been on the air, and a hundred thousand had applied for help); a segment on the seven o'clock news showing young Marines in Beirut, lined up at a telephone, waiting to call home with the news that they were okay—not among two hundred and eighty-nine of their buddies who had just been killed by a truck bomb at the airport; or, more recently, footage of a low fountain, with red-dyed water oozing thickly and steadily from its base, rather than being lofted to any height, in a Teheran cemetery where tens of thousands of Iranian Shiites go to mourn their kinsmen who have fallen in the ongoing war with Iraq, the

fountain evidently representing the endless bleeding of the kinsmen until their deaths are avenged.

Although we may never see them otherwise, our kin usually
materialize at the important moments of our lives, at our rites of
passage—our christenings, graduations, wedding days, retirements,
funerals. When we die, it is usually they who see to our burial
and split up our worldly goods, and when we are in trouble, they
can often be counted on in ways that even best friends cannot.
Although the cost-benefit ratio of having children may have gone
up and more people, particularly women, are finding that they
want to do other things with their lives than raise a family, the
noneconomic rewards of parenthood have not changed. As long
as we are unable to send perfect clones of ourselves into the world,
children are still our only immortality, the best hope that something of us (though *what* is completely unpredictable) will live
on after we are gone (the duration of fame, for those who manage to acquire a measure of it, being even less predictable). In
preliterate societies, particularly, children are often the only guar
antee that one's name will live on for a few generations. Having
children, moreover, can make one feel part of a continuum; one's
personal extinction seems less important when one believes that
one is going to join one's ancestors and when one knows that one
is passing the baton to an heir.

As long as there is a reason for having children, there will be
families, and as long as there are families and a durable form of
wealth for them to accumulate and pass on, human society will
probably continue to be stratified. (The prerequisite for nepotism—in the allotment of women, say—is even simpler: all that
is necessary is old men in power; while status consciousness and
territoriality don't seem to require even the presence of kin: they
flourish among single people in high-powered urban areas—in
New York, for instance, where questions like how important is
this person, what use is he to me, and do I go to his party, are
supremely important.)

Even though the kinship group has yielded to the state much
of its control over individual behavior, it is still usually waiting in
the wings, ready to take charge again should the state falter; and
when individual behavior is actually on trial, as the family law
professor Martha Minow pointed out to me, whether the court
is part of a national legal system or a group of village elders, there

is a strong probability that the testimony will be controlled by a kinship group, that the witnesses to whatever is trying to be established—whether the testator was of sound mind when he made out his will, for instance; whether the woman was indeed raped, or led the defendant on—are kin of the litigants, who have a familial interest in the outcome of the proceedings.

Some social scientists deny that the bourgeois family is in crisis, and claim it is stronger than it has ever been; and it is perfectly true that many American families *are* thriving, particularly in the country and on the lower end of the social scale. One respected intellectual historian with whom I talked went so far as to deny that the West had experienced a rise in individualism in the past few centuries, and that John Locke and the Enlightenment had done anything to promote individualism; the man couldn't even relate to my thesis.

In a new introduction to *Kinship and Marriage*, Fox argues that "kinship is [still] the most central of all social processes," and derides "the myth that kinship [is] a property of primitive societies and has been replaced by citizenship, or 'universalistic roles,' or whatever, in modern ones."

"The Weberian sociologists are always prematurely reading the obituaries of various irrational institutions—nationalism, religion, kinship," he told me recently. "But kinship is subversive, intrusive, and persistent. It keeps coming back. It's the most virulent institution of all. We belong to these small units, and it's absurd to think that they would go away.

"As far as I'm concerned," he went on, "we reached our peak as a species in the Upper Paleolithic, when we were the top carnivore, knocking off whole herds of mammoths. Now we're like a car with a cruising speed of eighty, doing a hundred and forty, and we can't keep that up for very long. We're still paying for the consequences of the Neolithic Revolution, when we went from being hunters to agriculturists—the Great Leap Backwards, as I call it, which sent us to seven days of backbreaking work. Since then what we've mainly perfected are ways of exterminating each other, most of the world is in a debased peasant condition, and you and I belong to an elite that lives on the back of billions condemned to dawn-to-dusk food gathering. In what sense is this progress? The cumulative advances of technology have fooled us into thinking that what has been happening is an upward movement, but most of the basic ideas are thousands of years old. I think the oscillation or cyclical theories of people like Toynbee, Spengler, Sorokin, Danilevsky, and Ibn Khaldun are closer to the mark than the notion of 'progress.' Our steady state, the 'environment of evolutionary adaptation,' as evolutionary biologists call it, in which humans have lived for ninety-nine per cent of their history, has been a kinship-oriented universe. We're pre-wired for dealing with it and not to be in it is a terrible deprivation. Now our evolutionary environment has become our self-centered urban culture. We've gone too far in the direction of gross individualism and state collectivism. We've stripped the self of its basic needs, and we've got to swing back to the center point. I think that we're already swinging back, that the period of individualism ushered in by Locke and the Enlightenment may have just run its course in the Me Decade."

What sort of comeback, I asked, did he think kinship was going to make? Were we going to have unilineal, cognatic, and double-descent systems again, like tribal people? "I think we will invent the systems we need," he said. "The beauty of kinship is its mobility, its protean nature. Lévi-Strauss in his inaugural lecture at the Collège de France looked ahead to a time when production has been completely taken over by machines and people no longer have to concern themselves with it, and he imagined us under this technological umbrella going back to a cool, crystalline society and getting into elaborate kinship systems, the way the Australian aborigines have in their abundant leisure as hunter-gatherers. Maybe we'll play with caste and new versions of endogamous exchange. Maybe, as the state fails us, we'll stumble back to small, supportive networks as a social necessity."

I asked if he thought that the ongoing modern-day struggle for equality and ever-expanding individual rights could possibly represent an unconscious attempt to undo the iniquitous effects of the Agricultural Revolution and to return to the sort of intimate egalitarian societies hunter-gatherers have had. "The trouble is we aren't an individualistic, egalitarian animal," he said. "We're a k-selection animal." A k-selection animal is one that has few offspring, to whom it devotes a great deal of attention; in other words, it goes for quality instead of quantity as a survival strategy, unlike such r-selection animals as fish or insects, which reproduce rapidly and in bulk because their habitat is ephemeral and their offspring are subject to heavy predation. K-selection animals want the best for their children.

K-selection is not to be confused with *kin selection*, the theory of W. H. D. Hamilton, discussed earlier, which proposes a genetic basis for kinship. Turning to that subject, I sounded Fox on the whole nature-nurture controversy, which has polarized the anthropological community and other disciplines. Considering that he "buys" kin selection for humans, and unlike many cultural anthropologists, has no trouble seeing an evolutionary connection between primate breeding systems and human kinship systems, I thought he was going to say something emphatic about the role of biological determination. His answer was surprising: "The whole genetic determinism thing is a red herring, a way to excuse ourselves for not being able to run our society. The entire controversy is largely beside the point. There's absolutely no reason for taking a rigid either-or stand. We humans have repeatedly demonstrated the ability to act contrary to our nature. Look at the modern Americans' diet and eating habits. Look at most modern cities. That people deliberately isolate themselves doesn't mean that they aren't doing it at their own peril, or that humans, given the chance, will not invariably try to live in the largest groups possible." (A statement that seems reasonable, except that one could point to the ongoing shrinking of kinship in importance and size, and argue that the opposite is true.)

What about all the bad things kinship is responsible for? It may not even be an exaggeration to say that most of the evil in the world is generated by or transmitted through families. "I'm not saying that kinship groups are the Garden of Eden, by any means— a mistake some of my colleagues have made. Of course they're full of double-dealing, favoritism, and oppression. All I'm saying is that they're *human*. We are creatures capable of being— and perhaps needing to be—both good *and* evil. It is not the evil *per se* that is our problem, however, but its context, the scale on which it operates. In the small-scale kinship worlds evil exists, of course; but it exists on a scale we can handle naturally, with our instinctive human emotional equipment. Sibling rivalry is commonplace and normal, and even if it is savage, the kinship network has traditional ways of dealing with it. But *national* rivalry is way off scale—especially with superweapons—and we still haven't figured out a way to handle it. Family oppression may not be easy or pleasant, but we can handle it. But class or state or racial oppression is a far more difficult proposition."

🌱

In the last twenty years or so there have been indications that the individualism which has been steadily intensifying in the West may have peaked, at least temporarily, and that people may be trying to return to a more kinship-oriented approach to living, or swinging back to it out of necessity (to the extent, as I say, that they have ever left it). The most recent censuses show that marriage is "in" again: only eleven per cent of the new American households formed in 1980 had married couples in them; in 1983, the proportion rose to seventy-one per cent. A recent television documentary called "Second Thoughts on Being Single" reported (according to its *Times* reviewer) that "loneliness seems to have become the great American disease" and examined "what could be called the companionship industry: singles bars, dating services, exercise classes to enhance attractiveness to the opposite sex—the plethora of enterprises that introduces men and women. [There] seems to [be] something sad about this. On the other hand, it can reasonably be argued that the new enterprises, impersonal as they may seem, are only new rituals taking the place of old rituals. Needs remain unchanged. Perhaps there is reassurance in that."

The "parenting" boom—the fashionability again of natural childbirth and breast feeding, the numerous books, lectures and courses on child rearing—is an indication that we are trying to recapture normal family life, as well as of how far out of touch with it we are; de Zengotita recently described it to me as a "hollow, affected reaction." Family therapy, which tens of millions of American families have experienced since its advent in the late nineteen-fifties, has done much to reunite the family. It replaces the traditional Freudian view of human behavior as dominated by powerful sexual instincts with a vision that we are "wired for attachment," as the family therapist John Pearce puts it. The family is no longer the enemy; it is the patient. "Since problems of personality always involve 'interactive behavior,'" Donald M. Scott and Bernard Wishy write, "the family therapist does not treat the single patient but draws family members into the treatment and moves from one to the other in clarifying difficulties. The family may be sick, not one member. The family setting also provides an opportunity to observe faces, body movements, and other indicators of 'response' of the members, not merely to hear single replies to the therapist's repeated question, 'What do you think of that?' " Parents with a "problem child," for instance, may be taught to observe their own behavior, to determine the "reinforcement contingencies"; the child's temper tantrums and abusive behavior may be inadvertently reinforced by the attention they elicit. "Family therapy is a corrective of the hyperindividualism encouraged by the precious, isolated patient-analyst relationship," according to Pearce. "Our point of view is that snatching people out of their milieu may be mischievous."

🌳

One of the prime causes of fragmentation and alienation in our society—geographical mobility—may be diminishing. The high cost of housing and the tight job market are, as mentioned before, encouraging young adults to return to their parents' home; and companies are responding by not transferring their personnel as readily as they did a decade or two ago. In fact, from the standpoint that resources are contracting everywhere and competition for them is increasing, the prognosis for the future of kinship— if the correlation between it and hardship is indeed a universal law—is excellent.

One indication that humans are "wired for attachment" and that the need to belong to a small group of intimates has not changed is the trend toward "chosen families." As actual family ties have weakened, more people have turned to living communally with "kindred souls." This trend was perhaps begun by the generation that came of age in the nineteen-sixties, who seemed almost to deliver the *coup de grâce* to kinship, first during that decade, with their wholesale rebellion against the values of their parents, and in the following decade with their own even more fickle attitude toward marriage.

In his recent book, *The Poverty of Affluence,* Paul Wachtel identifies what it was that members of this generation were reacting against. By the nineteen-fifties, as communities were fragmenting and religious faith was diminishing, Americans had begun to turn, as a sterile substitute, to accumulating more and more material things which they didn't need and which didn't make them happy—a societal neurosis which, according to

Wachtel, persists to this day. "Faced with the loneliness and vulnerability that come with deprivation of a securely encompassing community," he writes, "we have sought to quell the vulnerability through our possessions. When we can buy nice new things, when we look around and see our homes well stocked and well equipped, we feel strong and expansive rather than small and endangered."

The "countercultural revolution" began with unfocused rebelliousness of adolescents in the late nineteen-fifties, with the subversive, sexually explicit rhythms and lyrics of rock and roll, with the nihilistic humor of *Mad* magazine, which seemed to mock every aspect of the consumer society; with the early withdrawal of the "beat generation" into drugs, Zen Buddhism, and a marginal, self-destructive life style; with the emergence in the movies of the inarticulate anomie of James Dean. There was a "flavor of rebellion" to our generation, as one of my contemporaries recently reminisced. "It was cool to be alienated, to be slightly 'schizzed out,' to have a 'nervous breakdown.' " The ultimate act of alienation was to die, preferably by one's own hand, and a lot of people in movies, fiction, and real life checked out of the world almost as a statement, as Seymour Glass did in J. D. Salinger's "A Perfect Day for Bananafish."

By the mid-nineteen-sixties, what had started as "the gut reaction of a generation," as the journalist Robert Houriet wrote in *Getting Back Together,* a book about the hippie communes, had begun to take on the character of a movement, with its own voices to articulate its aims and its attitudes. In his song "The Times They Are A-Changin'," which was the movement's "Marseillaise," Bob Dylan spelled out exactly where parents now stood:

> Come mothers and fathers
> Throughout the land
> And don't criticize
> What you can't understand.
> Your sons and your daughters
> Are beyond your command
> Your old road is
> Rapidly agin'
> Please get out of the new one
> If you can't lend your hand
> For the times they are a-changin'

With a second paragraph as rousing as the beginning of *The Communist Manifesto,* Charles Reich proclaimed in *The Greening of America* the grand scheme of the movement, which promised both to free the individual and to restore to him, through the simple practice of peace and love, his lost sense of connectedness: "There is a revolution coming. It will not be like revolutions of the past. It will originate with the individual and with culture, and it will change the political structure only as its final act. It will not require violence to succeed, and it cannot be successfully resisted by violence. It is now spreading with amazing rapidity, and already our laws, institutions, and social structures are changing in consequence. It promises a higher reason, a more human community, and a new and liberated individual. Its ultimate creation will be a new and enduring wholeness and beauty—a renewed relationship of man to himself, to other men, to society, to nature, and to the land."

As the movement spread, "youths from the most privileged sectors of society seemed to be turning their backs on their birthright," Wachtel writes.

> The very people whom one would expect to be most eager to sustain the system in which they had grown up were withdrawing or opposing the system instead. Much of their protest and resentment was directed toward traditional political concerns such as civil rights and the war in Vietnam. Increasingly, however, they also expressed resistance to the values by which they were brought up and to the prospect of following in their parents' footsteps. The blandishments of the consumer society seemed to them pale stuff, and they felt an urge to seek a way of life that was richer, more meaningful, more deeply experienced. To many of them, life in middle-class America seemed to be experienced through gauze. Their successful parents seemed sadly limited, out of touch with themselves and other people, object lessons to avoid following at all costs rather than models to emulate.

As the relationship with parents deteriorated, many of these young people banded together, calling themselves, most commonly, "communes" or "families," and espousing such goals as economic self-sufficiency and harmony with the earth. Some experimented with group marriage; some developed home industries that sought to retain the integrity of individual craftsmanship; many rural communes took pride in growing their own food. By 1970, a survey by the *Times* had turned up two thousand communes in thirty-four states; the sociologist Benjamin D. Zablocki claimed there were three thousand. In addition to these large-scale, formal experiments, there were an unknown number of small, loose communal arrangements made up of several unrelated friends who were living under the same roof or on the same land.

What kept the countercultural revolution from making over American society was its failure to sustain its youthful sense of solidarity. The prevailing individualism and materialism of our society were too ingrained to be easily eliminated. There were also external pressures that made themselves increasingly felt during the nineteen-seventies. By 1976 the revolution had pretty much run its course. That year a *New York Times* article headlined "Many Rebels of the 1960s Depressed as They Near 30" reported a dramatic rise in the suicide rate for that generation; severe depression among those who had "dropped out" and were now, at a time of economic retrenchment, having trouble entering a competitive job market; fear of the possibility of not having any of the things their parents and grandparents had taken for granted and of not even having an adequate role in society; a narrowing of the generation gap and a growing mood of conservatism; widespread patterns of disillusionment and alienation as a result of having served in Vietnam, of the Watergate scandals, of society's failure to fulfill many of the dreams that had seemed attainable at the peak of the civil rights movement; and even, among those who had managed to find meaningful and well-paying jobs, a sense of guilt at having succeeded. "People spent the sixties trying to get closer to each other, getting to learn intimacy . . . ," one of the psychotherapists interviewed in the article said. "But now they find that somehow something is missing, that it just didn't work."

By the mid-nineteen-seventies most of the hippie communes had dissolved and their members had returned to society, although some of the most "together" ones, like Steven Gaskin's "Farm," in Summertown, Tennessee, are still going strong, and a dedicated minority of those who went "back to the land" have stayed there. While the commune movement has largely petered out, the trend toward alternative kinship and "chosen families" continues. The 1983 census counted three million households made up of unrelated people living together—primarily unmarried couples, roommates of the same sex, and elderly companions. The *Times* interviewed the members of some of these "nonfamily households" and reported that they were seeking not only to share costs but to have "the semblance of family," tribal attachment, and the sense of "coming home." The growing popularity of age-restricted communities for the elderly, and the number of ashrams and other non-Western religious communities that have established themselves in the United States, are further symptoms of this trend.

For many young Americans, whether or not they have spouses and children and close relationships with brothers, sisters, and parents, life has come to revolve around a circle of about a dozen or so "best friends"; they belong to a kind of chosen kinship group. A New York woman I know refers to her circle as a "corpus." These "corpuses" are not as stable as groups of blood relatives but they are on a similar "human" scale, and while one is in them they are totally absorbing; they are one's world. The relationships in them tend to be shifting; one is constantly breaking off with "best friends" one has outgrown and finding new ones who satisfy newly developing sides of one's personality. The interactions are mainly of a psychological, as opposed to a social, nature. One talks about why such-and-such a friend is insecure, why he can't keep girlfriends. It is the sort of universe that the writer Ann Beattie presents in her fiction: a bunch of friends who have got together for dinner or the weekend (perhaps a literary descendant of Kurt Vonnegut's "grand-faloon," a group of arbitrary size and composition: Vonnegut has all the members' last names beginning with the same letter), who seem to have seized on each other, more than for any other apparent reason, to keep the wolf of loneliness away, half of them miserable, most of them having trouble with extended commitments. Outside these groups there is nothing. "Society" and "community" are dead or vestigial. Real family is "too difficult," as the New Yorker with her corpus put it. There is only the mass culture, which one joins as soon as one gets into a car or hits the sidewalk and goes to the supermarket, the movies, or a restaurant; to which thousands of others like oneself, whom one does not know, but some of whose faces may have become familiar, also belong. Most of these people probably also have as their primary focus, besides their own nuclear unit, a similar corpus of around a dozen best friends.

✤

The linking up of the world by the jet airplane—thanks to which few of the most remote tribal people now take more than a week, say, for somebody in New York City to get to—has brought many people with the atrophied Western sense of kinship into contact with people whose traditional systems are more intact, and the Westerners have come to realize what they are missing. Americans don't even have to leave the West: the rich family life in Italy or France, say, can provide perspective on their individualism. The Peace Corps has been valuable as an educator of young Americans, who have learned that their society is a special case, with its high material standard of living, its abundant opportunities, and its isolation; while about two-thirds of the world's population still live in villages, in close association with large numbers of kin. A college classmate of mine, who joined the Peace Corps in 1968 and was sent to a small village in the hinterland of Cameroon to modernize its sewage and water-supply systems, recently told me that within a month of his arrival, he realized that it was he who needed help.

Other friends of mine, the Clynes, went to India to find themselves. When I first met them, in 1971, Bernie was a divorce lawyer with a busy practice, Penny poured out her abundant creative energies in an endless stream of music and art, and their son Peter was five. Although they owned two houses in Westchester and another one on Fire Island and threw great parties and had "groovy" friends, they gradually became disillusioned with the entire structure of their lives and finally separated. "Nothing had any value because we had done it all," Nada (the Indian name Penny has used since 1975) told me recently. "What I think was missing was an inner link with myself." In 1974 she became a follower of the Indian master of meditation Swami Muktananda; three years later Bernie quit his job and sold the house they were living in, and the whole family, reunited with the help of Muktananda's teaching, went to live in his ashram in Ganeshpuri, India. "Muktananda emphasized, beside self-knowledge, living in the world and honoring the traditions of your society, meeting your family commitments," Nada went on, "and that made me look at my marriage and consider what I was doing, or not doing. Several times, on trains, I met Indian women who had married men they hadn't even met, and they told me about the love that had developed between them and their husbands simply because they recognized that they were both in it together—and I thought about all the relationships I'd had with people who I thought were going to bring me happiness and fulfillment, and I realized that I could probably have had these things with any one of them; that the important thing was my own commitment."

People who have quarrelled with the Western notion of progress and have longed for something else have been making themselves heard since at least the eighteenth century. Rousseau, for instance, who was bitterly critical of the dehumanizing effect of the scientific revolution, maintained that civilization had a corrupting effect on man and praised the "noble savage," who was largely a projection of his own malaise and social ineptness in the highly mannered society of his time. Early in the nineteenth century a group of disgruntled Englishmen who called themselves Luddites and believed that the Industrial Revolution had been a great mistake and that if everybody went back to farming and handicrafts, life would be good again, went around making guerrilla raids on factories and systematically wrecking machinery. Meanwhile, in the upper strata of English society, men like Thomas Carlyle and Samuel Taylor Coleridge, appalled by the squalid conditions in which factory workers were working and living, deplored the reduction of human relations to the cash nexus and began to wonder how the social ills brought about by industrialization could be rectified. Carlyle became a conservative reactionary who wanted the government to abandon its laissez-faire policies and to return to the strong paternalism of feudal times; under the leadership of its "heroes," the most capable members of its ruling class, society would be well again. Coleridge became a romantic reactionary who wanted flesh-and-blood kinship itself reestablished as the basis of community. As the century progressed, nostalgia for the Middle Ages and its large, harmonious families (as life then was romantically portrayed in numerous novels of the *Ivanhoe* type) grew. Marx and Engels were appalled by the same misery Carlyle and Coleridge had seen, but they did not consider a return to flesh-and-blood kinship or to feudal organicism the solution (Engels, in fact, as we have seen, thought traditional kinship, with its patrilineal perpetuation of wealth, was the root of the problem); they wanted mankind to break through to a new stage, to a kinship of labor, in which everybody would work together and all property would be owned collectively. An egalitarian community with rich kin ties is still the vision of the postindustrial bourgeoisie, even though it seems scarcely able any more to maintain even a stable nucleus of parents and offspring.

It was also in the nineteenth century that interest in people whose consciousness and way of life had not developed along European lines intensified. The most sensitive and detailed descriptions of other societies—coming first from missionaries, explorers, merchants, and other travellers, and later in the century, with the emergence of anthropology as a scientific discipline, from trained ethnographers—suggested that much of value had been lost on the way to achieving the unprecedented prosperity and technological advances that Westerners were enjoying. "Primitive life" turned out to be much more subtle and loving than Hobbes had allowed when he characterized it as "nasty, brutish, and short." In fact many tribal societies, now that they were starting to be understood, seemed to answer the needs of man more fully, addressing not only his ego and his material well-being but his whole being. One of the most basic human needs is to feel that one has a place in the world, and perhaps the main thing that stands out in Westerners' descriptions of tribal people and also of more complex state-level agriculturists is how much better they provide this sense of connectedness, how much richer their family life, how much closer to each other and more secure in their identity the people seem.

The descriptions by Sir Richard Burton, for instance, one of the most widely travelled and perceptive of the Victorian ethnographers, are filled with favorable comparisons to what he viewed as the repressed, unnatural society of his native England, where, he once observed upon returning from a long sojourn abroad, "everything appeared so small, so prim, so mean, the little one-familied houses." In India, amazed by the "all-absorbing passion of the Hindu mother," he writes that to her "the child is everything. From the hour of his birth she never leaves him day or night. If poor, she works, walking about with him on her hip: if rich, she spends life with him on her lap. . . . When he is sick, she fasts and watches, and endures every self-imposed penance she can devise. She never speaks to or of him without imploring the blessing of Heaven upon his head; and this strong love loses nought when the child ceases to be a toy; it is the mainspring of her conduct towards him throughout life. No wonder that in the East an unaffectionate son is the rare phenomenon: and no wonder that this people when offensively inclined always begin by abusing one another's mother." But in the West, he continued, "the parents are engrossed by other cares—the search for riches, or the pursuit of pleasure—during the infancy of their offspring. In the troublesome days of childhood the boy is consigned to the nursery, or let loose to pass his time with his fellows as best he can, then comes youth accompanied by an exile, to school and college . . . there is little community of interests and opinions between parent and child—the absence of it is the want of a great tie."

One of Burton's contemporaries, Paul Gauguin, fled civilization and the sterile academic realism that had come to prevail in its art and found, or thought he found, among the natives and the dazzling colors on the island of Tahiti, in central Oceania, a sensual and spiritual wholeness that had eluded him in his native France (his own life on the island, however, was characterized by extreme isolation, poor health, and impoverished degradation). The paintings he made are paeans to the simplicity and calm of the island's people and to the lush beauty of its women.

One of his masterpieces, *Where Do We Come from? What Are We? Where Are We Going?*, portrays life from the cradle to the grave. "In the right foreground a baby lies asleep," he explained. "Next, three women are sitting. Two figures dressed in purple exchange confidences. An intentionally large figure, which defies perspective, sits with an arm upraised and looks in amazement at the two people who dare think about their destiny. A figure in the centre gathers fruit. . . . An idol with both arms raised in a rhythmical movement seems to be pointing to the mysterious Beyond. Finally, an old woman on the point of death appears to be reconciled and resigned to her thoughts."

The theme of "our relative cultural/human impoverishment"

runs through all the books of the contemporary anthropologist Colin Turnbull. "Perhaps I first tackled it backwards in *The Lonely African,* by trying to show how much loss we were bringing to the Africans in the name of 'progress,'" he has written to me. In his best-known work, *The Forest People,* Turnbull portrays the intimate communal life of the Mbuti Pygmies so compellingly that readers cannot help wondering whether they might have been better off born in such a society. In the last chapter of a later work, *The Mountain People,* he draws a disturbing parallel between our society and the Ik, a group of nomadic hunters in central Africa who, driven from their traditional hunting ground by the creation of a game reserve and now forbidden to hunt, have been reduced to desperate competition with each other for food and in their desperate struggle for personal survival have lost such "basic" human qualities as family supportiveness, cooperative sociality, belief, love, and hope. Turnbull observes Ik stealing food from the mouths of their parents, throwing their infant children out of their compounds and leaving them to fend for themselves, and abandoning the old, the sick, and the crippled to die without a backward glance. "Such interaction as there is within this system is one of mutual exploitation . . ." he writes. "The Ik are brought together by self-interest alone. . . . Does that sound so very different from our own society? In our own world the very mainstays of a society based on a truly social sense of mutuality are breaking down. . . . The very old and the very young are separated . . . [disposed of] in homes for the aged or in day schools and summer camps. Marital relations are barely even fodder for comedians, and responsibility for health, education, and welfare has been gladly abandoned to the state." And "The individualism that is preached with a curious fanaticism . . . is reflected in our cutthroat economics, where almost any kind of exploitation and degradation of others, impoverishment and pain, is justified in terms of an expanding economy and the consequent confinement of the world's riches in the pockets of the few. The rot is in all of us."

Turnbull's most recent book, *The Human Cycle,* spells out even more clearly what he feels Western society has lost. In it he shows how sensitive and supportive Mbuti Pygmies and the Indian and Tibetan societies that he has studied are to their members as they pass through the stages of life, from childhood, to adoles-

cence, to youth, to adulthood, and finally to old age—how a pregnant Mbuti woman, for instance, sitting in her favorite stream,
"sings to her unborn child about the forest in which it will soon
emerge"; how in most "primitive societies" a young girl's first
menstruation, instead of eliciting private confusion and shame, is
celebrated by the entire community in a solemn and joyous rite
of passage; how much better prepared for death the old people in
such societies are, having been taught from an early age to believe
that they are part of a single life force which came into being
long before they were born and will contiune to exist long after
they have gone, that they are remotely descended from animals,
that their family (as the Mbuti believe) is "a constantly expanding universe, beginning with the nuclear family and ultimately
embracing the whole forest, the entire extent of their experience
at any moment" (while we Westerners "rush toward the big zero,"
as I have heard our tendency to avoid coming to terms with our
mortality described). "If we measure a culture's worth by the
longevity of its population, the sophistication of its technology,
the material comforts it offers, then many primitive societies have
little to offer us, that is true," Turnbull writes in his introduction.
"But our study of the life cycle will show that in terms of a conscious dedication to human relationships that are both affective
and effective, the primitive is ahead of us all the way. He is working at it at every stage of life, from infancy to death, while playing just as much as while praying; whether at work or at home,
his life is governed by his conscious quest for social order."

Not surprisingly, Turnbull's thesis that progress has brought
more harm than good has not been very popular with people who
are grateful for what Western civilization has given them. *The
Human Cycle* was published within a few months of Brigitte and
Peter Berger's impassioned defense of the bourgeois family, *The
War Over the Family: Capturing the Middle Ground*, and Peter
Berger reviewed it scathingly, accusing Turnbull in his "protracted
lament about 'our' deficiencies compared with 'their' way of coping
with the human life cycle" of "grinding an ideological ax" and of
using anthropology "to denigrate Western civilization in comparison with allegedly superior or sounder cultures in faraway places."
"One wonders whether any group of human beings can be as
loving, joyous, and generally wholesome as the Mbuti are made
to be," the review goes on; ". . . pretending to be a diagnosis,

[the book] must instead be understood as a symptom of a specific cultural malady. . . . It is quite true that traditional cultures by and large have a stronger 'corporate' character than modern Western cultures; it is also true that this character preserves the individual from some of the alienations of modernity and provides a more intimate sense of belonging to the forces of nature. . . . There are many reasons for this," Berger writes. "But the one overriding one is that Western civilization, from its early beginnings on the shore of the eastern Mediterranean, has been moving toward the realization of the autonomous individual, of individual freedom and rights. The thrust towards freedom has been the glory of this particular branch of the human family; it has also been its burden. History exacts a price for every achievement. Our price has been, precisely, a greater loneliness within both society and nature. Is this price worthwhile? That is a very serious question, perhaps the most serious of our age." In the end, curiously, Berger seems to be asking the same question that Turnbull is.

⚘

During the latter part of the nineteen-seventies, when I began to visit non-Western societies, my reaction was similar to Turnbull's and many other people's: I began to wonder about the human cost of our emphasis on personal freedom and self-realization and of our "progress." In 1976-77 I spent eight months in Brazil, gathering material for a book about the Amazon. The warmth, the supportiveness, and the contented outlook of the people I came in contact with impressed me as deeply as the beauty and the intricacy of the landscape. I found this *calor humano*, or human warmth, as Brazilians proudly call this quality, which they have in abundance, in the unassimilated Cayapo Indian village of Mekranoti, where I spent a month. The days there began at dawn, with the women sitting in the middle of the village and chanting in the daylight in a rough a cappella chorus. For the rest of the day the villagers were almost always in each other's company, except, I was told, when one of the women went alone into the forest to give birth or when one of the men went *aybanh*, or berserk, and ran screaming into the jungle—the only outlet from his tight communal existence, as these Cayapo lacked alcohol or narcotics, unlike most Amazonian tribal people. When the man who had gone berserk returned, usually after several days, and resumed his life in the village, nothing was said; everybody acted as if he had never been gone. I witnessed a beautifully simple and open display of familial love: a woman crying with joy when her son returned from hunting in the forest. Such displays are common in kinship-oriented societies. The anthropologist Charles Wagley has titled a book about the Tapirape Indians of central Brazil *Welcome of Tears;* and Burton in the last century described a son meeting his pilgrim mother in Medina, "weeping aloud for joy as he ran around his mother's camel . . . standing on tiptoe, she bending double in vain attempts to exchange a kiss. . . ."

I also watched three boys kill a dog one afternoon for no apparent reason. Two held it down, while the third kept bashing it over the head with a rock. It struggled free and they ran after it with sticks. It was nobody's dog, so nobody stopped them. Although he has been accused of idealizing them, Turnbull reports similar gratuitous cruelty to animals among the Mbuti Pygmies: "The hunting dogs, valuable as they are, get kicked around mercilessly from the day they are born to the day they die." When, sickened, I went off by myself and sat down on a log, one of the women asked the anthropologist who had taken me into the village, "Why is he sad?" It would have been considered disrespectful for her to ask such a personal question directly. "In contrasting . . . the sense of community and belonging that were the lot of men born in prior times and the *lack* of connectedness in modern Western man, the *sundering* of ties he experiences, I do not mean to imply that people were necessarily nicer to each other," Wachtel writes. "Cruelty is not a modern invention."

Not knowing their language, I related to the villagers mainly through being able to recognize and "type" their personalities; my impression is that the basic human personality, with its balance of good and evil, and the basic human intelligence remain the same, whatever stage of cultural evolution the people in question have reached. The superb competence of the villagers as hunters, at everything they did, in fact, and their detailed botanical knowledge of the forest, led me to doubt that their failure to develop a more complex technology had anything to do with intellectual capacity.

A month later I fell in with some *caboclos,* the semiacculturated Amazonians of mixed Indian, African, and Portuguese ancestry who live along the many branches of the river system, many in roughly the time of Daniel Boone. Some of them didn't want me to leave and begged me to stay with them for months; I don't think it was because they had taken a special liking to me, but because they were simply very hospitable people. Whenever you enter a home anywhere in Brazil, in fact, you are usually brought a little cup of sweet black coffee, and the people will sit with you until you get up to leave, whereupon they will protest, "It's early," and implore you to stay longer, even if they are dying to get rid of you.

My own view of the effects of "civilization" and "progress" is not one of absolute corruption (as Rousseau argued) or of net loss (as Turnbull argues): the process of cultural evolution seems more like a trade-off. Some things are lost, others are gained. Before romanticizing the intimate communities of tribal people or of village peasants, one should consider what a limited world this can be, how tight a mould all the members are required to conform to, how completely their destiny is controlled by their elders, how often they dread having sorcery performed on them by their enemies or being ostracized as sorcerers themselves; how much they are plagued by irrational behavior, "demons," or (in the case of Pygmies little sparks that light up at night in the forest); not to mention the real diseases, against which they are relatively defenseless. The governments in most kinship-oriented societies have poor human-rights records; the individual's rights are not protected. In any small, insular community, there are usually long-standing rivalries and hard feelings among certain families.

The "life-term social arena" of Indian village life, as one anthropologist recently described it to me, can be particularly oppressive. "In traditional India, where marriages are arranged, neither bride nor groom has much to say about who, when, or even whether they will marry," the journalist William K. Stevens has written. "Often they do not know each other. After the wedding, the bride moves into the groom's house, where his parents, not the groom, rule. Her status is the lowest in the house, and can even amount to virtual servitude." V. S. Naipaul paints a similarly oppressive picture of the family organization of Indians on Trinidad, as "an enclosing self-sufficient world absorbed with its quarrels and jealousies, as difficult for the outsider to penetrate as for one of its members to escape. It protected and imprisoned, a static world, awaiting decay." It is not surprising, therefore, that many Indians today are eager to adopt the values of the West, and that those who emigrate to England or America do not generally return. Not only in India, however, but all over the world, wherever people are given the chance to leave small, close-knit communities, they are doing so. The most damning testimony in the debate over the value of traditional kinship versus individual opportunity is the choice that millions of people continue to make, the ongoing rural exodus and the increasing urbanization and Westernization of the world's population (although in many cases it is the possibility of finding work, when there is none at home, rather than a desire to escape from his family, that sends the country person off). But the alienation they find in their new social environment is real. People feel it; whether anything can be done about it is another question, and a very difficult one. Perhaps a good way to start for those who have known only an environment of alienation is to put themselves in other environments, where alienation is quite unknown and where they can gain an understanding of what they are missing.

🌲

Another indication of a yearning to reestablish old connections is the recent interest in family history and genealogical research, in "roots." A structural anthropologist might interpret this interest as a reassertion of the ancestral need to classify, especially to calculate the degree of relationship with one's kin, which has been denied by the reduction of kinship, but there is also a perfectly reasonable historical explanation. Periodic waves of intense genealogical activity can be found in the history of most countries. There was such a period in Elizabethan England, and again during the Victorian era, when many "new" families, lately risen to prominence and granted arms, sought to shore up their new gentry status by essentially buying "background." "Some of the accounts of these families stretched points," the genealogist Patrick Montague Smith explained to me delicately. "Many of them begin with a sentence like, 'The origins of this ancient family are lost in the mists of antiquity,' when in fact it could only be traced back a few generations. Lady Diana's ancestors, for instance, the Spencers, were spuriously derived by one of the heralds at the College of Arms from a medieval family called Desspenser."

Because we are a nation of immigrants, whose status has had to be redefined, Americans have been particularly concerned about their ancestry. The first craze for genealogy swept the country during the nineteenth century. It marked the beginning of bourgeois genealogy; before then only nobles had been preoccupied with their pedigrees or had had access to information about their forebears. Engravers did a brisk business in blank genealogical "trees," as thousands of American families combed public records for names to put on them, or hired the work out to specialists, who could supply such dignities as coats of arms or crests— "strange preoccupations for ostensible democrats," Scott and Wishy remark in their documentary history of the American family. The most fortunate were able to call themselves a "first family of Virginia" or "Mayflower descendants," or found a European aristocrat lurking on one of their upper branches. Mark Twain ridiculed the whole business of ancestry, yet it fascinated him. He wrote a novel called *The American Claimant,* and had "the rightful duke of Bridgewater" and "the pore disappeared Dauphin, Looey the Seventeen," fetch up on Huckleberry Finn's raft. Mark Twain's mother was a Lampton of Virginia, and the Lamptons were so obsessed with their alleged descent from the earls of Durham that they considered taking steps to claim the title when it fell vacant. When an Englishman once disdainfully asked him why Americans were so concerned with who their grandfathers had been, Mark Twain asked back why the English were so concerned about the identity of their fathers.

A good deal of fraudulent genealogy—the equivalent of the Japanese *nizekeizu,* centuries earlier—was perpetrated to cover up undesirable blood or to enhance marriageability. John Jay II (1817–94), for instance, an American Minister to Vienna, apparently overcome by a touch of vanity, commissioned some researchers in France to provide him with a bogus descent from a certain Baron le Jay. Not that his family was anything to be ashamed of. The Jays were prosperous Huguenot merchants who by then had married into some of New York's leading families—the Stuyvesants, the Van Cortlandts, the Livingstons; his grandfather and namesake had been the first chief justice and twice governor of New York. Jay's correspondence with his researchers indicates that the more expense money he sent them, the grander the title of his "ancestor" became. Later Jays went on to make actual marital connections with the European aristocracy and with other leading American families. Living descendants include John Jay Iselin, president of public television's Channel 13, John Jay Osborne, author of the best-seller *The Paper Chase,* and about two hundred others who are sufficiently proud of their connection to the first chief justice that they gather once a year at his homestead in Katonah, New York, now a national historic site. Some American families, like the Jay descendants, to whom the past has been good and who still have a stake in it, already knew who they were, genealogically speaking, well before the recent interest in "roots," and are often conversant with fairly complex networks of cousins, in-laws, and in-laws of in-laws. The main asset of such families is their "background." They can still trade on it. The descendants of the wealthy colonial landowner John Pell can trade on it quite literally. The terms of the sale in 1687 of part of Pell's manor to what eventually became the city of New Rochelle included payment to his descendants, in perpetuity, of one "fatte calf" per annum. The payment is still collected, sporadically.

A well-known British genealogist recently told me that episodes of heightened interest in ancestry usually follow periods of social mobility, migration up the social ladder, from country to town, or abroad. "The foundation of genealogical societies in Australia, New England, and South Africa all date to about a hundred years after the great migrations to these countries," he said. "Three generations later, the family begins to wonder why it moved." His own interest, however, was sparked by the "detective work," which he found "immensely satisfying." He was "not a believer that genealogy strengthens ties within the immediate family. On the contrary, it is usually an individual, selfish interest. People become obsessive about it. I know of cases where it has caused divorce." In *Debrett's Guide to Tracing Your Ancestry,* Noel Currier-Briggs and Royston Gambier describe "a characteristic syndrome of genealogists who, though reliable on other people's pedigrees, often get so hooked on their own family trees that they alter records to suit their delusions of grandeur." That genealogists themselves are susceptible to the snob appeal of an aristocratic forebear was recently brought home to me in a conversation with a prominent American member of the profession, who, apropos of nothing, dropped the name of "my fifth great-grandfather, the seventh Earl of Huntington." But perhaps it was only natural to him to be proud of the connection. I have noticed an involuntary tremor come into the voice of a man, even though he was not in the least bit stuffy and I am sure would have said, if I had asked him, that it was bad form to be proud of one's ancestors, as he spoke the name of one of his fifth great-grandfathers, a signer of the Declaration of Independence. (I resisted the temptation to ask him who his hundred and twenty-seven other ancestors in that generation had been.) I have heard of a man named Emerson who displays on his mantelpiece the complete works, leatherbound, of his distant ancestor, Ralph Waldo; and I am in correspondence with a retired schoolteacher in Maine whose last letter was signed "Drusilla H. Stengel, cousin of Casey and eighty-five years young." "Pride of birth has taken a bit of a hard knock, but it still fascinates everybody," Robin Fox said recently.

In 1961, when I was fourteen years old, my father got a job in London, and we lived for two years in a Flemish-style brick building in South Kensington, which happened to belong to the Society of Genealogists. To get to our flat, we climbed stairs past the society's "search rooms," which were full of musty tomes and had plaques on their doors that broke the material down into categories like "Knights, Kings, Commoners, Vermont, Massachusetts." My mother offered to replace or at least pay for the cleaning of the wallpaper in the stairwell, which had large red flowers on a gold background and had been designed by the multitalented Victorian William Morris. The society was dumbfounded by the suggestion. A heated exchange of letters took place between it and my mother. To settle the matter, the poet laureate, John Betjeman, connoisseur of Victorian interiors, was brought in to examine the wallpaper. Betjeman declared it a priceless gem and advised that it should not be touched. Our relationship with the society deteriorated even further after water I had left running for a bath overflowed and, seeping through the floor, dripped onto some irreplaceable parish registers in one of the rooms below. The staff, a brusque, desiccated lot, conscious of their role as the ultimate arbiters, the keepers of the lineages, was particularly long-suffering toward the Americans who provided much of their business. One afternoon a man who had come from Ohio expressly to find out which duke he was descended from—his family had a story about a ducal forebear centuries back—collapsed and died in front of

the building after discovering that his people had actually been
the village chimney sweeps.

Having no English blood that I knew of, I was unable to
make use of the facility. The closest to an English connection my
family could come up with was one of my second great-grandfathers, who, according to one account of his career, observed the
Battle of Trafalgar "with Nelson" as a visiting Russian midship-
man. Charged by my father to look into the matter, I went to the
Public Records office on Chancery Lane—one of the world's most
voluminous archives, with some fifty million individual documents—and was issued a card to the Round Room, where the pre-
Victorian records were kept. An attendant to whom I had explained my quest brought me the muster of Nelson's flagship
H.M.S. *Victory,* but the name of great-great-grandfather wasn't on
it. Maybe, the attendant suggested apologetically, he had watched
the battle from another ship. Several hours and dozens of musters
later, I found him enrolled as a supernumerary of provisions on
H.M.S. *Phoebe.* The *Phoebe* was at Trafalgar, I learned from a
history of the battle, but it "cruised to windward of the weather
column, and took no part in the engagement." At an early age
(fifteen), I had discovered two truths about genealogical research:
that it is tedious and is often disillusioning.

Twenty years later, I undertook to reconstruct the history of
my family, and I found a certain satisfaction in the genealogical
research the project involved, in resuscitating and making posthumous contact with forgotten forebears. Some of their names
sounded beautiful to me: Avenarius, Philippeus, Selivanov, Vitovt,
Lukianovitch; but I couldn't imagine anybody else being similarly
moved. Their names resonated in the depths of my being because
they were prenatal fragments of myself, my people. Tracing one's
ancestors may heighten one's own awareness of kinship, but it is
ultimately a private matter, a communing with personal spirits.
People whose self-esteem is boosted by belonging to "one of the
eight great families of Philadelphia," for instance, as I read in a
recent obituary of a woman whose social credentials seemed, even
in death, to have mattered more to her than anything else about
her, seem to me particularly deluded. The limited amount of research I have done has shown me how totally forgotten the great
men and famous beauties of their day usually are within a few

generations, that we are all "transitional characters," as my late
beloved paternal grandmother put it a few months before she died.
Far from adding in any way to my own stature, the knowledge
that one of my progenitors, for instance—a man who contributed
a little over three per cent of my genes—evidently played a significant role in the Russian military occupation of Poland early in
the last century pales before the depressing realization that five
generations later, there is no memory of the man, and very little
evidence that he even existed. I find it sobering that he has already
slipped into such oblivion. "Too often genealogy fits into the negative picture we have of it, of wallowing in one's ancestors' achievements," Hugh Montgomery-Massingberd recently told me. "You
see people at their most absurd when they take themselves seriously about it, and it's off-putting to those who might otherwise
get interested. The appeal of genealogy—or family history, as I
prefer to call it—for me is that it personifies history, which to me
is biography—not economics or graphs, but facts about people.
And since genealogy is the pursuit of truth, and the facts it un-
covers are so often embarrassing, it is really the *antithesis* of snob-
bery."

Members of other societies, whose bonds with their living kin
are stronger, have been uncertain what to make of the modern
Western fascination with genealogy. "As a counterbalance to their
immoderate cult of the future, Americans continually search for
their roots and origins," the Mexican poet Octavio Paz has suggested. Only a few Brazilians have traceable pedigrees as deep as
that of the anthropologist, writer, and present vice-governor of
the state of Rio de Janeiro, Darcy Ribeiro, one of whose Portuguese ancestors was given a choice between death and sailing with
Pedro Alvares Cabral, captain of the first European ship to sight
the Brazilian coast. "Brazilian culture is hedonistic rather than historically oriented," a young novelist in Rio de Janeiro named Julio
Cesar Montero explained to me recently. "Unlike people in Puritan cultures, we aren't interested in building up possessions or in
passing traditions to our children, as much as in living well. Americans puzzle me: they are obsessed with their ancestors, yet they
don't seem to care for the living members of their families. I
wonder if ancestor cults, like the myth that we can contact our
dead through mediums, which many Brazilians believe in, aren't
something we have concocted to combat our enormous solitude.

It's lonely to think that after a few generations probably nobody will remember you any more. Maybe the hope that they will be remembered, that they will live on in the memory of the race, makes it less lonely for some people, but the image of you gets so distorted with time that maybe you're better off being forgotten. I know only four generations of my ancestors, and I don't see how knowing any more could make me feel existentially any more comfortable. Sometimes I feel an overwhelming sense of fragility, as an astronaut must feel when he looks down at the earth and sees it as a little ball in the vastness of space. I didn't ask to be put here at this time. I'm an obstetric accident, forced to live at the end of the twentieth and the beginning of the twenty-first centuries."

The recent popularity of genealogy in England is a result of the growth of the country's middle class. The aristocracy was always interested in genealogy, and the pastoral farming classes were interested only in the present and the future. As most of their ranks moved up into the middle class, they became detached from and interested in knowing about their origins. The Society of Genealogists was founded in 1911, and most of the society's patrons today are lower- and middle-class English people, although the flow from former colonies continues unabated. "The twentieth century has been the age of the genealogy of the common man," Currier-Briggs and Gambier write. The recent genealogical renaissance in America is partly a shock wave of the great immigrations here from the Old World early in this century and late in the last one. It is partly due to the curiosity of the grandchildren of these immigrants. "What the son wishes to forget, the grandson wishes to remember," the immigration historian Marcus Lee Hansen has written. But the renaissance was also an offshoot of the political individualism and the upsurge of ethnic pride that asserted themselves during the nineteen-sixties and -seventies. It was part of a reaction against the American "melting pot," against the homogeneity and the anonymity of our postindustrial mass society, and it was tied to the attempt to erode the barriers of social and racial inequality, particularly to the civil rights advances that blacks were struggling for during that period. The publication in 1976 of Alex Haley's *Roots: The Saga of an American Family* and the airing of a television miniseries based on the saga the following winter were terrific catalysts, perhaps the single most important event of the renaissance. *Roots* was a runaway best-seller. It was what the writer Robert M. Pirsig has called a "culture-bearing book." It seemed to focus the mood of the society, to tell it something it needed to know—that every family, and by extension every*body*, has a history. It not only answered a psychological need of blacks (Haley had ghosted the *Autobiography of Malcolm X*, and was well aware of the black pride movement), it spoke to the mobile middle part of the society, which had been deracinated not only geographically but genealogically.

Six years after its publication, I called on Haley at the office of his Kinte Foundation in the dark-glass Warner Brothers building in Burbank, California. He was sixty-one then, a genial, unaffected man with a large, leonine face and gray curls. Curiously, after all he had done for the American family, and having himself been married twice, with three children and two grandchildren, he led a solitary, nomadic life now, he told me, commuting between "hideouts" he maintained on several continents. "The muse is a jealous lady," he explained.

Of *Roots* he said, "I could have researched it forever, but after nine years I decided it was time to sit down and write. It took a while to realize the significance of what I had, but when the story finally fell into place, I almost shook with its import. But still, when the book was published, in September 1976, nobody knew what it was going to do. At first the salesmen were wondering if it was even going to sell among black people, who are not known as great buyers of hard-cover books. But blacks bought it across the board; and then it took off wildly. Now it's in forty languages. The response still startles me. Everywhere I go, from Taipei to Marrakesh, people come up to me and start talking family. The thing worldwide seems to be family. Everybody has some lineage, some ancestry, some native land. 'If they can do it, we can.'

"Most American families start out by trying to escape the old country, the patterns and the imagery of it within themselves. The elders hold on, but the young do everything to forget. The first generation after Ellis Island, or wherever the family has entered, is totally intent on being Americanized. Then the third and fourth generations start to look back to the old country. With blacks there was even more reluctance to look back because of the odium of slavery. Until *Roots* came out, blacks were ashamed of their past. They were not a people associated with a history. Now they look back with pride and say, 'I'm descended from this slave on such-and-such a plantation.' " I repeated to Haley a remark I had heard a black man make to his son at the Los Angeles zoo, where I had taken my family just before coming to see him. We were all leaning over the zebra pits. "Back in the motherland, our people used to *ride* these zebras," the man said.

At the end of *Roots*, Haley relates how his mother "would abruptly snap something like, 'Oh, Maw, I *wish* you'd stop all that old-timey slavery stuff, it's entirely embarrassing,' " when his grandmother, sitting on the family porch in Henning, Tennessee, would launch into a narrative of the previous four generations of her family, which had been preserved and embellished and passed on orally. The narrative began with a man referred to as "the African," who was kidnapped by slavers on a river called Kamby Bolongo, brought on a ship to a place called "Naplis," and bought off the ship by a man named "Massa John Waller," who took him to a plantation in Spotsylvania County, Virginia. The African's name, before he was given the slave name Toby, was Kintay. A few words of his language survived in the narrative: he would point at a guitar, for instance, and say something that sounded like *ko*. Thirty years after he had last heard the narrative, Haley decided, largely as an exercise in black pride, to establish an identity for "the African" and to find out exactly where on the continent he had come from. All the old women who had talked the narrative on the porch in Henning were dead except the youngest, Cousin Georgia, now in her eighties; and the fragments of it she reproduced for him were all he had to go on. An African linguist told him that Kamby Bolongo could be the Mandinka words for the Gambia River, distorted in repetition by people unfamiliar with the language. "*Ko*" could possibly refer to the *kora*, one of the Mandingo people's oldest traditional stringed instruments. With these scanty leads and a young Gambian from another tribe, a Wolof, who knew Mandinka, Haley undertook to "cross the water," as the genealogist Timothy Beard has described the challenge that every American who is tracing his ancestors must eventually face (unless, of course, he is native American on all sides), usually the critical part of his quest. He flew to Banjul, the capital city of Gambia, where he found out about a professional caste of praise singers called *griots*, who on special occasions recite and act out centuries-old histories of villages, clans, families, and great heroes. Kintay, his informants told him, undoubtedly referred to the Kinte clan, one of Gambia's oldest and most important.

Returning to America, Haley started to work back the other way. In a census for Alamance County, North Carolina, taken just after the Civil War, he turned up his great-grandfather, the grandson of the African. In Washington he discovered that the archives of the Daughters of the American Revolution were an unexpected gold mine of information about life on the big plantations. "The material is kept in big accordion files," he told me. "The mistresses of the better-run, classic operations, like the Byrd plantation in Virginia, would conduct an annual inventory that was complete down to minutiae—every piece of hardware, every cow, piece of cutlery, slave. Sometimes they would gratuitously add a remark about a slave they knew well—usually a house slave—after his name; they would mention, for instance, a woman's 'cheerful, sunny disposition.'" A year later, his trip underwritten by the *Reader's Digest*, Haley went back to Gambia, hired a launch, and with a retinue of fourteen people, including three interpreters and four musicians, arrived in state at a village on the Gambia River called Juffure, where an old *griot* who specialized in the history of the Kinte clan was supposed to live. As the jet-black inhabitants poured out of their huts and "raked" him with their eyes, he writes in *Roots*, "a visceral surging or churning sensation started deep inside me." He became uncomfortably aware of the comparative lightness of his complexion, and felt "impure among the pure." The old man, whose name was Kebba Kanji Fofana, began to chant what seemed to be a formal epic about the generations of the Kinte clan, linking the births, deaths, and marriages to memorable natural events like "the year of the big water," highlighting such deeds as "he slew a water buffalo." After about two hours he came to the sons of a man named Omoro Kinte: "About the time the king's soldiers came, the oldest of these four sons, Kunta, went away from his village to chop wood . . . and he was never seen again." Haley felt as if his blood had "congealed." He had found the African!

At the Public Records Office in London, a few months later, he searched British military records to see if any units had been posted to Gambia around the time of Kunta Kinte's disappearance—the 1760s—and in the second week he came across a unit called "Colonel O'Hare's Forces," which was sent from London in 1767 to guard a holding center for slaves on the river, called Fort James. Then he started to look through old maritime records to see if any slaves had been shipped from the fort to Annapolis, Maryland—to which he had already figured the "'Naplis" of the narrative must have referred—and in the seventh week, on his 1023rd sheet of slave-ship records, he found that on July 5, 1767, a hundred and forty slaves had—on a ship called the *Lord Ligonier*, her captain a Thomas E. Davies.

Back in Washington, Haley confirmed at the Library of Congress that the *Lord Ligonier* had cleared the Annapolis customs on September 29 of that year, and at the Maryland Hall of Records in Annapolis he discovered her cargo: "elephants teeth," beeswax, bar gold, rough cotton, and "98 Negroes." Forty-two of them, in other words, had not survived the crossing. All that was left for Haley to do then was to get Kunta Kinte to Spotsylvania County, and this he did by turning up in Richmond, Virginia, a micro-filmed deed in which John Waller and his wife Ann transferred to Waller's brother William, along with other property, "one Negro man slave named Toby." The documentation was now complete: Haley had crossed the water. Later he would cross the water literally, spending ten days in the hold of a freighter called the *African Star*, trying to project himself into the "ghastly ordeal endured by Kunta Kinte, his companions, and all those other millions, who lay chained and shackled in terror and their own filth."

A number of discrepancies in Haley's saga have been pointed out. The London *Times* reviewed his Gambian research and proved to its satisfaction that he didn't find his relatives; it reported that some of his dates didn't jibe, and that the only slaves taken by the British in that part of Gambia were either criminals or were sold to them by the Mandingo king, who was active in the slave trade himself. Currier-Briggs and Gambier suggest that Haley "may have been misled about the actual village in Africa." Could his retinue have taken him for a ride? ("Did they have me appraised as merely another pith helmet?" Haley himself asks in *Roots*.) Others on pilgrimage to their place of origin have been "set up." When the British journalist David Satter, for instance, who is part Russian, was Moscow correspondent for the London *Financial Times*, he was taken to his ancestral village and marched in an elaborate procession to the cemetery to see the headstones which, he was told, marked his ancestors' graves. Withdrawing from the ceremony for a moment, he overheard two of the villagers talking about how the headstones had actually been planted several days earlier, in anticipation of his arrival, and remarking that nobody had heard of the people whose names had been forwarded.

Had the *griot* simply told Haley what he wanted to hear? Some *griots* can recite twenty generations of their patrons' ancestry, but the profession has fallen on hard times, and the authenticity of their information is questionable. ("He was making up numbers of years or days for each name as he went along and it did not matter to him in the least that he had given me different information [a few days earlier]," the African historian Donald Wright has complained of a *griot* named Jata, from whom he tried to learn about the Niumi, a precolonial Mandingo state at the Gambia's mouth.) The American part of Haley's research was clouded, too, by a plagiarism lawsuit, settled out of court.

I didn't bring any of this up in our talk, however. Haley was not a scholar, he was a storyteller, and a gifted, moving one. If his approach to history was a little like a *griot*'s (the names and dates didn't matter as much as the emotional impact of the narrative); if he had (inadvertently, he claimed) reproduced word for word several short passages from another book; if the saga of his family was partly fictional, a composite portrait drawn from the collective experience of many Africans who had been brought over as slaves—*Roots* was nevertheless a genuine achievement that hit home and demonstrated to American blacks, denied access to their heritage for so long, that they at last were "somebody." At the end of our conversation Haley spoke about the need for a comprehensive program of interviewing the old people of this and other young countries. "The true history of this country is written in the minds of older people," he said. "Every year two million people over the age of sixty-four die. It's imperatively important that their oral history be gathered. Each family's history is a tiny piece of the mosaic of the country's history. We've lost so much already."

PART II

THE
MOUNTAIN
OF
NAMES

9

The Kinship of Mankind

THE PUBLICATION AND AIRING OF *Roots* LIFTED THE MORALE OF many American families and made people curious about their own origins; the whole nation seemed to identify with Haley's quest. Patronage at the Mormons' Genealogical Library in Salt Lake City doubled, to an average of three thousand a day, and it has remained high ever since. "*Roots* made a marked difference in our organization," a spokesman for the church's genealogical department told me recently. "A lot of people had got interested in heritage a year before, because of the Bicentennial, but *Roots* pushed it over the edge. News media interest in us mushroomed. Since 1977 literally thousands of column inches have been written about us in newspapers big and small, from the London *Sunday Times* to the *Toledo Blade,* and hours of radio and tv time have been consumed." By February 1977, letters to the National Archives in Washington requesting information had tripled, and applications for permits to use the facility had jumped by forty per cent, to five hundred and sixty a week. Other genealogical repositories reported similarly dramatic rises in patronage. People began to track down and reunite with long-lost relatives. "I've heard of a hundred cases of white and black families from the same plantation having reunions," Haley told me. "We had one in 1979, at the former Murray plantation in Alamance County, North Carolina.

My maternal side was Murray." Haley himself was lecturing around the country about the importance of reunions. "There is something magic about the common sense of a blood bond," he told *Time* magazine. "It's not less magic for black, white, brown, or polka-dot. The reunion gives a sense that the family cares about itself and is proud of itself. And there is the assumption that you, the family member, are obligated to reflect this pride and, if possible, to add to it."

On February 14, 1983, a Wall Street lawyer named Richard Hewlett Valentine and his wife Nancy gave a black-tie party for a hundred and twenty of their namesakes. The surname Valentine dates from the Norman Conquest. The first American Valentine had settled in Virginia by 1642. "In time," the *Times* reported, "the Valentines intermarried with such prestigious families as Lowell, Hewlett, and Braxton and accumulated their wealth from ironworks, tobacco, department stores, Wells Fargo, pharmaceutical companies (Parke-Davis and Smith Kline Beckman), the Armour meat packing company, and Valentine Meat-Juice, an early American cure-all that is still sold, although as a flavoring agent." Most of the guests were unknown to their hosts and were meeting each other for the first time. "It's a shame we never really gave a darn about each other before this," said Mary Valentine Robins, of East Williston, Long Island. "As far as I know I'm the last Valentine in my line, but tonight, I think, marks the beginning of my search for my family and, perhaps, myself," said Eric Valentine, a publishing consultant. "Am I related to these particular people? I just don't know." And a Philadelphia Valentine commented, "It was quite interesting, but I rather doubt that we'll be exchanging Christmas presents."

Six months later, four generations of Risleys gathered to celebrate the anniversary of the family's arrival in America. Reunions have become popular in the working class. Two of my fellow members in the Katonah (New York) Volunteer Fire Department, for instance, go to them. Jimmy Carl gets together with the hundred or so descendants of his paternal grandparents, who came from Germany to farm in western Pennsylvania; one of his cousins got the idea from *Roots*. Carl feels that the U.S. Army has been the main agent of the family's dispersal in the last three generations. The reunion Joe Taylor attends, in Sylvania, Georgia, is in its third year.

Some working-class Americans have deep roots. I recently met a man who works at the city incinerator in Eastchester, a city in lower Westchester County near the Bronx where one would not expect much continuity—much of it has been built over repeatedly, and the population has a rapid turnover. Yet this man is sixth-generation Eastchester.

As the "roots" boom rehabilitated the image of genealogy, which had been widely regarded as a not-quite-exact science and a forum for bores, related businesses benefitted tremendously. Today, at a place on Forty-sixth Street in Manhattan called Heraldic Imports, almost anybody who walks in, not just a certified "gentleman," can have a coat of arms prepared for him, or at least for his surname; organizations like the Illegitimate Sons and Daughters of the Kings of Great Britain and Flagon and Trencher (Descendants of Colonial Tavern Keepers) have proliferated; and a retired schoolteacher in Sterling, Pennsylvania, named Beatrice Bayley compiles on speculation nationwide directories of people with "very rare" surnames like Mellecker and Sanjurjo—names with a frequency in the American population of one in two hundred and fifty thousand or less.

Another manifestation of the genealogical revival has been the new interest in family history. The idea that reminiscences of older people are of value and worth preserving had already been popularized with the publication in 1970 of the first of the "Foxfire" books, collections of Appalachian Mountain stories and lore from northeast Georgia. Editors impressed by the success of *Roots* sent writers on voyages of genealogical self-discovery—the more ethnic the better. Under the encouragement of Haley's editor at Doubleday, Paul Cowan, a roving reporter for the *Village Voice* and the grandson of an impoverished used-cement-bag dealer in Chicago named Cohen, wrote *An Orphan in History,* an account of his search for his Jewish roots and his eventual embracing of Judaism. A woman named Flory Fisher, who had been adopted as a child, was inspired by Haley to write a book about her search for her natural parents, and became a leading lobbyist for recently enacted legislation that gives some adopted children access to their birth records. Other writers' interest in their own families was not directly influenced by Haley but was perhaps symptomatic of the same societal yearning that *Roots* reflected and released. Burton Bernstein told of his father's flight from a shetl in the Pale of Set-

tlement to New York's Lower East Side, where he began by sell-
ing fish and gradually built up a profitable hair products business
that made possible the brilliant musical career of Burton's brother
Leonard. Kate Simon told of her Bronx childhood, Maxine Hong
Kingston of growing up Chinese-American in California ("Mem-
oirs of a Girlhood Among Ghosts," the book is subtitled). Gail
Lumet, daughter of the singer Lena Horne, told me recently that
she has got one generation away from Senegal and learned "a
bunch of history" while following her mother's side of the family
back in time. Multigenerational novels like *Ellis Island* and *The
Immigrants* trace the fortunes of fictional families as they "cross
the water" from the old country and establish themselves here.
Perhaps the fact that "the literary woods are full of family trees,"
as the critic Richard F. Shepard recently observed, is an indication
that, now that we are on our own more than we have ever been,
a suppressed ancestral genealogical propensity is reasserting itself.

   In 1977 an editor suggested that I write up the history of my
family, and I accepted the proposition not only eagerly (in homage to Haley, the working title of the project would become *Root-
sky*) but with a sense of urgency. My two grandmothers were
both nearly ninety. I had heard some of their stories, in bits and
pieces, of how they had got out of Russia during the Revolution
and started life over again in the United States, and of what their
life had been before—but never the whole story. Their pedigrees
and their husbands', I discovered, went back for centuries. One
afternoon, as I was studying them, I noticed a possible connection
between the Adamovitches and the Vitovts, which would have
meant that my parents' families had been related to each other
since the seventeenth century. Hearing that the Genealogical Society of Utah had the best collection in the world, I wrote to see
if they could be of help in confirming this connection, and asked
if anything had been written about the overlapping of pedigrees
in general. A few weeks later an amazing paper by Robert C.
Gunderson, called "Tying Your Pedigree into Royal, Noble, and
Medieval Families," came in the mail. According to Gunderson,
if you kept multiplying your progenitors by two every generation—doubling your parents, *their* parents, and so on—when you
reached the time of Charlemagne (ca. 800 A.D.) you would have
between four and seventeen billion of them. Each person's pedigree, in other words, experiences a sort of retrogressive Malthusian

population explosion. Gunderson has since revised his estimate, claiming that if you kept doubling every twenty-five years the pedigree of somebody born today, by the year 800 the final number would be more like two hundred and sixty-three trillion.

But obviously there were nowhere near that many people alive then, or at any time. What prevents the theoretical population implosion from taking place is another phenomenon, which Gunderson delightfully calls "pedigree collapse." Pedigree collapse is caused by cousins marrying cousins—intentional mating between close cousins and random mating between distant ones who don't even know they are related.

Close-cousin marriage has happened much more often than is generally supposed. In tribal societies the exogamic restriction is not usually applied to all one's blood relatives, but only to the "brothers" and "sisters" of one's kinship group; in a patrilineal society, for instance, there is nothing to stop one from marrying a matrilineal cousin or uncle; such a match, in fact, is often esteemed. The ideal is to marry out, but not too far out. In Japan, which has one of the world's most elevated consanguinity rates, arranged marriages between first cousins have been going on for centuries; and a survey made in 1964 found that a third of the marriages in the Sudra caste in Andhra Pradesh, in southern India, were between first cousins, and the proportion of uncle-niece matings—the classic avunculate alliance of tribal people—may have been as high as twelve per cent.

"If we could only get into God's memory," Robin Fox told me recently, "we would find that eighty per cent of the world's marriages have been with second cousins. In a population of three to five hundred people, after six or so generations, there are only third cousins or closer to marry, and you end up with generalized altruism because everybody is equally related. During most of human history the people in such finite, isolated communities have probably been the genetic equivalent of first cousins, because of their multiple consanguinity. In rural England, for instance, the radius of the average isolate or pool of potential spouses was about five miles—the distance a man could comfortably walk twice on his day off, when he went courting—his roaming area by daylight. Parish registers bear this out. Then the bicycle extended the radius to twenty-five miles, to include four or five villages. This was a big shake-up." Fox estimates in *Kinship and Marriage* that even in modern, much more mobile English society, the average isolate for any given individual, which is "to some extent determined by the previous marriage choices of his ancestors and consanguines," varies from about nine hundred to just over two thousand people—"the kind of variation in population size we find for the most elementary of elementary societies."

Elevated consanguinity has also been a feature of nonrural populations. In 1875, 7.5 per cent of all the marriages among Jews in England, who at that time constituted a closed, endogamous religious isolate, were between first cousins, about three times the rate among gentiles. In most of the world's upper classes, cousins have frequently married to keep wealth and power in the family, or because of a dearth of other acceptable mates. In a cemetery at East Hampton, Long Island, I recently came across a cluster of upper-class consanguinity: John Tyler, the American President, married Julia Gardiner; their son John Alexander, a veteran of the Civil and Franco-Pussian wars and a surveyor of Indian lands, according to his monument, married Sarah Griswold Gardiner, evidently kin to his mother; Sarah's parents—Samuel Euel Gardiner, the tenth proprietor of Gardiner's Island, and Mary Gardiner Thomson—seem to have been cousins as well. Marriage between close kin has been particularly common in royal houses, the extreme cases being the Egyptian pharaohs and the Inca kings, who had to marry their own sisters. By the nineteenth century, the Catholic Church had reined in the "forbidden degrees" of consanguinity within which royal marriages could not take place, except by special dispensation, and most of the people sitting on the thrones of Europe were cousins in many different ways, with their pedigrees in varying stages of collapse. The pedigree of Alfonso XIII of Spain (1886–1941), for instance, collapsed almost immediately: because of cousin intermarriage, he had only eight second great-grandparents instead of the usual sixteen.

Each time cousins marry, duplication occurs in their descendants' pedigrees, because as cousins they already occupy a slot there. The farther back one traces any person's genealogy the greater the rate of duplication grows, until finally, when there is more cousin intermarriage than input from new people, the shape of one's pedigree stops expanding and begins to narrow. Each person's complete family tree, in other words, is shaped like a diamond. In the beginning it expands upward from him in an inverted triangle, in the same formula as the one for exponential population growth, except that the rate of expansion is not as great because each person can have only two progenitors, while the progenitors in the triangle of descendants that spreads down from him can, of course, have more than two children who survive to parenthood. At some point, hundreds of years back, the rate of expansion peaks; the base of the inverted triangle is reached and, overwhelmed by "collapse," the pedigree starts to narrow again, eventually coming to a point at a theoretical first couple, "Adam and Eve." But whether one such couple existed, and where, and when, is impossible to determine; the answer to these questions requires, among other things, a subjective judgment about when we became human.

"Beginning about two hundred thousand to three hundred thousand years ago, forms of humans appear that might be called *Homo sapiens,* with a skull size comparable to that of modern man," Bodmer and Cavalli-Sforza write in *Genetics, Evolution, and Man.* One "reasonable hypothesis," based on a comparative study of skull metrics in widely distributed ancient and aboriginal populations and on present geographic variations in the frequencies of certain genes, holds that "the subspecies *Homo sapiens sapiens* may have expanded from a nuclear area (perhaps in western Asia) to all of the world during a period perhaps thirty to forty thousand years ago . . . replacing or mixing with earlier human populations, and initiating the rapid cultural change of the Late Paleolithic." That is about as specific as anybody can be about our ultimate ancestors without taking a religious leap of faith.

In a paper as mind-boggling as Gunderson's, the demographer Kenneth W. Wachtel (no relation to Paul that Paul knows of) creates a simple probability model for the progenitors of an English child born in 1947. By the time America was discovered, the child would have more than sixty thousand progenitors, and ninety-five per cent of the slots on his pedigree would still be filled by different people. At the twentieth generation, around the time of John Wyclif and the Peasants' Revolt, he would have roughly six hundred thousand progenitors, and a third of the slots would be filled by duplicates. Just before the Black Death, only thirty per cent of his mathematically possible 3,650,000 progenitors would turn up. Around the time of King John, the widest point of his pedigree, with about two million progenitors along the same horizontal line, would be reached; then the pedigree would start to narrow again. Each progenitor would be filling an average of sixteen slots, and the child would be descended from eighty per cent of the people in England. By the time of the Domesday survey, in 1086, five-sixths of the population would be his kin. At that point the rate of duplication would finally stabilize; there would always be at least a sixth of the population to which the child would never be related.

The pedigree of Prince Charles has probably been as exhaustively researched as anybody's—Gunderson has been working on it for the better part of fourteen years now, and there are others in England who have made it their life work. It illustrates this pattern beautifully. Charles is spared Alfonso XIII's fate of nearly instantaneous collapse because his ancestry is more diverse: he has a healthy dose of Scottish and English commoner blood, and most of his ancestors were actually from the Continent; but his collapse rate is still considerably greater than the average person's. In the seventeenth generation of his pedigree, for instance, when he should theoretically have 65,536 progenitors, cousin intermarriage has deprived him of all but about twenty-three thousand— only thirty-five per cent of the theoretical—of which Gunderson has identified only twenty-eight hundred—less than seventeen per cent. Of these twenty-eight hundred, Gunderson has discovered that "at least two thousand" of the descents are *from the same person:* Edward III, who ruled England from 1327 to 1377. Since his paper came out, the extremely cautious Gunderson has revised the figure to 1,995; but Charles's subsequent marriage and production of an heir has opened a whole new area of investigation for him: the pedigree of Princess Diana. "She has a lot more English and Scottish blood than her husband, and probably twice as many descents from Edward III," Gunderson told me recently.

The mathematics of descent have fascinated many people. "If we could go back and live again in all of our two hundred and fifty million arithmetical ancestors of the eleventh century," Henry Adams wrote of those with Norman-English blood, "we should find ourselves doing many surprising things, but among the rest we should certainly be ploughing most of the fields of the Cotentin and Calvados; going to mass in every parish church in Normandy; rendering military service to every lord, spiritual or temporal, in all this region; and helping to build the Abbey Church at Mont-Saint-Michel." And more recently the sociobiologist Edward O. Wilson has written, "The gene pool from which one modern Briton has emerged spreads over Europe, to North Africa, the Middle East, and beyond. The individual is an evanescent combination of genes drawn from this pool, one whose hereditary material will soon be dissolved back into it."

The genetic consequences of distant-cousin marriage, as we began to explain in Chapter Four, are negligible. Only "relatively recent consanguinity . . . is pertinent," Bodmer and Cavalli-Sforza write. ". . . In some human societies more distant consanguinities may have social significance [such as for membership in a blood-money group], but from a genetic point of view the connection between two individuals who have one great great great grandparent in common (fourth half-cousins) is . . . very tenuous indeed." The children of couples more closely related than fourth half-cousins, however, are at higher risk of inheriting a genetic disorder, particularly a recessive one. According to the geneticist Francisco J. Ayala, "the incidence of defective newborn children is about twice as high when the parents are first cousins as when the parents are unrelated." The more common genetic consequences of inbreeding include defects of the ear and eye, structural malformations, and various mental deficiencies ranging from idiotism to feeble-mindedness. There is also a greater chance of miscarriage; inbreeding can reduce reproductive fitness, in other words. (By the same token, plants with oversimilar genetic endowments can suffer from what the biologist Nicholas M. Waser has termed "inbreeding depression"—low seed production and low viability of the seedlings that sprout from the seeds.)

Dominant traits, like polydactyly, can spread in an isolated population, but as a consequence of drift, not of inbreeding. Some of the recently contacted Waorani Indians, who live in the remote Ecuadorian Amazon, have supernumerary toes and fingers; all the members of an inbred clan in the Hyabites tribes of Arabia called Foldi are polydactylous, and any twenty-digited baby born to them is regarded as the illegitimate issue of an adulterous mother, and is put to death. Rarely, inbreeding can cause a female who inherits from both parents two copies of a deleterious X-linked recessive gene (which would normally have been neutralized by the inheritance of one healthy copy of the gene) to express the trait; there are female hemophiliacs, for instance, but not very many of them.

The typical victim of inbreeding suffers from having inherited two copies of a deleterious autosomal recessive gene. There are probably many more of these genes than are presently known to exist because, to be expressed, they have to meet up with themselves again, which happens rarely in normal, outbred populations. The recessive for phenylketonuria, for instance, a metabolic disorder that often causes mental retardation, has an average frequency of one per cent, but only one in ten thousand babies is born with the disorder. Because unexpressed recessive genes are hidden from the process of natural selection, they cannot be swept as easily from a population as deleterious dominants, which are more exposed and disappear more quickly. A few recessives, in single dose, like the mutations for sickle-cell anemia and thalassemia, which are believed to confer some resistance to malaria, may have actually been advantageous and preserved by natural selection. "We suggest that modern European and American populations are now riddled with genes in the course of slow elimination," the geneticists J. B. S. Haldane and S. D. Jayakar wrote, and according to their colleague Bob Williamson, "each of us 'normals' carries twenty or so potentially lethal recessive genes, from whose lethality we are protected by also carrying a healthy, dominant version of the same gene."

Inbreeding, however, greatly increases the possibility that one of these recessives will meet up with itself, that two genes "identical by descent," which have passed down through different lines from a common ancestor, will double up and produce the trait. The more recent the couple's consanguinity, the greater the odds of their offspring being affected. The risk is determined by computing the average proportion of genes the consanguineous couple shares from the common ancestor or ancestors, which is the same as the probability that both will have any one of these genes in common. This value is known as the coefficient of kinship. A child shares half of his genes with one of his parents, and thus their coefficient of kinship is $\frac{1}{2}$; full siblings share a quarter of their genes through each parent, and thus their coefficient is also $\frac{1}{2}$. For uncles and nieces the value is $\frac{1}{8}$; for first cousins, $\frac{1}{16}$; for first cousins once removed, $\frac{1}{32}$; for second cousins, $\frac{1}{64}$; and so on. Once the probability that both consanguineous parents will be carriers has been computed, the odds that their child will inherit both of their copies then proceed according to the laws of Mendelian inheritance, outlined in Chapter Four: the child has a one-in-two chance of inheriting one copy and being only a carrier; a one-in-four chance of inheriting both copies and expressing the trait; and a one-in-four chance of being "clean." But often couples who are related in one way have other connections as well, and as Bodmer and Cavalli-Sforza put it, "the effect of multiple consanguinity is additive"; they may have a higher coefficient of kinship.

One afternoon, to get an understanding of how hereditary disorders can affect people's lives, I sat in on a case at the genetics clinic of Columbia-Presbyterian Hospital, in New York City, which involved a family from the Dominican Republic. Most other clinics restrict themselves to diagnosis and prognosis, but this one was proud that it had a psychotherapist, Yaakov Schechter, to help the parents of an afflicted child cope with their stress and guilt. Men are not very common in genetic counselling, because the burden of raising the child usually falls most heavily on the mother. The other members of the clinic—Phyllis Tatercka and Robin Schwarz—were women. The parents were both in their early twenties and both from Santo Domingo, the capital, where they had known each other before coming up to Spanish Harlem—José Moreno thirteen years ago (he drove a truck when he could find work), Josefina eight years ago. (Neither name is real.) Josefina became pregnant, and was encouraged at her prenatal clinic to be tested for the sickle-cell trait. One in fifty "Hispanics" (a category whose ambiguity may even exceed that of "blacks") is estimated to carry the gene, which is the best understood recessive—a "point mutation," caused by substitution of a single base pair of the genetic code, on the short arm of chromosome eleven. She tested positive. The next day José came in and he too was found to be a carrier. The joy of their imminent parenthood suddenly became a nightmare. The clinical expression of people who receive the gene in double strength is highly variable: some die in infancy, some are chronically debilitated, some have only mild anemic episodes and a normal life span. Fewer than a hundred thousand people around the world die annually from sickle-cell anemia.

There was still a seventy-five-per-cent chance that the child would be all right, and Corina, as the Morenos named their daughter, turned out to be healthy: after the bad luck of discovering themselves to be both carriers, they had pulled a miracle. God had decided not to punish them after all. "We were thrilled," Phyllis Tatercka told me. She had asked Josefina to bring her husband in to make sure he understood what had happened. ("The first thing we do," Phyllis told me, "is try to find out the patient's or the parent's perception of why they are here.") Corina was now three weeks old and in the pink of health. "Doing beautiful," Josefina told us, beaming. The nightmare was over, but José still looked shaken and confused.

Yaakov Schechter explained to José what the disease was, gave him a pamphlet called "The Family Connection—Sickle Cell Trait," and carefully described the inheritance of an autosomal recessive. We were all sitting at a small, round table in a small, white room furnished with a hospital bed and another small writing table beneath a shelf of thick genetics textbooks. The session was open-ended. No one got up until the questions in José's mind were fully answered.

The next step was to draw up the parents' pedigrees, which was done by Robin. Her deft diagram, with circles for women and squares for men, rose from Corina in an inverted pyramid as José and Josefina recalled the names and the health histories of their antecedents, suggesting that she had tracked mutant genes back through their possible carriers in many other families. "Most of the people who come in can't go back for more than three generations," Phyllis said later. "Sometimes the mother will not tell me who the father is or does not know, so the pedigree dead-ends right away on one side, and the information we get on adopted children is usually very sketchy, because parents are intensely interested in maintaining confidentiality."

It turned out that José's and Josefina's families had known each other for a long time in Santo Domingo, and that they were, in fact, second cousins, which meant that their coefficient of kinship was $\frac{1}{64}$.

Phyllis explained to the Morenos that should they decide to have another child, the odds of its being a carrier, affected, or clean would be the same as they had been for Corina. "Chance has no memory," she said, repeating a favorite expression among genetic counsellors. But José, avoiding everyone's eyes, including his wife's, shook his head emphatically and said that one child, whatever its sex, was all he had ever wanted and all he could afford.

"I think he feels that he has been labelled," Yaakov said afterward, "that he is not quite the man he thought he was. And the worst thing is that in most cases nothing can be done. Once the condition has been discovered in the parents, they can go ahead and take the risk, and early in the pregnancy, usually after fourteen weeks, the baby's amniotic fluid can be tapped. If the baby is found to be affected, the pregnancy can be terminated. In the future the couple can practice birth control, one of them can be sterilized, one of the parent's genotypes can be replaced by getting sperm from an anonymous donor or by finding another woman to conceive and have the baby; or they can get divorced. But what kind of solutions are these? There is a lot of frustration. That is why, as a geneticist, I realized I needed training in psychotherapy."

The director of the clinic, Arthur Bloom, had studied the genetic consequences of inbreeding on Grand Cayman, a Caribbean island northwest of Jamaica which was colonized in the eighteenth century and has about fifteen thousand inhabitants of mixed slave and English ancestry, who live in five isolated population centers. Their birth rate had been quite low, Bloom told me, and genetic problems had only begun to emerge in the most recent generations. "It takes a number of generations before the gene frequency goes up enough for disorders to become apparent clinically," he explained. "Each population center has its own spectrum. A lot of children in West Bay have San Filippo syndrome, a mycopolysaccharide-storage disease, usually lethal by adolescence, which is not seen on the East End. One per cent of the West Bay population is afflicted with a recessively inherited syndrome that includes retardation, ataxia, and disturbance of gaze, which we have called Cayman disease, and eighteen per cent are carriers, so it is a risky situation in terms of mating." (A comparable situation, but with retinitis pigmentosa, exists on Tristan de Cunha, a barren, formerly volcanic island in the extreme South Atlantic, too vertical for an airfield and fifteen hundred miles from the nearest other people, on the island of St. Helena. The several hundred inhabitants, who live in one of the world's most isolated communities, are descended from shipwrecked mariners and the remnants of an English garrison who began to settle the island after 1812. They have only seven surnames among them, and have meticulous genealogies and health histories, so that carriers of the disorder, which is characterized by constriction of the visual field and night blindness, can be identified and discouraged from marrying each other.) "Six in every thousand people on the East End are born deaf," Bloom went on, "which is the highest incidence known in humans. The normal incidence is one per thousand." The gene is recessive, but the deaf tend to marry "assortatively," so that half their children, on average, are born deaf, and the other half carry the trait. Bloom collected several eight-generation pedigrees that showed a steady rise in the frequency of congenital deafness.

The best-studied "unbending religious isolate," as Bloom describes it, is the Old Order Amish, more than forty-three thousand of whom live in the United States and Canada, eighty per cent of them in Pennsylvania, Ohio, and Indiana. Most are descended from the followers of a Mennonite bishop named Jakob Ammann who in the 1690s broke with the Swiss Brethren and started his own sect. The main immigration, to Pennsylvania from the canton of Berne and from Alsace-Lorraine, began no later than 1727 and lasted until about 1770. The genealogical records of the Amish are extraordinarily complete. Most of them can trace their complete ancestry, on every line, to the first immigrants. The Fisher genealogy has data on more than thirty-six hundred families and embraces the entire Amish population in Lancaster County, Pennsylvania. The descendants of Barbara Hochstedler include 15,556 parental pairs and their children. The Bitsche, Eash, Gnagey, Hershberger, Hertzler, Kauffman, Lantz, Lapp, and Mast families have also published extensive genealogies. Eighty per cent of the Amish in Lancaster County have only eight surnames. The Amish are a "peculiar people," who keep to themselves. They do not proselytize and they forbid marriage to outsiders. Some leave the fold, but very few enter it. "A strong system of sanctions, including excommunication and shunning (*Meidung*), helps maintain the group," the geneticists Victor McKusick, John A. Hostetler, and Janice A. Egeland write at the beginning of a book called *Medical Genetic Studies of the Amish*. Passages of Scripture like II Corinthians 6:14, which reinforce the society's aloofness, are frequently repeated: "Be ye not unequally yoked together with unbelievers: for what fellowship hath righteousness with unrighteousness? and what communion hath light with darkness?" By restricting themselves to transportation by horse and buggy, the Amish limit their breeding range to about thirty miles, and because of their tight extended-family networks they tend to be more successful at farming than the modern farmers around them, despite using only horses. Reciprocal work agreements, even those between nonrelatives, are generally cemented by the exchange of work horses. The average level of consanguinity among the Amish may be at the level of third or fourth cousins; of the six hundred and twenty-seven marriages involving descendants of Johannes Schwartz and his wife Anna Ramseyer, who lived in Berne, Indiana (the only such data available), 21.5 per cent were between second cousins or closer consanguines. The price for the Amish's endogamy has included the Ellis–van Creveld syndrome, cartilage-hair hypoplasia, two recessive types of dwarfism, albinism, familial agoitrous cretinism, muscular dystrophy, lateral sclerosis, and von Recklinghausen's neurofibromatosis. Not surprisingly, there is a great interest in illness among them. The *Budget,* for instance, a weekly that caters to the sect, runs long, detailed accounts of genetic illnesses sent in by members of Amish families from all over the country.

The hereditary houses of Europe have repeatedly intermarried, forming a political, as opposed to a geographic or religious, isolate. Ferdinand and Isabella of Spain, for instance, who backed the first two voyages of Columbus, were second cousins on one side, but the houses of Aragon and Castille, to which they respectively belonged, had previously intermarried so often that their cumulative coefficient of kinship was much higher than $\frac{1}{64}$. One of their daughters—"mad Joanna"—was insane. Another, Catherine of Aragon, married Henry VIII. Five of Henry and Catherine's children were stillborn or died within several months, and only Mary, who became known as Bloody Mary, lived to marry her first cousin. Some idiots who were kin to Philip V of Spain were painted by Velásquez, and I once saw, during a trip to Europe as a child in the late nineteen-fifties, in the Schloss Ambrass, near Innsbruck, Austria, a portrait of a hapless Hapsburg princeling with hair radiating from the center of his face; whether this condition was a consequence of inbreeding I have no idea. Most of the defective children of the European royalty and nobility were not painted or exhibited. Francis Galton wrote in the last century of "a large number of milder cases [than idiotism or imbecility; cases of what he went on to describe as "hereditary silliness"] among private families and kept out of sight, the existence of whom is, however, well known to relatives and friends." One serious case was that of the eldest son of the Earl of Strathmore some generations back who, according to the writer Jean Goodman and the genealogist Sir Ian Moncreiffe of That Ilk, was born early in the last century "in a hideous form with a massive body covered with matted black hair, tiny arms and legs, and a head sunk deep into his barrel chest. Obviously such a creature could not inherit the title and he was kept in a secret room [in Glamis Castle, the setting of *Macbeth*] and exercised on the roof at night. He was believed to have lived to well over a hundred and died in the early part of this century. To keep the dreadful secret only four men at any one time were allowed to know of the Monster's existence. They were the Earl, the family lawyer, the agent to the estate and the eldest son [Moncreiffe presumably means the *next* eldest son], who was shown the Monster, the rightful Earl, on the day that he came of age."

Some old European families, like the Obolenskys and the Troubetzskoys, who have been princely since the time of Ivan the Terrible, have intermarried for centuries without apparent genetic consequences. Serge and Lyuba Troubetzskoy, of Syosset, Long Island, are the products of five generations of Obolensky-Troubetzskoy intermarriage. Lyuba was an Obolensky, but her mother, a Troubetzskoy, was Serge's first cousin. "He teases me that I used to call him Uncle when I was little," she told me recently. In other families dwarfism has periodically cropped up. Cavalli-Sforza recently told me that the former King of Italy, Victor Emmanuel III, was "so small that if his napkin fell he couldn't get back into his chair, so he tucked it under his legs to avoid embarrassment. The army had to lower its minimum height requirement so he could be a general." Cavalli-Sforza isn't sure what form of dwarfism the king suffered from, but thinks it was probably a recessive one, as it had been produced by inbreeding. "The coefficient of kinship of the European royalty is high," he said, "but not as high as in artificially bred cattle or laboratory mice, which have a ninety-five per cent overlap and are practically homogeneous." (Contrary to widely held opinion, inbreeding has had nothing to do with the "royal hemophilia" that has so far afflicted nine male descendants of Queen Victoria, including the Tsarevitch Alexis Romanoff and an uncle of the present King of Spain, the Prince of the Asturias, who hemorrhaged to death after a car accident in 1938. The original mutation, which was inherited by one of Queen Victoria's four sons and two of her four daughters, is believed to have occurred in the X chromosome of her father, Edward, Duke of Kent. When Victoria was born in 1819, Prince Edward was fifty-two, and the germ cells of older men are more prone to some types of mutation. The execution of Tsar Nicholas and his family and the untimely death of two afflicted Prussian princes have eliminated the mutant gene from Victoria's Hesse line, but it may still be carried recessively by some of her English and Spanish female descendants. Males expressing the gene have a deficiency of clotting factor VIII, which produces severe bleeding at the slightest provocation.)

Inbreeding levels are sensitive to political and technological change. At the beginning of the nineteenth century, for instance, after the Napoleonic Code had abolished primogeniture in Central Europe, first-cousin marriage increased in Italy as a means of keeping property in the family. But on the whole, inbreeding has not been a problem in Catholic countries, because of the Church's ban on marriage within the third degree of relationship, or between second cousins, which lasted from 1550 to 1917. Since the end of the nineteenth century, with the diffusion of local populations brought about by the Industrial Revolution, the West and the developing world have seen a decrease in consanguineous marriage. The Mormons have a relatively high level of inbreeding for the United States, but still no more than one per cent of their marriages are between first cousins. The world is becoming increasingly panmictic—a healthy development both medically and sociopolitically.

❋

"The human species is young, perhaps not more than ten thousand generations old, and the major geographical races diverged from each other about fifteen hundred generations ago, at most," the population geneticist Richard Lewontin has written in *Human Diversity*. ". . . If anything is clear about the direction of human evolution, it is that the early differentiation of people into local groups, while still very much a part of our biological diversity, is on the decline. The unifying forces of migration and common selection through common environment and common culture are stronger than they have ever been." Most geneticists are in agreement that, as the science writer Guy Murchie explains, "no human can be less closely related to any other human than approximately fiftieth cousin, and most of us are a lot closer . . . [that, in other words] the family trees of all of us, of whatever origin or trait, must meet and merge into one genetic tree of all humanity by the time they have spread into our ancestors for about fifty generations." The "family of man" which has been posited by many religions and philosophies—it was a central concept of the Enlightenment—actually exists.

The main point about our universal interrelatedness is not that we are all descended from some common ancestors. The notion that a primordial couple are the mother and father of us all begins to seem like a romantic oversimplification when one considers that most of our genome had evolved before we separated from the apes, that "the chimpanzee and the human share about 99.5 per cent of their evolutionary history," as the zoologist Richard Dawkins has written. The main point is, rather, that each of us contains genetic contributions from practically everybody who ever lived. All it takes for widely divergent populations to merge genealogically is migration by one person. "A single indirect genetic contact between Africa and Asia in a thousand years can make every African closer than fiftieth cousin to every Chinese," Murchie writes. "Surprisingly, this may happen without any natives of either continent doing any particular travelling at all, but simply in consequence of the wanderings of nomads in intermediate territory." And Lewontin remarks that "a very small amount of migration—as little as one migrant individual exchanged between groups in each generation—is quite sufficient to prevent differentiation between groups by genetic drift [whatever divergences would be caused by the random fluctuation of gene frequencies within the groups if they were completely isolated]."

In other words, everybody belongs to one enormous pyramid of descendants that fans down from the first humans, and at the same time everybody has a separate, personal pedigree diamond.

History can be seen as a mosaic of billions of overlapping pedigree diamonds. The kinship group to which we all belong—"the family of man," which anthropologists would describe as a kindred—extends indefinitely in every direction. Some genealogists have started to play with this notion, so that a new vogue in genealogy is *horizontal* genealogy. By charting the overlap in the pedigrees of recent American political figures, for instance, the genealogist William Addams Reitwiesner has discovered that Hamilton Jordan, former President Jimmy Carter's top aide, and former Florida governor Reuben Askew are eighth cousins once removed; that Carter and former President Richard Nixon are sixth cousins (both descended from a New Jersey Quaker named Richard Morris, who lived before the American Revolution); that Nixon and Vice-President Bush are tenth cousins once removed; that Bush is a seventh cousin of Elliot Richardson, attorney general in the Nixon Administration, as well as being a kinsman of Ernest Hemingway and of the nineteenth-century plutocrat Jay Gould; and that the California senator Alan Cranston has in his constellation of known kin, through common descent from a man named Robert Bullard, who lived in Watertown, Massachusetts, in the early sixteen-hundreds: Queen Geraldine of Albania, Richard Henry Dana, Emily Dickinson, George Plimpton, the Dow chemical family, Julie Harris, and Margaret Mead. "The more you dig, the smaller the world becomes," the *Times* reporter who interviewed Reitwiesner observed.

The extent of our multiple interrelatedness is brought home even more dramatically, however, by traditional, vertical genealogy. "It is virtually certain . . . that you are a direct descendant of Muhammad and every fertile predecessor of his, including Krishna, Confucius, Abraham, Buddha, Caesar, Ishmael and Judas Iscariot," Murchie writes. "Of course, you must also be descended from millions who have lived since Muhammad, inevitably including kings and criminals, but the earlier they lived the more surely you are their descendants."

The political implications of this great kindred to which we all belong are exciting. If everybody became aware of this multiple interrelatedness; if the same sort of "generalized altruism" Fox describes as prevailing in small communities, and which may embrace larger groups—a tribe, say, but to a large extent still ends abruptly when national boundaries are reached—could prevail over the entire human population; if this vision of ourselves could somehow catch on—then many of the differences that have polarized various subpopulations from the beginning of our history, the result of adaptation to disparate climates and of genetic drift within geographically or culturally segregated populations (differences that are, for the most part, literally only skin-deep), would seem secondary. The problems we have with each other would become, as it were, internal.

10

The Mountain of Names

How big is the human family? We know that close to five billion people are alive today, but how many others have there been? According to the most carefully reasoned estimates, between sixty-nine billion and a hundred and ten billion people have lived since the appearance of humans. The figures are based on an exponential growth curve interpolated between "benchmark estimates," or key points at which there are data about the size of the world's population; the disparity in them is the result of differences in estimated birth rates and life spans, and in the date of origin for "humans." Although the ascent of the curve is at first, and for many millennia, so gradual that it is largely lost in the thickness of the draftsman's pen, the final tally is significantly affected by when one decides to begin the curve. Creationists, who start the human race with the placing of Adam and Eve in the Garden of Eden six thousand years ago, and who believe that in about 2700 B.C. a worldwide flood killed off everybody then alive except Noah and his family, come up with a considerably lower figure of fifty-one billion for the total number of people ever. Most historical demographers begin their curves a million years ago. Erect, tool-using hominids—the australopithecines—are thought to have lived as long as three and a half million years ago; the genus *Homo* is perhaps one and a half million years old;

archaic *Homo sapiens* was around four hundred thousand years ago, and our race, *Homo sapiens sapiens*, begins to appear in the fossil record only about forty thousand years ago—so the choice of a million years ago is something of a compromise. The demographer Edward S. Deevey has estimated that between a million years ago and twenty-five thousand years ago, a total of thirty-six billion Paleolithic hunter-gatherers lived in average generations succeeding each other about every twenty-five years, thirty-five thousand times. Ten thousand years ago—the consensus date for the beginning of settled agriculture—some five to ten million people were alive; the figure is based on study of the territorial requirements of contemporary hunter-gatherers and on a guess at how much land was available for human exploitation, after considering geological evidence for how far down the icecaps had advanced at that time, and reconstructing the climate and rainfall patterns.

By the beginning of the Christian era, when most people had shifted from wild to domesticated plant and animal food—which greatly increased the means of subsistence—and had become village farmers or city dwellers, the human population had risen to within an "indifference range" of two hundred million to four hundred million. This slightly more informed guess, the demographer Ansley J. Coale has explained, is based on surviving information about censuses in the Roman Empire; on imperial Chinese records; on a "tenuous estimate" by historians of the population of India around them; and on "a crude allowance for the number of people in other regions." By 1750 there are much more extensive written records, and the world's population can be estimated within twenty-per-cent of accuracy to have been around eight hundred million. At this point the curve, which for thousands of years has shown little more upward mobility than a straight, horizontal line, begins to rise steeply.

The growth rate of a population is the difference between its birth rate and its death rate, and beginning about 1750, a number of developments combined to reduce mortality in the West, thus causing comparatively unrestrained growth. To begin with, as Coale explained it to me, "there was a more abundant and more regular supply of food because of an extension of cultivation, particularly in America; because new foods from the New World—potatoes and maize—caused an agricultural revolution in Europe;

and because transport improved. Water supplies were cleared up and sanitary habits changed: people started to bathe and to wash their hands more regularly, including doctors. By 1825 one or two genuine medical innovations, like the smallpox vaccine, had begun to have an effect. Doctors stopped healing their patients by bleeding and purging, and in the latter part of the nineteenth century germs were discovered and anesthetics were invented. Real curative medicine did not begin until after 1930, with chemotherapy (sulfas) and antibiotics (penicillin). The reduction in mortality affected growth in two ways: by prolonging life, it led to a larger population from a given stream of births, and by allowing more women to survive to procreative age, it enlarged the stream of births."

By the late nineteenth century, between seventy-five and eighty-five per cent of women in industrialized countries were surviving to the mean childbearing age of twenty-eight (which is about the current proportion in the Third World). This was a tremendous improvement over the life expectancy not only of women but of everybody who had lived before. Coale estimates that until "the modern era"—for all but .02 per cent of human history, in other words—family size (including parents) averaged eight people, with the sexual breakdown of the children about even; but only one of the three females survived to the "middle age of parentage." The early deaths depressed the growth curve but figure significantly in the computation of the total people ever, because the question of how many people have lived is, in effect, a question of how many were born. Since 1750 the growth rate has risen from .56 per thousand to more than seventeen per thousand (with almost forty per thousand in prodigiously fertile Kenya), and the world's population now stands at about 4.7 billion. Nearly a billion of these people were born after 1970, and four to seven per cent of all the people who have lived are alive today.

Of all the people ever alive, between eighty-five and ninety-two per cent lived, died, and slipped into complete oblivion without even leaving their names. The loss of their identities, like the extinction of a species, is irreparable. There is no "catalogue of catalogues," such as Jorge Luis Borges has written of, in which we might hope to find the names of everybody who has lived. Such records as were kept of human populations in the past were ravaged by various agents of destruction. The Black Death of 1360, for instance, not only killed half the people in London; fires set to fumigate the victims' quarters destroyed many of the documents with which they and their ancestors could have been identified. The earthquake of 1906 destroyed most of the birth and marriage records in San Francisco, enabling some Chinese immigrants to claim citizenship as native-born Americans. During the bombing of Exeter in the Second World War, all the wills from south-western England, which had been gathered there for safekeeping, were destroyed. Professor Lo Hsiang-lin, who had built up in Canton a priceless collection of gazetteers and clan genealogies, which he was forced to leave behind when he fled to Hong Kong from the Communist takeover, later heard from a friend that his collection had appeared in a bookstore which, unable to find another market, had sold them to a grocer for wrapping paper.

But record loss is not the real problem. Most of the historical human population was never recorded. It has been estimated by the Acquisitions Section of the Genealogical Society of Utah that existing records of the dead name on the order of only six to seven billion people, almost all of whom lived after 1500.

The practice of conducting a regular, comprehensive census is a recent development in most of the world, although the Babylonians appear to have been doing it as early as 3800 B.C., and the Romans were inveterate census takers. Census is a Latin word, and there is information about the periodic assessment of adult male Roman citizens and of their property, which was instituted by the sixth king, Servius Tullius, around 550 B.C. and continued until the Empire fell, although none of the material has survived. Roman citizens were ranked by how much land they owned: a senator had to own eight hundred thousand sesterces, an equestrus four hundred thousand; a poor man was a *homo sine censu*. The census was taken every five years, and at its close an expiatory sacrifice of an ox, a sheep, and a sow was offered. In 158 B.C., 328,000 citizens capable of bearing arms were enumerated. At the time of Caesar Augustus, the census was expanded to take in the whole Roman Empire; one recalls how, in the Gospels, Joseph and Mary had to go to Bethlehem to be counted among the descendants of David.

Fragments of Chinese censuses in the fourth and fifth centuries A.D. have been found in the Tunhuang Caves in Kansu Province; the demographer D. Durand has discovered records of or references to about a hundred censuses between 2 A.D., when the Golden Age of the Western Han Dynasty was drawing to a close, and 1912, when the last Ch'ing emperor abdicated.

The Japanese were keeping track of themselves, with land registers that contained additional household information, by the seventh century, but the practice stopped when the society became feudal in the next century. During the repressive Tokugawa Shogunate, from 1634 to 1871, peasants (as we have seen) were not allowed to use surnames, contact with the outside world was forbidden, and people who had converted to Christianity were put to death. The Inquisition Records (*shumon cho*) from this period, however, are as complete as most modern censuses; they provide, in fact, the earliest "Grade A" data, in which vital statistics were gathered for nearly a whole population.

The first post-Roman censuses in the West were Scandinavian: Finland in 1635, Iceland in 1703 (a very thorough one, it lists entire households). The first federal census in the United States was taken in 1790, and there has been one every ten years since, but until 1840 only heads of households were listed; the rest of the family appeared only as numbers in age and sex columns, and no Indians were counted until 1860. Recent American censuses have probably undercounted by one to three per cent, and because the information dates so quickly, the census will be taken at five-year intervals beginning in 1985. Because of time limitations on use of the raw data, the 1910 census has only just become available.

Russia did not conduct a comprehensive census until 1897, and there have been only four since. The 1897 census seems to have been conducted rather like one of the annual Christmas bird counts by the Audubon Society. It was all done in one day, January 28 (the reasoning was that people were most likely to be at home in the dead of winter), by 150,000 census-takers who filled over thirty million data sheets. Even temporary residents and people who were temporarily abroad were counted. The 1897 census was a notable improvement over the "revisions" of taxable "souls" (everybody not in the nobility) started by Peter the Great. The first revision had begun in 1719 and had dragged on until 1727. The twenty-three million souls counted in the tenth revision are estimated to have been only thirty-five per cent of the Tsar's subjects in 1859. Nikolai Gogol's character Chichikov pulls off a brilliant swindle by buying for a pittance "dead souls"—the names of serfs who had died since the last revision—from provincial land-owners and mortgaging them as living property to the State Bank; Gogol got the idea from an actual swindle he read about in a newspaper.

Most of the people in sub-Saharan Africa did not get counted until after the Second World War. The first census in the Sudan, in 1953, is of questionable accuracy (as is the first modern census in China, also taken that year). Nigeria's 1963 census was apparently grossly overcounted. The first census in South Africa was not made until 1965. Some people, including the citizens of Saudi Arabia and Yemen, have never been counted. In 1981, at the request of some anthropologists, I took photographs and wrote down the name, age, and clan of some BaLese tribespeople who live in small villages in the Ituri Forest of northeastern Zaire, several days from the nearest road. It was the first time their existence had been documented.

The age of modern vital record keeping is widely considered to have begun in 1538, when Thomas Cromwell, Henry VIII's Vicar General, ordered the parish clergy to enter on books every christening, wedding, and burial (although the Japanese, with Buddhist necrologies going back to the thirteenth century, and the Vatican, which Cavalli-Sforza told me has Italian baptismal records that begin before 1538, might not agree). Some of the 10,894 ancient parishes in England and Wales did not begin their registers until 1700, but most of the other European countries, following the British example, had started to keep parish registers by the end of the sixteenth century. The usefulness of these records varies by country (one scholar recently ranked the German ones as "most meticulous," the French ones as "a hodgepodge," and the Spanish ones as "even less detailed and more difficult to evaluate"); but parish registers, in general, are the meat and potatoes of European genealogists. In South Africa, the registers of the Dutch Reformed Church go back to 1652, but the christening records are not available for inspection because many Afrikaners have native ancestors whom they would rather not publicize; a recent study found that the possibility of any Afrikaner with an ancestor in South Africa before 1750 not having black blood is minuscule.

Being restricted to local Protestant, Catholic, Jewish, or Orthodox congregations, the parish registers are far from comprehensive;

by the end of the seventeenth century they covered, optimistically, only half of the European population. It wasn't until the governments got interested in who was born and died that the percentage rose to perhaps seventy per cent. The first civil records were begun in France in 1792, and they are ninety-five to a hundred per cent complete. In the United States, most states did not begin to keep birth records until after 1900. The bread and butter of American genealogists are the probate and land records, which have been kept since the beginning of colonial history.

The names of people who lived before there were parish or civil records, before the age of modern record keeping, are in short supply. Great Britain, because it has a relatively stable history (no one, after all, has invaded the island since 1066) and a remarkable capacity for accommodating social change, has accumulated the greatest volume and diversity of records from the Middle Ages. It has peasant land transactions to the twelfth century; wills from 1316 on; family histories of London merchants in the aldermanic class back to 1300; rosters of yeomen in fifteenth-century Leicestershire. But most of its records before 1538 are of its aristocracy. Throughout the world, wherever names from before 1500 have survived, they are almost always of the tiny minority that belonged to the country's hereditary elite.

✣

Of the six to seven billion names of the dead which various societies are thought to have generated for various reasons, about a billion and a half have been collected and stored in a climate-controlled, nuclear-bomb-proof repository twenty-two miles south of Salt Lake City. The rest are still at large, scattered around the world in a multitude of forms. Some exist, as we have seen, only in the minds of elderly remembrancers. The names in Utah are contained on about a million and a quarter rolls of microfilm. Each roll has an average of twelve hundred exposures, each exposure reproduces an average of two pages of written record, and each year forty to fifty million more exposures are taken by a hundred and three cameras specially designed for filming genealogical records, which are operating in forty countries. One camera, for instance, is in Haridwar, India, filming the pilgrim registers described earlier. Its operator is a local under contract who can get the work done a lot more cheaply than an American could. From

time to time oral pedigrees from the island of Tonga, taped and
transcribed by a man named Tavita Mapa, are shipped to the
Granite Mountain Vault, as the repository is called.

The Vault was built by the Genealogical Society of Utah—
a name the Genealogical Department of the Church of Jesus
Christ of Latter-Day Saints uses because governments and other
churches are sometimes reluctant to deal with the Mormons. No
genealogical archive or primary testament of human passage is
remotely comparable. It is the closest there is, and the closest there
will be, to a "catalogue of catalogues" for the human race.

The reason for its existence has to do with the Mormons' religion, with their belief that the family is eternal and all-inclusive,
and that each church member must seek out his ancestors and
posthumously perform certain ceremonies for them so that they
can all meet again in the Celestial Kingdom. The multimillion-
dollar operation, which employs some of the most sophisticated
records-processing technology in existence, is really an extension
of the church's missionary program.

🌱

New York State during the first half of the nineteenth century was a "religiously fecund atmosphere," as the former Mormon Fawn M. Brodie has written in a fascinating biography of
Joseph Smith Junior, the prophet and founder of the Church of
Jesus Christ of Latter-Day Saints, called No Man Knows My History. Between 1814 and 1830 the Methodist Church split four
ways, and there was even greater schism among the Baptists, who
broke up into Reformed Baptists, Hard-Shell Baptists, Free-Will
Baptists, Footwashers, and other groups. In nearby Vermont, "half
a dozen hills away" from where Joseph Smith spent part of his
childhood, Isaac Bullard and his pilgrims practiced free love and
communism, regarded washing as a sin, and wore only bearskin
girdles. In New York State itself, Ann Lee, the mother of the
American Shakers, called herself the reincarnated Christ, whirled
dervishlike, spoke in "tongues," and was reputed to indulge in
promiscuous debauchery and to practice infanticide; Jemima Wil-
kinson proclaimed herself "the Christ" and the "Universal Friend"
and appointed as her chief aide the prophet Elijah; as a result of
William Miller's prediction that Jesus would visit earth and usher
in the millennium in March 1843, thousands auctioned off their

property and bought ascension robes; and although Miller lost face after 1845 when after two recalculations Christ had still failed to appear, his Adventists, Brodie writes, are "still an aggressive minority sect"; while John Humphrey Noyes, founder of the Oneida community described in Chapter Six, preached that the millennium had already begun. Faith healers and circuit-rider evangelists went from town to town, "preaching in great open-air camp meetings where silent, lonely frontiersmen gathered to sing and shout. The Revivalists knew their hell intimately—its geography, its climate, its vital statistics—and painted the sinner's fate so hideously that shuddering crowds surged forward to the bushel-box altars to be born again." Some were seized with "the jerks"; others, seized with "the barks," went crawling on all fours and vocalizing like dogs.

Many frontier families belonged to no church, and a crusade was mounted by ministers of various Protestant denominations to convert the unconverted. Starting in New England, the crusade swept down to Kentucky and in 1820 it reached the "burnt-over" district of western New York. Hundreds of people in the little settlements of Palmyra, Macedon, Manchester, Lyons, and Ontario, persuaded that the end was at hand, "confessed that the Lord was good" and became "hopeful subjects of divine grace" at revival meetings, according to an account in a Rochester newspaper.

But the Smith family of Palmyra did not join any church. Both parents were antinomian. Joseph Senior looked to his own dreams, which his wife called "visions," for guidance. Her father, according to Brodie, "in his old age fell into a kind of senile mysticism, with lights and voices haunting his sickbed." Her uncle, Jason Mack, became a "seeker" and set up in New Brunswick "a quasi-communistic society of thirty indigent families whose economic and spiritual welfare he sought to direct." Her boy, Joseph Junior, a pamphlet published by the Mormon Church recounts, wanted to join one of the newly formed congregations, but he didn't know which. Retiring to the woods, he had the first of a series of encounters with an angel named Moroni, who told him that there was no true church of Christ upon the earth, and that he should join none of them. In 1827 Moroni presented twenty-two-year-old Smith with two golden tablets containing, in what he termed "reformed Egyptian" hieroglyphs, the story of the descendants of the lost tribe of Lehigh, who fled Israel to avoid being conquered by the Babylonians and travelled by barge to South America, where they divided into two groups—the Nephites, a "fair and delightsome people," who were farmers and temple builders; and the Lamanites, "wild and ferocious, and a bloodthirsty people," who in 420 A.D., having gradually moved north, fought to the death in the valley of Cumora, near what became Palmyra. This great battle explained the burial mounds in the vicinity, which had fascinated Smith, who had spread the rumor that treasure was buried in them and had persuaded friends to accompany him on digging expeditions. The mounds are thought by archaeologists to have been left by certain Upper Mississippian Indians who, well before the arrival of white men, had a Festival of the Dead in which they exhumed the bones of recent ancestors and reburied them all together. The Lamanites won the battle, but their descendants, the Indians, were blighted with dark skin for turning away from the Lord. The theory that the Indians were remnants of the ten lost tribes was widely held in the United States and Europe; William Penn, Roger Williams, Cotton Mather and Jonathan Edwards had all espoused it, and the twentieth-century archaeologist Edward V. McMichael has written, "The idea of an extinct mysterious race of Mound Builders flourished in the nineteenth century, and included all manner of theorizing by early writers—on very little evidence—that the Mound Builders were the Welsh, the Ten Lost Tribes of Israel, or other strayed European types. However, all skeletal remains of mound-building Indians, while sometimes slightly variant from the historic groups, are essentially the same 'Old Mongoloid' racial type. That historic Indians knew little or nothing about the mounds is not surprising, since most had abandoned mound building for at least five hundred to a thousand years."

Smith translated the story on the tablets into English with the aid of some "spectacle-like instruments," also received from Moroni, and it became known as the Book of Mormon; Mormon was a Nephite prophet who had condensed the history of his people into the form on which it appeared on the tablets. Moroni, the last Nephite prophet, and a series of other heavenly messengers empowered Smith to restore the gospel of Christ, to reestablish the authority of the priesthood, which had been removed from the earth after the death of the twelve original apostles, and to found the true Church of Jesus Christ, which Smith did on April 6, 1830. Three years later, the phrase "of Latter-Day Saints" was added. "Thus Mormonism began as a restoration of primitive Christianity with a strong eschatological-millennial flavor," Ward J. Roylance writes in his guide to the state of Utah, and Brodie describes Mormonism as "a real religious creation, one intended to be to Christianity what Christianity had been to Judaism: that is, a reform and a consummation."

As his church was getting started, Smith began to wonder about all the people who had lived before him—how were they going to get the true gospel and be saved? Searching in the Bible for direction, he found in I Corinthians 15:29 a verse which seemed to imply that, although none of the denominations and sects active in western New York were doing anything for the dead, baptism for the dead had gone on in the early church, and in I Peter 3:18–20, he noted how Jesus, when he came back from the dead, told the apostles that he had been preaching the gospel to "spirits in prison." On February 16, 1832, in Hiram, Ohio, the structure of the hereafter was revealed to Smith in a "glorious vision." It consisted of three levels: the terrestrial, the telestial, and the celestial (a coincidence which, later in the century, would facilitate the conversion of the Catawba Indians in the Carolinas, whose heaven also happened to be three-tiered). The highest level is the Celestial Kingdom. On April 3, 1836, in Kirtland, Illinois, Smith reported that the prophet Elijah had visited him, fulfilling a prediction of the Old Testament prophet Malachi that, according to the Mormon translation, Elijah would come to "turn the hearts of the fathers to their sons, and the children to the fathers, lest the whole earth be smitten with a curse." He began to expound to his followers what he called the "new and strange" doctrine of Baptism for the Dead, which Elijah had given him: the dead could enter the Celestial Kingdom only if certain sacraments, or "proxy ordinances," were performed in the temple on their behalf; and the living could not be saved without their departed kin. Smith was extending the idea of the family so that it included not only all of one's living relations but all of one's ancestors. "It is doubtful whether Joseph sensed the truly staggering implications of his endowment system," Brodie writes. "Upon his church now rested the burden of freeing the billions of spirits who had never heard the law of the Lord."

Having brought in everybody from the past, he then considered how Abraham and Isaac and Jacob and the other early patriarchs had been blessed with "seed as numerous as the sand upon the seashore," and how necessary it was to build up the living church membership as quickly as possible because it was already under heavy persecution; and these considerations led him, after a revelation from the Lord on July 12, 1843, at his new headquarters in Nauvoo, Illinois, to advocate "the plurality of wives" and to tell his followers that it was their religious obligation to procreate. A man's posterity, he said, would constitute his kingdom and his glory in eternity, and the more children he had and the more of his dead he saved, the larger his kingdom would be. Not only that, but if the man had been righteous, he would go on reproducing after death; the Lord would empower him to have "spiritual children." And the Lord would give him and his family their own star, where they could all live together blissfully forever.

On April 7, 1844, at the funeral of his friend King Follett, Smith said that "the greatest responsibility in the world God has laid upon us is to seek after our dead." Two months later, Smith's "earthly dispensation," as Mormons say, came to an end when an angry mob broke into the county jail in Carthage, Illinois, and killed both Smith and his brother Hyrum. They were being held on charges of destroying the press of the *Nauvoo Expositor,* which had printed names of women Smith had allegedly seduced with the promise of making them his "spirit wives."

By then his followers had already converted to polygamy and begun to trace members of their families and to do "temple work" for them, so that they could all be united in the Celestial Kingdom. This work is still a central part of the religion, and each Mormon has spent hours, months, or years, depending on the depth of his commitment, tracking down his ancestors and taking their names to the temple. Gradually the work has expanded; since 1939, when microfilming of American records began, the ordinances have been performed for *all* the dead, not just traceable relatives of living church members. In 1982, 7.4 million names of the dead were extracted from microfilms by volunteers at five hundred and eight "stakes," as the Mormons' parishes are called, around the world, and there were about 1.2 million "patron submissions," the result of genealogical research that church members had done on their own. These names were fed into an IBM

30-81, one of the most powerful computers on the market, to make sure that work had not already been done for them. Six to eight per cent of the extracted names, and ten per cent of the patron submissions, "duped out." The rest were "cleared" for temple work.

There are about five million Mormons, and those who are nineteen or older—old enough to be elders (if they are men) and to perform the proxy ordinances—are encouraged to go to one of the forty-one temples in the world at least once a month. The temple is where the needs of the dead are taken care of, and where private covenants with the Lord are made and renewed; the regular Sunday worship takes place in the meetinghouse in each stake. Only Mormons in good standing, who have obtained a "temple recommend" from their bishop (the equivalent of a parish priest), can enter the temple, and nobody is supposed to talk about what goes on inside. Near the door, if they have not brought along the name of an ancestor, they receive the name of somebody of their own sex, who has been cleared by the computer—Josefina María Ximenes, let us say, whose name was recently extracted from a parish register filmed in Coixtlahuaca, Mexico, which had recorded her marriage on August 25, 1748, to a man named Juan García. Then they change from their street clothes to their "temple garment," which Brodie describes as "an unlovely and utilitarian suit of long underwear," with holes at the nipples, Masonic squares and the Masonic compass cut into the garment's breech, and a slash across the abdomen "symbolic of the disemboweling that would be the fate of anyone who revealed the sacred secrets." (The most pious wear this garment continuously, under their street clothes.) Proceeding into the sanctum, whose beauty is said to be breathtaking, they choose one of the three ordinances for Josefina.

The first is Baptism. Nobody, living or dead, can enter the Celestial Kingdom unless he has been "born of the water and of the spirit." A living person can be baptized wherever there is water deep enough for complete immersion—in a river, even in a swimming pool—but baptism for the dead can happen only in the temple. Children who died before the age of eight do not have to be baptized; they go automatically to the Celestial Kingdom. Baptism is for the remission of sins, and children are not considered to have reached "the age of accountability," to know right from wrong, until their eighth birthday. (The Mormons, in other words, do not believe in original sin.) The second ordinance, called "the Endowment," is a series of "oaths and covenants" that one makes with God on behalf of the dead person one is sponsoring, that one will live "at a certain level of performance." Brodie describes the Endowment as "camouflaged fertility worship." The rite includes purificatory washing and anointing of the entire body, including the "vitals," by a member of the same sex. Smith, who became a Mason of the Sublime Degree in 1842, was fascinated by Masonic ritual—its costuming, its grips, its passwords, its keys, its oaths, its "veiled phallicism," according to Brodie. The Endowment used to run about two and a half hours, a regular temple-goer told me, but "a very pleasurable movie about the Creation, with professional actors," is now shown at most temples, and has cut the ceremony to about an hour and a half.

The last and most important ordinance is the "Sealing," in which members of families are bound together "for time and all eternity"—woman to husband, child to parent, generation to generation. The temple-goer may seal his own ancestors or dead provided by the computer; he is also free to seal people whose names he has found in genealogical records, as long as he has checked them first with the computer. The work on one's family is done in bits and pieces, two generations at a time, over one's lifetime. When there are breaks in the chain, one does research. Living couples may also be sealed in the temple. Such "celestial" marriages, which are also "for time and all eternity," are very hard to undo; the parties must petition the president of the church himself, Spencer Wooley Kimball, and satisfy him that they were wrong for each other and should never have been sealed in the first place. Sometimes a couple may not be able to get along, but neither party wants to jeopardize the status of his immortality, so they just separate.

Partly because what goes on in the temple is so secret, a good deal of controversy surrounds the proxy ordinances, as it surrounded the church's early practice of plural marriage. Some, angered to learn that the Mormons had been meddling with their ancestors, have accused the church of "spiritual kidnapping"; but the church is careful to explain that the dead have "free agency" to accept or reject the ordinances, just as the living have the right to choose whether to join the church or not. The church is also

scrupulous about observing the "rights of privacy" of next of kin.
No birth records are sent out for extraction until they are ninety-
five years old, which more than complies with every country's
statute of limitations. Anybody submitting a name from records
less than ninety-five years old must get permission from the person's next of kin, and nobody who has died less than a year before
will be considered, for two reasons: to give the next of kin, who
may still be in mourning, a chance to "settle into the idea of
whether they want to do this," as a spokesman for the society recently explained to me, and to give the dead themselves a chance
to be exposed to the gospel in the spirit world; the Mormons believe that if you were not susceptible to the gospel in life, you
will not be, initially, in the hereafter. "We're not striving to make
people mad or unhappy, but we are anxious to do all the good for
them we can," Henry E. Christiansen, long-time "trouble shooter"
for the society, recently explained to me. "Once in a while a few
people get indignant. There are two areas of objections: from people who have different religious opinions, and from people who
are sensitive about the vital statistics of their immediate family being made known." In a few cases, people who had been born out
of wedlock have been removed, at the request of a descendant,
from the International Genealogical Index of names cleared by
the computer, which is made public—although legally, as Val
Greenwood, the society's counsel, explained, "the dead have no
rights. In a court of law the next of kin would be hard pressed to
make a case." "It used to be that we wouldn't do work for sui-
cides or murderers," another member of the society explained, "but
then we thought, what about guys who went to war and shed
innocent blood? They had to obey the law of the land." (The
Mormons believe very strongly in obeying the law of the land.)
"So now we just do all we can; we provide the vicarious ordinances for everybody, and leave it to the Lord to decide if there
will be forgiveness."

Over the years the Genealogical Society, which was officially
incorporated in 1895, has grown into a full-blown institution with
a salaried staff of about five hundred and about four hundred volunteers. Productivity is closely monitored; industry is an important Mormon virtue. The church's symbol is the honeybee (or the
deseret, as honeybees are called in "reformed Egyptian"). A person who starts in at the society as a clerk-typist can work into a

supervisory or other management position; or stay at the same job and work through various grades of seniority and salary level; or be fired. The working environment at the society's headquarters in Salt Lake City is unusually healthy: nobody smokes and there are no coffee wagons, although candy is dispensed by machines on each floor. Occasionally one catches a pretty young secretary in a Little-House-on-the-Prairie dress stifling a yawn at her desk. The organization is always evolving new ways to keep up with the material. Chairs shuffle; new sections and divisions are created; old ones are merged or phased out. The society is not immune to the intrigues and power plays that seem to go on in every human institution, and its bureaucracy sometimes gets carried away with itself, but I was unable, in the three weeks I recently spent as its guest, to find any employee for whom the processing of dead people's names was just a job. It seemed, on the contrary, a joyous communal effort.

At first I thought the whole idea of going to such lengths to improve conditions for the dead was a little naïve, and maybe even a little crazy. Other aspects of the religion are certainly hard to reconcile with what most people have been taught. But then I thought of all the parallels. Many societies believe that one cannot proceed until one's ancestors have been taken care of (see the sampling of other beliefs about the dead given in Chapter Two), and no society (even where the communist dogma of oblivion has been imposed) has been willing to accept that after death there is nothing.

I did find philosophical differences among the employees, though. One man, who had become an expert in the culture whose genealogical records he was responsible for acquiring, condemned the "narrow, expedient-type approach" of some of his colleagues, who were interested only in submitting "as many names as possible, because they think the more names they submit, the more it will guarantee their salvation. I think we owe the dead more than that," he said, with visible emotion.

Mormonism has its critics, including feminists, who object to the traditional domestic and procreative role expected of its women members. The critic Edmund Wilson, who studied the development of Christian thinking as revealed by the discovery of the Dead Sea Scrolls, felt that the religion was a fraud, something Joseph Smith made up as he went along, rather than the natural accretion by a society of moral values and understanding. But whatever the genesis of their beliefs, the Mormons have not only survived, unlike most of the sects that appeared at that time in American history; they have also gone on to establish a virtual theocracy in Utah and are one of the nation's healthiest, most fertile, most cohesive, and most prosperous enclaves.

❦

One cloudless August morning not long ago, having driven across the desert in a rented car from Reno, Nevada, to Salt Lake City the day before, I presented myself at the office of Thomas E. Daniels, the Genealogical Society's public-relations manager. The society takes up one of the wings and the bottom five stories of the Church of Jesus Christ of Latter-Day Saints Office Building, which is right off Temple Square and is the tallest building in Utah. A clean-cut, young-looking man of fifty-one, Daniels was already three times a grandfather, with three more grandchildren on the way, and he projected a fatherly gentleness not often found in public relations. "This is where the real action is," he explained. "The Vault is just the storage and developing arm of our Micrographics Division." There used to be tours of the Vault, he explained to me, but the society became worried about vandalism and breath damage to the microfilm. Since 1967 the Vault, like the cave at Lascaux, France, has been closed to the public.

One of the first things Daniels did was arrange a tour for me, to put the society into context. My guide was a tall, elderly man named C. Laird Snellgrove, who had been for fifty-three years in a family ice-cream business started by his father during the Depression, and who had recently, he told me, stepped down as president to "give my sons their turn at the tiller." The quality of Snellgrove's ice cream is generally conceded to be unsurpassed in Utah.

As we took in the view from the twenty-sixth floor of the Church Office Building, Snellgrove told me that the peopling of Utah had begun just below, in the summer of 1847, when a hundred and forty-four persecuted "saints," who had crossed the Mississippi a year and a half earlier in search of a place where they could practice their religion in peace, had dammed what is now called City Creek to irrigate the crops, planted hastily in torched sagebrush, which had got them through the first winter. The Lion

House and the Beehive House—the two adjoining gabled residences where Brigham Young lived with nineteen of his twenty-seven wives and governed the Kingdom of Deseret, which later became the Territory and finally the State of Utah—were a hundred yards from the tower. In the next block, walled in a ten-acre square, were the church's most sacred monuments: the Tabernacle, which is shaped like a halved egg, flipped over, and is famous for its choir; and the Temple, which is made of thick blocks of gray granite and looks indestructible. Brigham Young wanted it built strong enough to withstand the great conflagration before the millennium, Snellgrove explained. The lines of the Temple—six principal spires, surrounded by three tiers of lesser spires, with a gilded Angel Moroni standing on the tallest spire and blowing a long trumpet to proclaim the restoration of the gospel—were "given" to Young in a vision. The vision took forty years—until 1893—to execute.

Later in the morning, Snellgrove took me into Temple Square. Outside the South Gate, a pretty young woman who had lost her faith thrust some literature on me. Snellgrove looked pained but said nothing. I put the flier in my pocket and read it later; it attacked the "barbarian" rituals in the Temple. A sign inside the gate said, "Literature received outside gates is not part of Temple Square." Snellgrove showed me a monument to the "handcart companies," made up of people proselytized in Europe the century before—tradesmen, mostly, who had immigrated with their families and set out from Iowa on foot. Young had had the idea that newcomers should walk to Zion as a demonstration of their faith. Many of them died en route, and lie buried in the Great Plains. It has been suggested that the robustness of present-day Mormons may be partly due to this winnowing process, much as the robustness of American blacks has been attributed to their descent from the heartiest of the enslaved West Africans, who survived the ocean crossing and later hardships.

At 12:30 Snellgrove and I went to the daily organ recital in the Tabernacle. We sat in the VIP gallery with an elderly man surrounded by three nervous men in their thirties; they turned out to be William Casey, director of the Central Intelligence Agency, and his Secret Service escort.

In the days that followed, Daniels or people he sent me to see explained how raw genealogical material that comes in from all over the world is processed. I was allowed to learn about every aspect of the operation except its budget, which I was only told is "in the millions" and is raised by the tithing—each Mormon's contribution to the church of ten per cent of his earnings. Statements by the society's director, George H. Fudge, a dour man whose faint, residual English accent (he emigrated from Manchester when he was a young man) contrasted with the Utahn twang of most of his associates, that each roll of microfilm costs between fifty and a hundred dollars to acquire, and by Daniels that each roll has an average of twelve hundred exposures, and that about fifty million exposures are taken a year, would suggest that somewhere between two and four million dollars are spent annually just to get the material; and acquisition is only the first step.

The society's Field Services Division, which is in charge of acquisition, has divided the world into five areas: the United States and Canada; Latin America; Western Europe; Central and Eastern Europe; and Asia and the Pacific. Each area has a "records specialist," who is responsible for negotiating for permission to film records that qualify. Priority is given to countries that have historically produced the most Mormons—England, Germany, and Scandinavia—and to records in imminent danger of destruction, like the colonial records of Ceylon (present-day Sri Lanka), whose acquisition, the records specialist Monte McLaws told me, amounted to "a race against time and worms. Some of the Dutch *tambos*, or registers of the school enrollment and the landowners in Ceylon, go back to the 1600s. When the British took over in 1861, they cranked up civil registration—births, marriages, deaths —right away. The names were simultaneously entered in Sinhalese, Tamil, and English, but the Sri Lankans can't afford to protect the registers, and they are just falling apart. Some of the pages crumbled to dust as we turned them, and on others the ink had eaten through, so we were filming holes—what would have shown through if we had held the pages to light."

When negotiating with a government, a church, or a library for permission to film its material, the records specialist offers a number of incentives: technology—the first microfilm laboratories in Poland, for instance, were built in 1967 by the society; hard cash; a free print of everything that is filmed; and a guarantee that the original films will be preserved in the Granite Mountain Vault as permanently as is humanly possible. The specialist plays down his theological motives and usually identifies himself as an employee of the Genealogical Society of Utah rather than of the Mormon Church's Genealogical Department; if asked why he wants the records, "I explain that because of spiritual commitments to our family and our progenitors, we try to identify them and to perform certain sacraments on their behalf, and leave it at that," the records specialist for Central and Eastern Europe, Dennis Neuenschwander, told me.

Most archivists are more than willing to collaborate. In Neuenschwander's sector, most of the material in Yugoslavia, Greece, and most of Scandinavia had been filmed; Hungary had been finished in the nineteen-fifties. The Soviet Union was still "a hard nut to crack," he said. "It is safe to assume that everything is in the state archives: all the religious material—Armenian, Orthodox, Moslem, Lutheran, Jewish, Baptist, Old Believer—and whatever nobility records have survived. From the time of Catherine the Great, someone called a marshal of nobility kept track of the noble births, deaths, and marriages in each district, but many of these records were destroyed during the Revolution. We still don't know what there is, or whether it is being kept as the central, state, or city level, because there are very few lists or indexes; the archivists simply don't publish. As for being able to get in to film, that is still under discussion. The archivists are friendly but noncommittal."

The prospects for filming in the People's Republic of China were better. In 1980 a Chinese delegation had come to the society's World Conference on Records, obviously with the aim of sniffing out the operation, and its report had been favorable. The society had just received permission to film the First Historical Archives in Peking, which contain many of the imperial records. "The administration of the imperial household was like a city within a city, and its records are voluminous," John Orton, who had just returned from China, told me. Orton had been able to see some of the rest of the country, and "there appeared to be more records than we have given the Chinese credit for. During the Cultural Revolution of 1966, when many records were burned, people were able to fortify their archives and to stave off the Red Guards. Many of the genealogies of the richer clans were saved because multiple wood-block prints of them were made. I even saw a mud-block print."

The constitution of India prohibits publicizing cause of death, so the society has been able to film only part of the country's civil records—the marriage entries. In Switzerland, where the society had been filming off and on since 1950, the Lutheran parish registers of the provinces of Graubünden, Neuchâtel, Ticino, and St. Gallen, which went back to the late seventeenth century, had been acquired, but the Lutheran Church had recently brought pressure on the National Archives not to release the rest of them to the society. (The records of the meticulous, traditionally neutral Swiss, who haven't had a war on their own soil since the ninth century, are, as one would expect, excellent.) The Dutch Reformed Church of the Afrikaners in South Africa had been no more cooperative; it wouldn't even allow a private Mormon into its archives. The Vatican had turned the society down. So had Haiti. Uruguay, after much importuning, had finally let it in. Cuba was being approached through a third party—the Sandinistas. Attempts to get to the Coptic Church records in Cairo, and to the Catholic records for Armenia and Anatolia, which were in Istanbul, had so far been fruitless. The society had been proceeding circumspectly in Western Europe, especially in France, because the Council of Europe had recently become sensitive about the confidentiality of old parish registers and about such records being used for purposes other than those for which they had originally been kept. During the nineteen-thirties the Nazis began to collect civil, parish, and synagogue records in Germany for the purpose of "race research"—to find out who was of "the pure blood" and who was not. After they had begun to exterminate Jews, the same records were used to identify them, particularly matrilineal Jews who might otherwise have escaped their notice. Consanguinity with anybody who had belonged to the faith was enough to make one Jewish, just as anybody in the United States with any visible or traceable African ancestry is considered "black."

As country after country fell to the Nazis, its genealogical records were microfilmed and sent to Germany, and in light of this history the Council of Europe's wariness about "trans-border data flow" is understandable. But Vance Standifird, the director of field services, told me that the French Commission on Data Privacy had just come and inspected the operation, and "determined that what we are doing is proper and worthwhile."

In England there is a different problem, one of decentraliza-
tion. Most of the parish registers are still *in situ,* so the records
specialists have to go from church to church and negotiate with
each one individually. Although the society has been filming in
England since the end of the Second World War, the work is
only about a third done. The society has been lobbying vigorously
for a bill to be brought before Parliament which would nationalize
the registers and have them all brought to one place. This would
save the society a lot of time and money.

The most perishable and anthropologically important records
are, of course, the ones that have never been written down—the
genealogical chants of the Bedouins, of *griots,* of Indonesian and
South Pacific islanders whose oral traditions are still alive. (Even
on Tory Island, a small island off the northern coast of Ireland,
Robin Fox has found older men "who styled themselves quite consciously *isloinnteori*—genealogists"—and who could recite seven
generations of bilateral descent for every native on the island,
which provided "the framework for the articulation of land ownership and inheritance.") Many of these traditions are dying out;
the younger generation has been modernized and has found new
forms of evening entertainment more exciting to them than reciting pedigrees, and the adoption of the European system of land
tenure on such islands as New Zealand and those of Western
Samoa has obviated the need for traditional genealogical title de-
fenses.

Sadly, the society's oral genealogy program, which started in
1968 and spread into thirty-eight countries, with five hundred
hours of tape and twelve hundred separate pedigrees, was on bor-
rowed time. "The time it took to win the people's trust and to get
them to start reciting—a lot of the chants are sacred—wasn't justified by the number of names we were acquiring," Fudge explained. "Sometimes we had trouble finding people who knew the
dialect. It's one thing to have somebody mumbling into a tape recorder, and another thing to try to transcribe it. And frequently,
as with the *griots,* there was a problem with how accurate the information was in the first place."

One man who was familiar with the program told me that it
was being dropped because of internal politics, that "management
is too English-parish-register-oriented," that there had been pressure from what he called the "Maoists" in the society—the more

dogmatic, ideologically pure Mormons, who were interested only in saving as many souls, living or dead, as possible. The decision to ax the oral genealogy program means that many of the ancestors of the world's tribal people—whatever the less than one hundred thousand natives of the Amazon Valley can remember of their ancestry, for instance—will not be recorded. Their dead will be "lost souls," as far as the Mormons are concerned.

After permission to film material has been obtained, "listers" go in and itemize each record. The listers are followed by the cameras (in remote parts of the world the listing and filming functions can overlap). The camera was specially developed by technicians at the society. Unlike industrial microfilm cameras, it is portable. The whole apparatus—including strobe lights and a collapsible mount with a tray for displaying the material—fits in two small suitcases. It is foot-operated and it takes pictures as fast as the operator can line up the next exposure. The film—sixteen millimeter, silver-based—is delivered through regular mail and by the United Parcel Service to the Granite Mountain Vault, and there it is developed. Vesicular copies, which are cheaper to make, are sent to the donors of the material, and to the stakes for extraction. Originally the extracting of names for temple work from the microfilmed records, which began in 1960, was done in-house, but in 1977 the work was farmed out to volunteers in the various stakes, who had each been trained to decipher the antique scripts of a particular language. This greatly expanded and streamlined the extraction process.

One afternoon Daniels took me to a darkened room on the third floor of the tower, where a facet of the operation known as Extraction Audit went on. Half of the room was piled high with parcels that had come in from the stakes. The parcels contained hundred-foot rolls of microfilm, each in a round steel can the size of a small tin of pipe tobacco, and yellow "extraction" cards the size of computer punch cards, on which the names of the dead on the films had been entered. In the other half of the room thirteen women were sitting at free-standing microfilm readers, each hunched over her own triangular cocoon of light, checking extraction cards against microfilm. Each name had already passed through three extractors at the stakes; now the quality of *their* work was being checked. Because it was impracticable to review each entry, the women spot-checked a hundred and twenty-eight names randomly selected by computer from every batch of two hundred and eighty-one to five thousand names.

The room was completely silent. Two of the women were pregnant. One woman was going over a christening performed in Córdoba, Argentina, in 1865; another had on her screen a Catholic parish register from Westphalia, Germany, open to the year 1691. Another was auditing the extraction of records of a man who had been married in Rougement, Switzerland, in 1778. There were people in the room who could read Arabic, Chinese, Japanese, Russian, Greek, and Mexican Indian dialects. A woman named Lynette Stroud, who was expert in English, Scandinavian, German, French, and American paleography, showed me a chart of all the scripts, or "hands," she had to know to read English parish registers before 1754: bastard hand, secretary hand, printed secretary hand, engrossing secretary hand, sloped secretary hand, Chancery hand, King's hand, remembrancer's hand, pipe office hand, legal hand—all of which were illegible to me. "After 1754," she said, "it gets normal."

Occasionally mistakes slip through, because, say, an extractor in Barry, Missouri, is not personally familiar with the local surnames in Hertfordshire, England, or because the entry is only half-legible, so the surname is misconstrued. This happened to the Bickleys of Shoreditch, Hertfordshire, who went into the computer as Buckley. Material that fails the audit is sent back for reextraction.

A few blocks from the Church Office Building, under heavy security, the church's IBM 30-81 stores and processes in a system code-named GIANT, for Genealogical Information and Names Tabulation, the names of about sixty-nine million of the dead. The purpose of GIANT, besides collating the names alphabetically and geographically, is to catch duplicates. The input for GIANT is entered by employees and volunteers in the society's Data Entry Section, who man 4-Phase Model 470 minicomputers, and the tapes from them are taken by messenger to the main frame. There are also nine data entry centers around the country on which preaudited names, generated by extraction or patron submission, are entered on DATAMARK 16/220 microcomputers and sent to GIANT on tapes through the mails or by United Parcel Service. "We went to the computer in 1969," Reynolds Cahoon, the director of Projects and Forward Planning, explained to me one afternoon. "Before that the work was done manually. Church members submitted 'family group sheets' containing three generations of their ancestors or, less often, of other people whose pedigrees they had traced—a couple, their parents, and their children. By 1970, when we were fully computerized and the file was declared static, we had eight million family group sheets, with about thirty million names." The names, typed on file cards and alphabetized by surname, are kept in a room on the fifth floor of the tower which resembles the card catalogue of a large library and is called the Temple Index Bureau. Eventually, Cahoon said, everybody in the T.I.B. would be transferred to "a son of GIANT."

Once they have been accepted by GIANT, the names are run through hundreds of "program modules"—"proprietary software" designed by the society's own resident "wizards." But not all the names are accepted. To begin with, the name is entered with a request that it is in need of "uniquely qualifying information." Usually the name, its associated event (most frequently birth, christening, marriage, or death), the event date, and the event place are enough to identify the person uniquely, but different names, dates, and places have different "uniqueness factors." "Reynolds Cahoon is a uniquely identifying name," Cahoon explained. "John Smith is not. Each name is assigned a statistical uniqueness factor that has been determined by studying demographic records and learning the frequency of its occurrence. Obviously, if you know the names of the person's parents or children, too, that is even more uniquely identifying. [A new concept, I thought: shades of uniqueness.] The uniqueness factor of a place depends on its size and population. Dates become increasingly unique the more complete they are, with the year, month, and day being most specific. The earlier the date, the less unique it is, because the probability increases that somebody else has already found that they were descended from the same person and has submitted his records." ("Uniqueness" decreases with time because, as we saw earlier, the probability of being related to any given individual increases, and because the number of records of available people to use for genealogical research decreases.) "The uniqueness factor of the year 1500, for instance, is .003. The uniqueness factor of 1980 is 2.68."

Once the name is entered (transliterated, if necessary, into Roman letters; sometimes patron submissions arrive in Arabic,

Greek, Cyrillic, and other alphabets that GIANT doesn't recognize), the computer standardizes its spelling—Cahoon, for instance, would be grouped with Calhoun—and both the standardized and the actual spellings are compared with the three million seven hundred thousand surnames and the one million one hundred thousand given names in the catalogue of the names subsystem. One afternoon a large, jovial woman named Esther Smith, who is one of the senior name evaluators, pulled a few microfiche cards from the catalogue to show what she was up against. Microfiche is a type of microfilm which has multiple microimages in a grid pattern. The microimages on these cards were all versions of the name Ann. There were over two hundred spellings, from names that had come in or had been found in publications. "Sometimes you get a little aspiration, and the name is spelled Hannah," she explained. "I've even had Annah. Most of these are phonic spellings. For Americans, you don't have to go back too far before people couldn't read or write. It wasn't that they weren't intelligent, but that their educational opportunities were limited." In the Netherlands, and among Dutch immigrants who refused to anglicize their given name to John, Ann is a man's name. Ambrose had ninety spellings, and eighty-six variants for Alphonso had been found in the United States alone. "This is the melting pot," Ms. Smith explained. "The most common first names worldwide are John and Mary. There's a derivative of them in just about every country."

A common problem for Americans of non-English descent who are trying to "cross the water" is the surname change which often took place in the generation that immigrated. GIANT is programmed to recognize some of the most common ones, like Smith for Schmidt, but sometimes the new American surname is so wildly different from the original that unless one happens to know what one's people were called in the old country, or is lucky enough to find the old name on one of the published passenger lists—a major source for people who are trying to cross the water—the genealogical trail ends at Ellis Island or at whatever other port of entry one's ancestors came to. I told Ms. Smith about a classic case—the sweet old émigré who was my grandmother's photographer (my grandmother was a portrait painter). Shortly after the Russian Revolution he landed at Ellis Island, a penniless refugee, and produced his immigration papers, which identified him as Nicholas Kotzubinsky. The admitting officers suggested he change his name to something simpler and more American-sounding, and so, straining to remember his schoolboy English, he wrote down Kobins. The official read the K as an R, and for the rest of his life Kotzubinsky was known as Nicholas Robins. Ms. Smith reciprocated with the story of an Armenian named Harrigian who came through Ellis Island in 1910 and was made Harrigan. The children of his first marriage were officially registered as Harrigian, but those of his second were Harrigan; by then he was tired of explaining that he wasn't Irish. There was a terrible row between the half-siblings when he died. The first set of children buried him in Salt Lake City with a headstone identifying him as Harrigian, the second hired a stonecutter to remove the second *i*.

These stories led to the subject of people who go around using names that are not their real ones, either because they are on the lam or because they don't know their real names. I told Ms. Smith about a rather spectacular case that resulted from concealed paternity and involved a man in Washington, D.C., who was of Mexican and black-American extraction. Until the age of twenty-one he had gone by the name of Roger Irving, but when he came of age his mother sat him down and told him that his real name was Quaco Clautterbuck.

The problems that arise with event places are handled by a team of geographers in the Evaluation Section, also on the third floor. Birth and christening records are most useful as locators because by the time he got married or died the person may have moved to another place altogether. "Place" is broken down into town, county, and country, unless the country is the United States or Great Britain; so many of the names extracted or submitted by patrons are from these countries that each American state and each British county is treated as a country in itself. The computer compares the entered place with the standard spellings in its locality catalogue, to see if it is dealing with a new place or with one it is already familiar with. In the latter case, both the actual and the standard spellings are entered. Once the town has been identified and located, it is given a code, which consists of its actual geographical coordinates. This locates the event place much more effectively than a town-county-country label alone would, because place names are notoriously misleading.

One afternoon I called on Brent Barlow, the senior geographer, to learn about some of the problems that cross his desk. He began by fishing from his wastebasket a scrap of paper on which somebody had written the word Nestrid. "It's really Naestved, a town in Denmark," he said. "Just that was enough to be a problem. Some Irish place names are horrible. Their Gaelic spelling is foreign even to English ears. Then there are the many places with the same name. Think of all the Santa Claras, Santa Cruzes, and Santa Rosas in Latin America, or take Washington, Pennsylvania: are you talking about Washington County, or one of the townships in the county? Sometimes the town can't be located, because it's a corrupt phonic spelling, or it no longer exists, like Sutter Settlement, in the Territory of Nevada, which disappeared when its silver mines gave out; or the town of Kensico, New York, which is now under water, behind the Kensico Dam.

"Amalgamation is another problem. In Tokogawa Japan, before 1867, for instance, there were over seventy thousand villages. Now there are only twenty-five hundred. The others have all been absorbed by megalopolises like Tokyo, Kyoto, and Nogawa. In the Communist countries, a lot of places have been given new names—like the city Dnieperpetrovsk, in the Ukraine, which used to be called Ekaterinoslav, or the province of Simbirsk, on the Volga: now it's called Ulyanovsk, because Lenin, whose surname was Ulyanov, was born there. When we can't find a place for the individual, we leave the town and the coordinate blank and process him on a 'fourth level'—just by his county, state, or country.

"Many of our headaches are from border changes. The fact that New York City was once known as New Amsterdam doesn't make any difference because they both have the same coordinates and they are both in the same jurisdiction. It's when the jurisdiction changes that the trouble starts. Like Poszn, a county in Poland, was Posen, a province in Prussia, when it belonged to the German Empire. You have to be aware of the problem places."

Once the name, event place, and event date have been evaluated, the dead person is given an overall uniqueness factor, and if this is below a certain threshold, the entry is rejected. If it is high enough, the person is qualified to be processed. The next thing to discover is whether temple work has already been performed for the person, or whether he has already been "cleared" for it. His entry is matched against all the people who are already listed in

the Genealogical Mass Entry File, as GIANT's data bank is
called, and his event gets a "hundred-and-ten-year edit," to make
sure that he is really dead. If the individual is from one of the
"high submission" areas—England or America—a request is generated to check the Temple Index Bureau. If a duplicate is found
in either place, he "dupes out." If he "clears," he joins the Genealogical Mass File, and his name is included in a packet that is sent
to one of the temples. Every two or three years the International
Genealogical Index, the public part of the Genealogical Mass File,
is updated with the names of the newly cleared dead. The index
lists all the people in the file except those whose next of kin have
filed a rights-of-privacy petition to have the person's name remain
confidential, and those from records about which there are restric-
tions—those the society was allowed to film, for instance, but not
to circulate. Entries after the person's name monitor the progress
of his soul: when he was baptized, endowed, or sealed, and where.

That refined computer technology had been put in the service of down-home millennialism from the century before seemed
unique in the annals of human versatility, but Daniels had no
trouble explaining it. "People don't understand why they invent
things," he said. "All things that are conceived are conceived in
the preexistence." (Another original Mormon doctrine: the mortal
body is a "probationary state" between the "preexistence"—in
which we existed for eons as God's "spiritual children," but were
unable to feel pain or joy—and eternity.) "Maybe this is paro-
chial, but I see modern technology as coming on primarily for the
Kingdom of God and secondarily for secular purposes."

One afternoon Dennis Neuenschwander spoke excitedly
about the possibility of replacing microfilm with videotape: the
camera was lighter and smaller, and no strobe light was necessary,
so the field apparatus would be much more portable. On videotape the records would take even less space, and they could be
transmitted to the branch libraries as electric microwaves instead
of having to be copied and sent through the mail.

Nobody was more impatiently forward-looking than Reynolds
Cahoon. "This system is over ten years old," he complained of
GIANT. "It's dying and it needs to be replaced. It was written
before high-level languages and data-base management systems
came on. They have evolved greatly and our whole theory of
names processing is going to change. People aren't like airplane

parts. The matches aren't perfect. They don't always have the same name all their lives"—vide Roger Irving/Quaco Clautterbuck. "I think we should move toward making humans more efficient in doing the job. At the moment the system is 'batch-process'—a thousand names are entered at a time. I think we should make it 'interactive,' with different people entering one name at a time."

But that would slow down the redemptive work, and the society is already worried that it is falling hopelessly behind. Each year about fifty-five million people around the world die, but only three to four million of the dead have proxy ordinances performed for them in Mormon temples. Each year many more names are filmed than are extracted, slightly more are extracted than are cleared (7.4 million to seven million in 1983), and many more are cleared than are saved. This "overage" assures that even if the society were given access tomorrow to all the available genealogical records in the world, it would be busy for years. A few years ago, dedicating a new temple in Washington, D.C., President Kimball spoke about the pressing need to "catch up": "The day is coming not too far ahead of us when all temples on the earth will be going day and night. There will be shifts and people will be coming in the morning hours and in the night hours and in the day hours, and we must reach the time when we will have no vacations, that is, no temple vacations. . . . [But there will be a corps of workers working night and day almost to exhaustion] because of [the importance of the work and] the great number of people who lie asleep in eternity and who are craving, needing, the blessings we can bring them."

Most of the names in the International Genealogical Index are those of commoners who lived between 1500 and 1875. If a person who is "medieval" (pre–1500) or "royalty" (a category that includes the various hereditary nobilities) is submitted, the case is referred for special handling to the Royalty Identification Unit. Most of the royal and the more prominent noble pedigrees are well-travelled avenues of descent, and the rates of duplication—and of fabrication—among people endeavoring to connect to them are particularly high. Realizing this problem, the society created the Royal Identification Unit in 1972, and put Robert C. Gunderson, who has been tracing royal pedigrees since he was a teenager, in charge. In 1982 Gunderson and his two assistants, Miss

Rachel Kirk and Mrs. Tina Plaisir, personally cleared fourteen thousand names for temple work and rejected many others as duplicates or as fraudulent. Gunderson is probably one of the world's most productive genealogists, although his work is not widely known; he seldom publishes—though when he does his papers, such as "Tying Your Pedigree into Royal, Noble, or Medieval Families," which introduced the concept of "pedigree collapse," are memorable—and he confesses to being a poor correspondent. "I'd rather spend my time on the charts," he told me.

"I probably would not be in the least bit interested in genealogy if it wasn't for my religious beliefs," he said. "We Mormons believe that to be resurrected and to inherit a degree of glory, you have to do *nothing*. You *will* receive immortality, and we know that it will be a marvellous inheritance because the Bible says that a day with the Lord is as a thousand years with man. Even on the bottom rung—the telestial—you will be an angel." ("Even 'liars, sorcerers, adulterers, and whoremongers' would inherit telestial glory," Brodie writes, "and only a handful of unregenerates called the 'sons of Perdition' were to be eternally damned.") His answer began to "reach to a streak of gladness," as I once heard the sermon of a black Baptist preacher described. "Jesus Christ said that if a man could just glance into the telestial, he would commit suicide to get there. But angels can't have posterity increase, and if you enter the upper third—the Celestial Kingdom—you can create *spiritual children* besides those born to you in life. Man is that he might have joy, and joy is expanding and having children, providing for others, and helping them to reach their capabilities. The joy of parenthood is teaching your children to cope with life. The joy of temple work is helping people go to the Celestial Kingdom prepared. Without baptism by authority, without receiving through endowment the gift of knowledge which is an essential part of the progression, and without entering into the everlasting category of marriage, you wouldn't be happy there; you'd be like a drunk in a swank place, or somebody who was out of his social element. If I didn't have these beliefs, I probably wouldn't be in the least interested in genealogy. I'd probably be out making money.

"I landed my first job here in 1964, and as soon as the Royalty Identification Unit came into existence, I started collecting the descendants of Edward IV. It was an impossible task to begin with—after four or five generations there are more than you can count—so I took a bigger bite and went four generations further back, to Edward III. All Americans with British ancestry are probably descended from Edward III, although many of the connections we've looked at haven't held up. At the same time I started working backwards, from Prince Charles. A lot of his maternal ancestry is lost, because the wives weren't named, but after fourteen years I've got him related to Edward III almost two thousand different ways. If you just kept plugging away at these two pedigrees you would eventually run into everybody in history, and you would provide a structure that *everybody* could tie into. That's why I'm involved in royalty."

Mrs. Plaisir had been extracting and lineage-linking names from Nordic sagas going back to 260 A.D., and another extractor was doing the Xius, a noble Mayan family who had never reigned, but who went back to the tenth century, were prominent in the fourteenth, and had traceable descendants until the nineteenth. I asked if anything was being done about early figures like Moses, Socrates, and Helen of Troy. "At this point we aren't involved with biblical or historical people before 200 A.D. We consider that Moses and all of the prophets have done all their own work, and other biblical figures will be done in the millennium, under the direction of the Lord."

We got on the subject of fraudulence, a frequent problem with "royal" connections, as we have seen. "There are two very common myths in American families," Gunderson told me. "One has three brothers coming to America together. One brother settles in New England, the other in the mid-Atlantic states, the third in the South. I've heard that for a hundred families. It might be true for one of them. The other myth has a woman, made pregnant by a duke or a prince, migrating to America. Having the father be royalty makes the illegitimacy more acceptable." In his paper on the subject, Gunderson explains that there are "three main avenues" by which "the more common among us" can connect into royalty or nobility: illegitimacy, descent from younger sons, and marriages of unequal status; and he identifies four kinds of illegitimacy: recognized, circumstantial, traditional, and fraudulent (in which "the connection has . . . definitely been forced").

I spent a couple of days combing books and microfilm for my dead and, with the help of a "reference consultant" in the Scandinavian Reference Section, turned up a Finnish side of the family nobody had known about. Meanwhile, thousands of other people were engaged in similar odysseys. Occasionally the silence that filled the library's public stacks and reading rooms would be broken by a muffled gasp from somebody who had made a break-through, but I witnessed no outbursts, although shortly before my arrival a woman hot on the trail of her antecedents had apparently kicked the shin of a reference consultant who wouldn't surrender a restricted record she needed. For its first fifty years the Genea-logical Society had been a membership society. Then, in 1944, it had opened its archives to the public. Patrons of the library had been required to sign a register, but with the doubling of patron-age after *Roots*, this policy created such a bottleneck at the en-trance that it was abandoned. "There are all kinds of people in here," Fudge told me, frowning, "and we have no idea what they're up to." Security guards watch for anything out of the or-dinary, and an electric eye at the exits, programmed to detect a metal strip inserted in the bindings, picks up any of the library's books that are being walked off with.

In an aisle of the French section, I struck up a conversation with Raymond La Pointe, an "imported Californian" who worked as a medical technician for the Department of Corrections in Vacaville and was trying to cross the water from Quebec to France. Three families named Audet had immigrated to Quebec in the seventeenth century, he told me, and their three home-steads had formed a triangle. His ancestors had lived at the apex of the triangle, and to distinguish them from the others they be-came known as the Audets de la Pointe; in 1670 the Audet had been dropped altogether.

A little later I sat down at a reading table next to a man named Frank Czito, who was in seventh heaven. In one day he, his wife, and their two children, working as a team, had gone back a hundred and forty years. Czito had emigrated from Hun-gary eight years earlier and was still struggling with English.

"We come from Santa Monica," he told me. "We heard there is big library in Utah where you can find everything about Hun-gary. We would like find our old family—what from and what kind of class. In Hungary," he said, pressing to his breast a mili-tary book called *Magyaroroszag tiszti es Nevtara*, in which he had discovered that one of his grandfathers had attained the rank of general, "we never can touch this kind of book because of *cenzura.*" The way he was hugging the book reminded me of something the Indian historian B. N. Goswamy has written: "There is a peculiar tug to the heart when you come face to face with the record of your family. The signatures and names of well-loved persons no longer alive . . . remain intensely human, possessed of a warmth which is denied to many sources of history."

Besides the personal rewards of making contact with long-forgotten ancestors and the sense of security to be derived from "seeing how everything fits and belongs," as a woman I talked to put it, genealogy has two practical uses. Lawyers working on inheritance cases and professional genealogists retained by lawyers and probate courts use the library regularly. This type of research is known as forensic genealogy. When a person dies intestate— without a will—his estate passes to his next of kin. In the standard Western inheritance pattern, the first in line is the spouse, who usually gets half of the estate; next are the descendants: children, grandchildren, great-grandchildren; then the ascendants: parents, grandparents, and so on; then come the siblings, and their descendants; then the aunts and uncles, and their descendants, who are first cousins to the decedent, first cousins once removed, and so on; then on up to the great-aunts and the great-uncles, if they are still living; then out to the next line, to the second cousins, who share a set of great-grandparents with the decedent, and so on. Except in the case of the spouse, who unless she is a consanguine of the decedent shares no genes with him, the order of heirship is similar to the coefficient of kinship.

In New York State, if no first cousins (of any remove) or closer relatives can be found, the estate reverts to the state—a law which the genealogist Timothy Beard deplores because, as he told me recently, it reflects the poverty of the American conception of the family. But in Texas any relative, no matter how distant, is a potential heir, and a large fortune like that of the late Howard Robard Hughes, Jr., valued at from a hundred and fifty-eight million to 1.1 billion dollars (Hughes's holdings were so diversified by the time of his death, on April 6, 1976, that their exact worth is still undetermined), can attract all sorts of claimants. It is eight years now since Hughes died, but not a penny of his estate has yet been distributed. Harris County Probate Judge Pat Gregory, who is hearing the case, told me recently that the settlement of the estate is still "two or three years down the road," pending a decision by the United States Supreme Court on whether Hughes's legal domicile was Texas, California, or Nevada. Texas and California are fighting over the inheritance taxes one of them might get on Hughes's estate; Nevada has no inheritance tax, and has no interest in the decision. All the other litigation has been resolved.

Judge Gregory has ruled that none of the wills purportedly made by Hughes (on the order of forty have been filed in Texas and Nevada, and new ones still surface periodically) are authentic, and he has ruled that none of the people claiming to be Hughes's wives, children, brother, or sister have valid claims upon the estate. In 1976 he appointed the Houston lawyer O. Theodore Dinkins, Jr., to serve as attorney *ad litem* to protect the rights of all unknown legal heirs. Dinkins hired the Houston genealogist Mary Smith Fay to investigate the Hughes family, and the search for the legitimate heirs began. "The maternal, Gano, side of the tree was fairly well established," Mrs. Fay has written in a recent article for the *National Genealogical Quarterly*, "but the Hughes family was quite a different story." Eventually, however, the heirs were determined to be twenty-two in number: five on the Gano side, and seventeen on the Hughes side; and the two sides agreed to divide the estate into two "moieties," with the greatest share going to the highest line of living heirs in each moiety.

Hughes was an only child, but his father was one of seven children. One of Hughes's uncles, Rupert, a well-known novelist, biographer, and movie director, was married three times, and there was bitter litigation about his legitimate descendants. A coalition of about four hundred second, third, fourth, and fifth cousins tried to show that Rupert's daughter Elspeth, who had died in 1945, was not his real daughter, because he had been sterilized, they claimed, by simultaneous cases of mumps and German measles contracted when he was fourteen or fifteen. Another group of about a hundred and sixty cousins argued that Rupert and his first wife had had a son who had died young and had a daughter named Lenora or Leila, who had drowned in a swimming pool in Los Angeles in about 1921, and that Elspeth, who was, they claimed, Rupert's daughter from a previous marriage or liaison with the woman who eventually became his third wife, was secretly substituted for her, and thus was illegitimate. On September 4, 1981, a jury of six, with Judge Gregory presiding, ruled that Elspeth was the real, legitimate daughter of Rupert Hughes, and that her three daughters would therefore inherit a share of the estate; that Avis (Bissell) Hughes MacIntyre and her late brother Rush (Bissell) Hughes were the adopted children of Rupert Hughes by "estoppel": Hughes had never legally adopted them, but he had taken them in and let them use his surname; that therefore they (or their heirs) were also entitled to a share of the estate; but that the plaintiffs—the second, third, fourth, and fifth cousins, who were next in Rupert's line—were entitled to nothing, because in Texas first cousins, including equitably adopted children, take precedence. In the most recent development in the case, the heirs have got together and agreed to pay the actress Terry Moore $390,000 to drop her appeal in a Nevada probate court; she claimed that she and Hughes had secretly married aboard a yacht in the late forties and that she was thus entitled to a wife's share. The suit was denied in both Texas and Nevada.

Each of the states has a law of perpetuities, which prevents a man from bypassing his immediate descendants and "trying to rule the world by perpetuating his ego as far down his tree as he can get it," as a Maryland estate lawyer recently described it to me. The limiting clause in most of the statutes is "lives in being plus twenty-one years and nine months" (or "a period of gestation"). In other words, twenty-one years and nine months after the death of the last of your next of kin who was living when you died, in your estate must "vest" on your next of kin. Theoretically, by leaving your estate in trust to the next of kin of a one-year-old grandson or great-grandson, for instance, you could hold up the inheritance for a hundred years or so, and if a lot of money and real estate were involved, you *could* almost "rule the world," or at least create a lot of posthumous havoc. Such a situation has arisen in Brazil with the estate of a millionaire of the last century named Domingo Faustino Correa, who made his will four days before he died, in 1873. Brazil did not have a law of perpetuities, and to spite his nieces and nephews (Correa himself was childless), who seemed a little too eager for him to go, Correa provided generously for his slaves and mistresses, but fixed the will so that none of his kin could inherit anything for a hundred years. At the time of his death Correa owned what are now virtually the entire downtowns of Pelotas and Rio Grande, two coastal cities in the very south of Brazil, with respective populations of a hundred and fifty thousand and a hundred thousand. His real estate included miles of beach, a six-hundred-foot waterfall, and what is now a ninety-thousand-acre forest preserve, and it spread over into neighboring Uruguay. Tens of thousands of people have been squatting on it for decades, and his gold bullion has been sitting in banks in Uruguay, Chile, and Argentina. In the past hundred years, southern Brazil has grown and developed prodigiously, and the value of Correa's real estate and gold has doubled and doubled again. For many years they were worth more than Brazil's entire foreign debt; currently the estate is appraised at about twelve billion dollars. Correa had eight brothers and sisters, who were all prolific, and after a hundred years their progeny is uncountable. About four thousand claimants so far, possessing a total of a hundred and seventy-eight surnames, seem authentic. Each stands to inherit about three million dollars, if the estate can ever be settled. A lawyer named José Cicero Biglia, in the city of Campinas, has been tracing Correa's next of kin through the vital records of bishoprics and justices of the peace. Some of the lineages from his siblings are already ten generations long. In 1981 the *New York Times* reported that the case had "already generated sixteen thousand pages of paperwork," and that the state had "just appointed a judge to inventory all the properties, sell them at assessed value, bank the proceeds, and eventually divide them up among those people who can prove their direct descents," but as with the Hughes estate, nothing has yet been settled on any of Correa's heirs.

🌱

The second practical use of genealogy is that it can further the understanding of hereditary disease, and no group has been more valuable for this than the Utah Mormons, for a variety of reasons besides the excellence of their records. The size of the population—about a million descendants of about twenty thousand pioneers presently live in Utah—is ideal for genetic research, because it is "large enough . . . to insure that genes of interest are represented with samples large enough to give significant results," as the population geneticist Mark Skolnick, who studies it, has written. "Most of the gene pool comes from an initial population of New England and Midwestern origin, augmented by three waves of migration from the British Isles, Scandinavia, and

Germany," he explains. Because the pioneers who founded the population were largely unrelated and their collective coefficient of kinship was very low, dominant and recessive modes of inheritance are easier to distinguish among their descendants than they are in highly inbred religious isolates like the Amish, the Hutterites, and the Mennonites, in which it is sometimes unclear whether the trait which is being expressed is a dominant that has spread by genetic drift, or the result of two recessives identical by descent meeting up with themselves again in the offspring of a consanguineous union. The present and historical desire of Mormons to have large families is a major asset, because large numbers of offspring give greater statistical power. For much of the past century the Mormons produced more than eight children per couple, and the present fertility rate in Utah (28.6 live births per thousand people in 1980) is very close to double the national rate. Before 1890 polygyny was practiced by probably five to ten per cent of Mormon men, some of whom had dozens of children by multiple wives. The presence of plural marriage in many of the Mormons' pedigrees gives the geneticist who is seeking to identify male or female input an unusual control: when children of the same father but different mothers express the same trait, it is obvious which parents contributed the gene or genes; one variable is ruled out.

Another advantage of the Utah Mormon population is that it has not had a great deal of new genetic input since 1880, when the last wave of European migration had arrived. "In-migration is the bugbear of demographic studies," a demographer at Brigham Young University told me. Most of the descendants of the pioneers are still in Utah. In their comparative immobility and clannishness, they resemble another good population for medical-genetic research, the French Canadians, whose population since it arrived in 1700 has doubled nine times and increased five-hundred-and-fifty-fold, without appreciable admixture. On the other hand, there is enough social and environmental heterogeneity within the Utah Mormon population—some live in the urban centers along the Wasatch front, others in rural communities in the mountains and in the desert—that "one can study the variability of gene expression against the natural background which occurs," Skolnick writes. ". . . The variety of occupation, social status, and variable adherence to prescription against coffee, tobacco, and alcohol insure that many potential gene-environment interactions are represented."

In 1974 the Genealogical Society allowed Skolnick to Xerox about a hundred and seventy thousand of the family group sheets in its Patron Section. The scientist chose only those in which at least one individual was listed as born or died in Utah or along the "Pioneer Trail." The data were fed into a computer, which "lineage-linked" about a million and a quarter individuals on overlapping pedigrees with an average depth of six to seven generations. Certain medical patterns, such as an excess of early death clustering in a particular family, were already apparent from demographic analysis of the genealogical information; other patterns emerged when demographic analysis was combined with supplementary medical information. The medical information about the study population was obtained from a variety of sources: from the Utah Cancer Registry, death certificates going back to 1900, and other vital records; and from discharge diagnoses (about two hundred thousand annually) at each of the state's thirty-eight hospitals which may soon be added to the data base. In addition, the scientists also interviewed many of the families themselves. "Large segments of these [computerized] pedigrees remain in Utah," Skolnick writes, "and others can be studied easily at annual family reunions, a Mormon practice. At one visit to an isolated town we drew blood on a hundred and eighteen members of one pedigree in a single day." The families were on the whole very cooperative, out of respect for research and out of a sense of obligation to their kin: they understood that if something in the family had to be checked, it was for the good of their offspring, and some of them volunteered medical information that had not been picked by the other sources.

All the medical information was also fed into the computer and linked with the genealogical data, and as a result Skolnick and his associates were able to construct a more detailed medical-genetic profile of a large population than has ever been assembled, and to further understanding of several specific disorders, particularly breast cancer, early heart disease, and hemochromatosis, a rare, recessively inherited disorder of metal metabolism, in which the body holds on to too much of the iron it absorbs from food or alcohol.

✤

Considering that the church doesn't accept the theory of evolution, it seemed magnanimous of the Genealogical Society to release its family group sheets to geneticists. Some Mormons, Gunderson told me, were "kind of torn" about the church's strict adherence to "creationism," but Tom Daniels was not among them. "Darwin and all that stuff," he said to me one afternoon as we drove south from Salt Lake City, "we don't buy it at all. It's a godless theory." He also had misgivings about genetic engineering, about the day, which would seem to be not very far off, when a defective sequence of DNA could be replaced by a remodelled virus-like particle that would instruct a cell to function correctly. Perhaps the time might even come when people could identify and delete specific ancestral contributions and break away from their families completely, or at least in a purely physical sense, and those who wanted to be free-floating individualists could ad lib themselves into the sort of people they had always wanted to be. "I don't think the Lord will let them get that far," Daniels said.

With all the dinosaur bones and the pre-Cambrian rock that are exposed in Utah, it seemed to require a special fervor to believe that the earth was only six thousand years old and not the culmination of a succession of inconceivably ancient and protracted geological and biological processes. The creationist argument is based partly on a rejection of carbon dating as a valid method for determining the age of organic material. "Carbon dating is theoretically correct only if the atmospheric bombardment has been constant over the ages, also, if radioactivity of the elements is constant," Thomas Milton Tinney, the Mormon who has traced himself in a hundred and fifty-five generations right back to Adam, explains in his privately printed genealogy, a copy of which I came across at the New York Public Library. "Prior to Adam and Eve partaking of the forbidden fruit in the Garden of Eden, there was no death, or radioactive decay. The atmosphere at the time of the patriarchs was different from what it is today. There was no rainbow prior to the world-wide flood; also the process of decay and degeneration was slower as can be noted by the age of longevity of the early PATRIARCHS." Daniels suggested to me that "when the Bible says that God created the world in six days, six different stages of considerably longer duration, rather than six literal twenty-four-hour time periods, may have been meant." Then he repeated the same Scripture Gunderson had cited as an indication of the delightfulness of the telestial kingdom: "A day with the Lord is as a thousand years with man."

A few miles south of Salt Lake City, as we drove below the western flank of Traverse Mountain, Daniels pointed out the shoreline of old Lake Bonneville, which is thought to have originated during the last Ice Age and at its high point to have flooded Salt Lake Valley under a thousand and fifty feet of water. Most geologists who have studied the lake have calculated that it lasted until about ten thousand years ago, but I wasn't going to argue with Daniels about it. He was taking me to the Vault, which very few Mormons and hardly anybody outside the faith have been allowed to visit in recent years. A special meeting of the society's management had reviewed my request for the visit, and Daniels had evidently spoken in my favor, because a few days later, when I met Elder Royden Derrick, who at the age of sixty-one had been called from a thriving steel company he had founded to serve the church full-time and was now the society's president, he thanked me for being "objective."

Refusal to accept Darwin had certainly not prevented the Mormons from leading healthy, productive lives. Chase Peterson, president of the University of Utah and a church member, had shown me a study comparing the citizens of Utah, who are among the healthiest people in the country, with the citizens of Nevada, who have among the highest incidences of cirrhosis of the liver and lung cancer and a sixty-three-per-cent death rate between the ages of forty and forty-five. Since the desert environment, the average income, and the medical care in the two states are not appreciably different, the dramatic contrast in the health of the two populations is probably due to differences in life style and "internal environment." "Utah is inhabited primarily by Mormons, whose influence is strong throughout the state," the study, which is by Victor R. Fuchs and is part of a book called *Who Shall Live?*, explains. "Devout Mormons do not use tobacco or alcohol and in general lead stable, quiet lives. Nevada, on the other hand, is a state with high rates of cigarette and alcohol consumption and very high in-

dexes of marital and geographical instability. The contrast with
Utah in these respects is extraordinary." Daniels felt that the
Mormons' religion itself promoted good health, too. "When you
have a culture which feels that it has the truth, it can result in a
very sanguine feeling," he told me. "The people are not encum-
bered with a lot of problems because they have a mechanism for
solving them. When a loved one dies there's grief, but it's not
total loss, because we know that we'll be with them again. The
family orientation causes less parent-child strife, less stress in that
department. We live by Exodus 20: 'Honor thy father and thy
mother, that thy days may be long upon the land which the Lord
thy God giveth thee.' Contention is a definite source of unsettled
health."

After we had been driving for about half an hour, we turned
up Little Cottonwood Canyon, one of the seven sheer-walled cavi-
ties cut through the Wasatch front—the spectacular westernmost
chain of the Rockies—by torrents that rush down into Salt Lake
Valley. At the mouth of the canyon a verdant suburb called Sandy
had sprung up on an ancient glacial moraine. "Some polygamists
live in one of those ranch houses, so I'm told," Daniels said, indi-
cating a group of houses below us. "They seem to be quite prosperous. The old man sends his wives out, so they have multiple
incomes. The law leaves them alone." As we climbed the steeply
rising floor of the canyon, the houses stopped and the walls of
rock narrowed. Vegetation reached up wherever it had found a
footing: fir, spruce, and lodgepole pine had colonized the angled
strata of the shadier right-hand wall and scrub oak, box elder, and
sagebrush filled the cracks in the left-hand one, which was bathed
in strong light. After about a mile, we turned left, on an unobtru-
sive dirt road that led to the foot of a seven-hundred-foot cliff, part
of a blister of hot fluid that had seeped into the 800-million-
year-old slate, quartzite, and welded sandstone of the lower canyon
during the uplift of the Wasatch Mountains; had cooled, crystal-
lized, then been stripped by erosion and exposed. Much later the
cliff had been exfoliated by a series of glaciers, so that it overhung
in places. The rock was white and very hard, predominantly feld-
spar, sprinkled with black slivers of hornblende and platy sheets of
biotite mica. It was similar to granite and was called quartz monzonite. Daniels told me that a few years earlier a young man had

tried to climb the cliff but had fallen to his death; that mountain goats were sometimes spotted on the ledges across the canyon; and that one morning somebody who was driving up to the Vault had come upon a cougar in the parking lot.

At the base of the cliff there were four large portals which looked somewhat like tunnel entrances and were protected by plate glass and steel grilles. We parked, got out, walked over to a bunkerlike building to the right of the cliff—the personnel entrance—and went through a door. The air inside was much cooler: sixty degrees instead of ninety-five. Daniels faced a closed-circuit television camera and said, "Tom Daniels and party." A voice in a suspended loudspeaker answered, "Okay, sir, you're expected," and we were buzzed through a second door. We went through an open iron grille and turned left, down a corridor of sheeted, corrugated, heavy-gauge steel which led into the mountain. At the end of the corridor a man in a booth gave us identification tags, had us sign a register, and buzzed us through a third door into a room where two women in orange smocks were opening parcels full of steel cans. Each carton, of which dozens had been stacked against a wall, contained eleven cans. Soon a large man who looked to be in his early thirties—Herbert White II, the group manager of the Granite Mountain Records Vault—emerged from an office in one of the portals and greeted us warmly. Like many of the male employees of the Genealogical Society and many of the male Mormon missionaries, White was dressed in a three-piece suit, but his manner was completely informal. He said to call him by his nickname, Moose. He told us that the facility had been built between 1958 and 1963 at a cost of two million dollars, high enough above the canyon floor—the altitude at the portals was six thousand feet—to be out of danger from spring floods; that it was probably nuclear-bomb-proof, although he hoped that would never have to be demonstrated, and maybe even capable of surviving the millennium, which the Mormons believe is not only imminent but overdue. "The Book of Revelations says that the earth will be levelled, valleys will be raised, there will be a follow-up of the Flood, and all the just deceased will be resurrected," Moose said. "We don't know what the Lord has in mind. Maybe he won't even need these records—He must know who has lived and when—but the purpose of this facility is to give them the best protection we can for as long as we have control of them. That is the commitment we make to our donors. And when you think of what has already been lost—the Dutch records when the dikes burst in the fifties, for instance, the Nicaraguan records when Managua was hit by the earthquake a couple of years ago, the Buddhist necrologies that are destroyed whenever Japan is struck by a typhoon, all the European records that went up in smoke or were blown to smithereens in the last war—you wonder if the biggest travesty to mankind wouldn't be to lose its history."

Moose explained that we were in the shipping and receiving section, and said that we should imagine we were one of the three hundred rolls of microfilm which had just been received from Frankfort, Germany. The first thing the girls in the orange smocks did, after opening the cartons, was to "marry" the number on each can to its computer punch card, which had already been sent over by the bibliography unit at headquarters; the status of each roll is monitored by computer throughout processing. Then the cans are taken to the laboratory part of the facility, where they are opened in darkness by technicians in blue smocks, who re-move the film and wind it on an Allen M-70 processor, which looks something like a miniature car wash and can develop ninety feet of silver film per minute. First the film is dunked in two "banks" of developers, then it is immersed in a bank of "stop-bath" clear-water rinse, then it goes through two banks of thiosulfate fixer, then it is rinsed in five more banks of clear water. Most processors have only four banks of wash, but the Allen M-70 was custom-built for the society with an extra bank, to make sure that any residual spots of thiosulfate, which could attack the emulsion and destroy that portion of the film, leaving what are known in the trade as "measles," are removed. Then the film proceeds into a "squeegee" system, in which whatever droplets of wash still cling to it are sucked off. From there it goes into a "dry box," and from there it is wound on a take-up spool. Then the film is taken to the negative evaluation area, where test patterns are run on randomly selected frames to determine whether their density and their reso-lution are within standards. If the image is too light or too blurry, if there is poor contrast, or if a certain number of lines per milli-meter are not measured by the evaluators' sensitometer, second- or third-generation prints of the film won't "read." Some "cosmetic" problems can be corrected by settings on the duplicators, but if the frames are not within standards, there is no alternative but to send the cameraman back to film the records again. The master film is silver-based, and if it passes muster, working prints of it are made, from which three positive copies are run off by either silver, vesicular, or diazo duplicators. The vesicular duplicators in that month alone had already copied three million feet of film. One print goes, as promised, to the donor (which happened at that moment to be the San Francisco County Clerk); another, if the records are considered in the "heavily used" category, is put in circulation at the Genealogical Library, and a third is sent upon request to one of the branch libraries for extraction. On an average day at the Vault sixty-five thousand rolls of microfilm are in the system—being developed, copied, stored, or sent down to headquarters for geographic cataloguing.

Moose led us through a sort of lobby, past a piano with an open Mormon hymnal over the keyboard, past a row of framed likenesses of the church's twelve presidents, four of whom had been named Smith, and into the air-intake portal, where the large particulates in the incoming air are trapped in filter bags, and the smaller dust particles are extracted by carbon filters. On most days, automatic atmospheric adjustments are made by a Kathabar humidifier. The humidity in the canyon that day, for instance, was only nine per cent, but at least thirty-per-cent humidity has to be maintained for optimal microfilm storage. Elsewhere in the facility, ion-detection and smoke-detection alarms were ready to sound off at the outbreak of fire; a strain meter, composed of hollow quartz rods suspended by piano wires and encased in Styrofoam sheeting, monitored the monzonite as it expanded or compressed in concert with neighboring or remote shifts of the earth's crust. The meter is sensitive enough to have picked up, for instance, in March 1979, shock waves from an earthquake in Mexico which measured 7.1 to 7.2 on the Richter scale. It is almost six hundred feet inside the mountain, in one of the six storage chambers. The chambers are two hundred feet long and they open to three three-hundred-and-fifty-foot corridors that run straight into the mountain at a very slight incline, so that water which might become trapped in them can run off. The entrances to the corridors are protected by three steel doors. The doors weigh seven, fourteen,

and seven tons respectively and were made by the Mosler Safe
Company. The central door is opened at eight in the morning and
shut at four forty in the afternoon. Two combination locks must be
dialled to open it. Moose wouldn't tell me how many people knew
the combinations. Above each door is an air vent whose covers,
mounted on spring-loaded blast locks, will automatically seal shut
in seconds if there is an explosion outside. Once the door and the
vents are shut—in the event of, say, a nuclear holocaust—Moose
reckons that the master films in the chambers, which are sealed
off by yet other doors, will last "almost for eternity." The chambers
are under five hundred feet of solid rock, with scarcely a fracture
in it, the natural temperature in them hovers between fifty-nine
and sixty-two degrees, and the relative natural humidity at around
thirty per cent—perfect for indefinite storage. He opened the door
to A-vault, one of the two chambers that had film in them. (The
other chambers were still empty or were stacked with processing
equipment. C-vault contained backup computer tapes from
GIANT of financial and church-membership records.) We peered
down a narrow aisle flanked by solid monotone walls of regula-
tion-gray metal cabinets which tapered toward the vanishing
point. Each wall was eighteen drawers high and eighty-eight cabinets deep, and there was another row on either side of them. Each
drawer held seventy-five rolls of thirty-five-millimeter microfilm,
and each roll contained from thirteen to two thousand pages of
records, or the equivalent of three to six large volumes. A hundred
years of the London *Times* would have taken up less than two
drawers. Each chamber had room for 885,400 hundred-foot rolls
of thirty-five-millimeter film, and as of that month there were, according to a bulletin board in A-vault, 1,267,518 rolls in storage
(fifty-three weeks later there were 1,318,210 rolls), some of them
dating to 1939, when the filming began, and containing in all
about a billion and a half names of the dead—a figure that Moose
warned was a sheer estimate, because many of the rolls had not yet
been extracted.

Although the view down A-vault was not particularly awesome, it slowly dawned on me that I was in the presence of one of
the modern wonders of the world. When I imagined myself an
extraterrestrial, or one of the next species to inherit the earth, coming upon this chamber after the human race had destroyed itself,

it *was* awesome. I sensed that Daniels, too, was moved, although he must have seen the monotone walls of drawers many times before. He said quietly and with a straightforwardness I had come to admire, "In here are the names of a billion and a half people who have walked the earth in the last four hundred years." A few minutes later we were outside again, in the bright land of the still living.

Acknowledgments and Further Reading

This book is a synthesis of ideas and information from scores of people, but to have named them all would have slowed down the text intolerably. Some gave me long telephone tutorials on their subject. Others I came to know only through their books or articles. I am particularly grateful to those who were kind enough to review parts of the manuscript or, in the case of Robin Fox, the whole thing, and to suggest changes or cuts. My main literary concern was to transmit faithfully and clearly what these people have taught me.

The central idea—that there are two types of societies in the world: one kin-centered, the other self-centered, and that the self-centered societies have paid a considerable price for their progress—has been developing in my mind since 1971, when I made the first of many visits to the Third World. I am, of course, by no means the first person to have perceived the distinction or to have written about it. The history of the idea is traced incompletely in Chapter Eight, "The Return to Kinship."

Three books were constantly referred to throughout the project: Robin Fox's *Kinship and Marriage: An Anthropological Perspective* (Cambridge University Press, 1984); Pierre F. van den Berghe's *Human Family Systems: An Evolutionary View* (Elsevier, 1974); and L. L. Cavalli-Sforza and William F. Bodmer's

The *Genetics of Human Populations* (Freeman, 1971). Fox was
an invaluable source, sounding board, and critic, as was Cavalli-
Sforza, who reviewed the sections on genetics. William Shawn of
The New Yorker and John Herman of Simon and Schuster provided equally valuable counsel and support. John Bennet of *The
New Yorker* came up with the title. Many of my colleagues on
the magazine—as bright and well-informed a group of people as
I know—made suggestions and contributions. The habit of starting the day with a mug of coffee and the *New York Times* served
me well: in its pages I found abundant confirmations of the very
trends that I was becoming aware of.

To simplify the following, I have sometimes not reacknowl-
edged sources already named in the text, and have often not acknowledged more than once sources that were used repeatedly.

For Chapter One, "The Need For Kinship," I talked with
Richard Wrangham, George Schaller, Irven DeVore, Robert F.
Murphy, Napoleon Chagnon, Thomas de Zengotita, Helen Fisher,
and Lyn Carson. Wrangham reviewed the chapter. I read the
chapters by Robert L. Trivers and Robert K. Selander in *Sexual
Selection and the Descent of Man,* edited by Bernard Campbell
(University of Chicago Press, 1972); Robin Fox's "Primate Kin
and Human Kinship," in *Biosocial Anthropology,* edited by him
(Malaby Press, 1975); Peter G. Voit's "Gorilla Society," in *Natural
History,* vol. 93, no. 3; "Elephants Reveal Their Social Lives to
Lone Researchers," in the Nov. 15, 1983, *New York Times;* E. O.
Wilson's *Sociobiology* (Belknap Press, 1975); W. H. D. Hamil-
ton's "The Genetical Theory of Social Behavior" (I and II), in
the *Journal of Theoretical Biology,* 7(1):1–52; Richard Dawkins's
The Selfish Gene (Oxford University Press, 1976); Richard
Wrangham's "Mutualism, Kinship, and Social Evolution," in *Current Problems in Sociobiology,* edited by the Kings College Sociobiology Group (Cambridge University Press, 1982); Joan Stephen-
son Graf's "Whose Tribe Are You?" in *Science Digest,* vol. 91, no.
11; Napoleon Chagnon's "Natural Selection Theory and the Evolution of Human Kinship and Reproduction Systems," in *Sociobiology* 6(1), 1981; Fox's "Alliance and Constraint: Sexual Selection and the Evolution of Human Kinship Systems," in *Sexual
Selection and the Descent of Man* edited by Bernard Campbell (Aldine, 1972); de Zengotita's paper on Jonestown, published in

French in *Le Genre Humaine*, III, 1982; and Anthony Wagner's *Pedigrees and Progress* (Phillimore, 1975).

For "Traditional Kinship" I talked with Owen Lovejoy, Judith Bruce, Jack Goody, Daniel Gross, a Bedouin scholar who wanted his information and his tribe to be anonymous, Jeanette Waken (who reviewed all the sections having to do with Arab kinship and genealogy), Charles Donahue, William Miller, George Hamawy, Nicholas A. Shoumatoff, Orville Schell, and Gregory Gubler. Two textbooks were very useful: *Anthropology: The Study of Man*, edited by E. Adamson Hoebel (McGraw-Hill, 1958); and *The Study of Anthropology*, edited by David E. Hunter and Phillip Whitten (Harper & Row, 1976). I read the catalogue to a 1984 exhibition at the American Museum of Natural History, "Ancestors: Four Million Years of Humanity," by Ian Tattersall and Eric Delson; Boyce Rensberger's "What Made Humans Human?" in the April 8, 1984, *New York Times Magazine*; "Theory of Man's Origins Challenged," in the Sept. 4, 1984, *Times*; Ira L. Reiss's *The Family System in America* (Holt, Rinehart and Winston, 1974); "Income Gap Between Races Wide as in 1960, Study Finds," in the July 18, 1983, *Times*; Elise Boulding's *The Underside of History: A View of Women Through Time* (Westview Press, 1976); Helen Fisher's *The Sex Contract* (Quill, 1983); Robert F. Murphy's "Canela Kinship and the Question of Matrilineality," in *Brazil: An Anthropological Perspective*, edited by Maxine L. Margolis and William E. Carter (Columbia University Press, 1979); David J. Parkin's *Palms, Wine, and Witnesses* (Chandler, 1972); Sally Falk Moore's "Chagga 'Customary' Law and the Property of the Dead," in *Mortality and Immortality: The Anthropology and Archaeology of Death*, edited by S. C. Humphreys; Stuart A. Queen and Robert W. Habenstein's *The Family in Various Cultures* (Lippincott, 1961); William J. Smole's *The Yanomamo Indians: A Cultural Geography* (University of Texas, 1976); Napoleon Chagnon's *The Fierce People* (Holt, Rinehart and Winston, 1968); Jacob Black-Michaud's *The Cohesive Force: Feud in the Mediterranean and the Middle East* (St. Martin's, 1975); M. J. L. Hardy's *Blood Feuds and the Payment of Blood Money in the Middle East* (Beirut, 1963); "Northeast's Blood Feud Spills into Rio for 30th Death," in the Nov. 9, 1981, *Washington Post*; "Brazil Takes Over Town Racked by a Blood Feud," in the

Nov. 18, 1981, *Times;* Richard Leakey's *Origins* (Dutton, 1977); James G. Frazer's *The Belief in Immortality* (reprinted by Dawsons, 1968) and *The Golden Bough* (New York, 1941); "A Very Special Marriage," by Nirmala Shotam, in the May 5, 1980, *Silver Kris Magazine;* Arthur Waley's *The Nine Songs* (Allen and Unwin, 1955); Marvin Harris's *Cows, Pigs, and Witches* (Vintage, 1975); Ignaz Goldhizer's *Muslim Studies* (Aldine, 1966); Ashley Montagu's *Immortality, Religion, and Morals* (Hawthorn, 1971); and Fawn M. Brodie's *The Devil Drives* (Norton, 1967).

For "Stratification and Pedigrees" I talked with Robert Bianchi, Monte McLaws, Gregory Gubler, Kenji Suzuki, Elwin Jenson, and James Russell. I read Edward O. Wilson's *On Human Nature* (Harvard University Press, 1978); Timothy Beard's *How to Find Your Family Roots* (McGraw-Hill, 1977); Harold E. Driver's *Indians of North America* (University of Chicago, 1961); Sigmund Freud's *Totem and Taboo* (Norton, 1952); B. N. Goswamy's "Pilgrimage Records of India: A Rich Source for Genealogy and Family History" and S. A. I. Tirnizi's "Genealogical Records of Medieval India," both in the proceedings of the Genealogical Society of Utah's 1980 World Conference on Records; Hui-chen Wang Lin's "The Traditional Chinese Clan Rules," in monographs of the Association for Asian Studies; D. J. Steel's *The Descent of Christian Names,* in the June 1962 *Genealogist's Magazine;* Gregory Gubler's "Characters and Ancestors," in *Genealogy Digest,* vol. 10, no. 1, and vol. 13, no. 2; Arkon Daraul's *Secret Societies* (Octagon, 1961); and Fetaui Mata'afa's "Oral Family Traditions in the Pacific Islands" and Vernice Pere's "The Story behind the Legend of the Maori Canoes and the Descending Maori Chiefs," both in the Utah Genealogical Society's 1980 proceedings.

For "Types of Inheritance" I talked with Victor McKusick, Richard Lewontin, Kenneth Weber, Martin Kreitman, Peter Bingham, R. J. Herrnstein, Paul Wachtel, and John Pearce. Wachtel and Pearce reviewed the section on psychological inheritance. I read *The Metabolic Basis of Inherited Disease,* edited by John B. Stanbury et al. (McGraw-Hill, 1983); Victor A. McKusick's *Mendelian Inheritance in Man,* sixth edition (Johns Hopkins University Press, 1983); Cavalli-Sforza and Marcus W. Feldman's *Cultural Transmission and Evolution* (Princeton University Press, 1981); Cavalli-Sforza's "The Transition to Agriculture and Some of Its Consequences," in *How Humans Adapt,* edited by Donald J. Ortner (Smithsonian Press, 1983); Cavalli-Sforza's letter to the editor following the publication of Herrnstein's "IQ Testing and the Media," in the August 1982 *Atlantic Monthly;* and Cavalli-Sforza et al.'s "Theory and Observation in Cultural Transmission," in the Oct. 1, 1982, *Science.*

For "The Aristocracies of Europe" I talked with Henry E. Christiansen, Ignacio Medina (who graciously put me up in Seville for several days; I am grateful to his cousin Inigo de la Huerta for introducing us), Robert C. Gunderson, Jack Goody, Charles Donahue, Dudley Fishburn, David Sulzberger, the Earl of Gowrie, Hugh Montgomery-Massingberd, Sir Ian Moncreiffe of That Ilk, Patrick Montague-Smith, Robert Lacey, Anne Somerset, Timothy Beard, and two prominent British genealogists who wanted to be anonymous. I read *The Jewish Encyclopedia;* Arthur Kurzweil's *From Generation to Generation* (Morrow, 1980); Dan Rottenberg's *Finding Our Fathers: A Guide to Jewish Ancestry;* Elsdon C. Smith's *New Dictionary of American Family Names* (Harper & Row, 1973); Barbara W. Tuchman's *A Distant Mirror: The Calamitous Fourteenth Century* (Knopf, 1978); Nikolai Tolstoy's *The Tolstoys* (Morrow, 1983); Simon Winchester's *Their Noble Lordships* (Random House, 1982); Roy Perrott's *The Aristocrats* (Weidenfeld and Nicolson, 1968); Robert Lacey's *Aristocrats* (Hutchinson/BBC Publications, 1983); Christopher Simon Sykes's *Black Sheep* (Chatto & Windus, 1982); Mark Bence-Jones and Hugh Montgomery-Massingberd's *The British Aristocracy: Titles and Forms of Address,* fifth edition (Adams and Charles Black, 1939); two of Jack Goody's books, *Succession to High Office* (Cambridge University Press, 1979); and *The Development of the Family and Marriage in Europe* (Cambridge University Press, 1983); and *Family and Inheritance,* edited by Jack Goody, Joan Thirsk, and E. P. Thompson (Cambridge University Press, 1976).

For "The Rise of Modern Individualism" I talked with David Landes, Howard Gadlin, Charles Donahue, Peter Gay, James Weed, Tobias Schneebaum, Henry Holzer (who provided me with the texts of several important individual-rights decisions), Karen Kolvard, Sally Falk Moore, Martha Minow, Lionel Tiger, Paul Wachtel, and Michael McGuire. I read A. Macfarlane's *The Origins of English Individualism* (Oxford University Press, 1970); Steven Lukes's *Individualism* (Oxford University Press, 1973); J.

Bronowski and Bruce Mazlish's *The Western Intellectual Tradition* (Harper & Row, 1960); David Riesman, Nathan Glazer, and Reuel Denney's *The Lonely Crowd* (Yale University Press, 1950); *Life's Picture History of Western Man* (Time Inc., 1951); Brigitte and Peter Berger's *The War Over the Family: Capturing the Middle Ground* (Anchor Press, 1983); a chapter of de Zengotita's doctoral thesis titled "The Functional Reduction of Kinship in the Social Thought of John Locke"; Philippe Ariès's *Centuries of Childhood* (Knopf, 1962); "Elderly Choose Retirement Community Living," in the April 5, 1984, *Times*; *Household and Family in Past Time*, edited by Peter Laslett (Cambridge University Press, 1972); David M. Potter's *The People of Plenty* (University of Chicago Press, 1954); Richard F. Applebaum's *Theories of Social Change* (Markham, 1970); *Man Alone: Alienation in Modern Society*, edited by Eric and Mary Josephson (Dell, 1962); Frances Fitzgerald's profile of Sun City Center, Florida, in the April 25, 1983, *New Yorker*; "Many Women in Poll Value Jobs as Much as Family Life," in the Dec. 4, 1983, *Times*; Landon Y. Jones's *Great Expectations* (Coward, McCann and Geoghegan, 1980); "China Cracking Down on Progeny of Powerful," in the Jan. 17, 1984, *Times*; *Prospects for Soviet Society*, edited by Allen Karsoff (Praeger, 1968); Richard Burton's *The City of the Saints*, edited by Fawn M. Brodie (Knopf, 1963); David Livingstone's *Missionary Travels and Researches in South Africa* (Johnson, 1971); *America's Families*, edited by Donald M. Scott and Bernard Wishy (Harper & Row, 1982); Christopher D. Stone's *Should Trees Have Standing?* (William Kaufmann, 1974); Ludmilla Thomas's "The Littlest Defector," in the March 18, 1983, *National Review*; "Pregnant Drug User Taken to Court," in the April 27, 1983, *Times*; "Missouri Court Rules Out a Fetus Is a Person," in the Aug. 18, 1983, *Times*; "Son Given Up for Adoption Pursues His Family Records," in the April 8, 1984, *Times*; "Mothers Find the Children They Gave Up," in the Aug. 29, 1983, *Times*; my book, *The Capital of Hope* (Coward, McCann and Geoghegan, 1980); V. S. Naipaul's *The Middle Passage* (Vintage, 1981); Paul L. Wachtel's *The Poverty of Affluence: A Psychological Portrait of the American Way of Life* (Free Press, 1983); David C. K. McClelland and Hendrik Hertzberg's "Paranoia," in the June 1974 *Harper's*; Douglas Madsen and Michael T. McGuire's "Whole Blood Serotonin and the Type-A Coronary-Prone Behavior Pattern," in press; "Heart Attacks and Behavior: Early Warning Signs Are Found," in the Feb. 14, 1984, *Times;* and "When Running in Pairs Leads to Pairing Off," in the March 21, 1984, *Times.*

For "New Patterns of American Kinship" I talked with Jack Goody, James Weed, Paul Bohannan, Carolyn Peters, Stephanie J. Ventura, and Ronald Smothers. I read the *Statistical Abstract of the United States 1982–83* (U.S. Bureau of the Census); "A New Generation Finds It Hard to Leave Home," in the Jan. 15, 1984, *Times;* Anatole Broyard's review of Phyllis Rose's *Parallel Lives* in the Oct. 26, 1983, *Times;* "Queens Grandmother Wins $10 Million Lotto," in the March 20, 1984, *Times;* "Sex in America: A Conservative Attitude Prevails," in the Oct. 4, 1983, *Times;* Letty Cottin Pogrebin's *Family Politics* (McGraw-Hill, 1983); Sandra Sanneh's unpublished paper "Polygamy and Social Change"; "Stepfamilies Share Their Joys and Woes," in the Oct. 29, 1983, *Times;* Vera Muller-Paisner's article, "Stepfamilies: A Bid to Come to Terms," in the June 5, 1983, *Times;* "Couple Wins Court Battle to See Grandson," in the Jan. 27, 1984, *Times;* "Single-Father Survey Finds Adjustment a Problem," in the Nov. 21, 1983, *Times;* "Single Mothers by Choice: Perils and Joys," in the May 2, 1983, *Times;* Stephanie J. Ventura's "Trends in First Births to Older Mothers," in *Final Data,* vol. 31, no. 2, supplement (2); "Sharp Rise in Childbearing Found Among U.S. Women in Early 30's," in the June 10, 1983, *Times;* Audrey Redding and Kurt Hirschorn's "Guide to Human Chromosome Defects," Birth Defects Original Article Series, vol. 4, no. 4; "Birth Defects" and "Genetic Counselling," both National Foundation–March of Dimes pamphlets; "Childbirth After 35: Dispelling Myths," in the Nov. 27, 1983, *Times;* "Sperm-Bank Baby Joy to His Mother," in the Sept. 6, 1983, *Times;* "Jersey Mother Held in Drowning of Two of Four Missing Children," in the Nov. 30, 1983, *Times;* Elmer P. Martin and Joanna Mitchell Martin's *The Black Extended Family* (University of Chicago Press, 1978); Andrew Billingsley's *Black Families in White America* (Prentice-Hall, 1968); "Breakup of Black Family Imperils Gains of Decades," in the Nov. 20, 1983, *Times;* "Heading a Family: Stories of 7 Black Women," in the Nov. 21, 1983, *Times;* "Experts Plan to Address Ills of Black Family," in the Sept. 13, 1983, *Times;* two letters under the heading "Black Families: Beyond the 'Deficit Model,'" in the Dec. 6, 1983, *Times;*

"Concern for the Black Family: Attention Now Turns to Men," in the Dec. 31, 1983, *Times*; Lionel Tiger's "Productive Prosperity/Reproductive Depression: The Decline of Intimate Bonds," in *The Phenomenon of Change*, edited by Lisa Taylor (Cooper Hewitt Museum, 1984); Nan E. Johnson and C. Shannon Stokes's "Family Size in Successive Generations: The Effects of Birth Order, Intergenerational Change in Lifestyle, and Familial Satisfaction," in *Demography*, vol. 13, no. 2; "Divorce's Stress Exacts Long-Term Health Toll," in the Dec. 13, 1983, *Times*; "Today the Single Woman Is Setting Up House in Style," in the Nov. 17, 1983, *Times*; Eva Hoffman's review of Barbara Ehrenreich's *The Hearts of Men*, in the Aug. 16, 1983, *Times*; David Halledstein's *The Peter Pan Principle*, excerpted in the Oct. 1983 *Esquire*; and "Lonely Singles Try to Find Romance at Department Store," in the Nov. 14, 1983, *Times*.

For "The Return to Kinship," I talked with Thomas de Zengotita, Greg Gubler, Lino Lipinsky, and Timothy Beard. I read "Patient's Bid to Refuse Food Termed Suicide," in the Dec. 6, 1983, *Times*; "War-Scattered Korean Kin Find Their Kin at Last," in the Aug. 18, 1982, *Times*; William K. Stevens's article on arranged marriage in India in the Aug. 1, 1983, *Times*; "Many Rebels of the 1960s Depressed as They Near 30," in the Feb. 29, 1976, *Times*; Raymond Chamet's *Gauguin* (Barnes and Noble, 1966); Colin Turnbull's *The Mountain People* (Simon and Schuster, 1972) and *The Human Cycle* (Simon and Schuster, 1983); Peter Berger's review of *The Human Cycle* in the April 10, 1983, *Times Book Review*; and Charles Reich's *The Greening of America* (Random House, 1970).

For "The Kinship of Mankind" I talked with Thomas E. Daniels and Timothy Beard. I read "A Clan Called Valentine Gathers for the First Time," in the Feb. 13, 1983, *Times*; "Family That Grew with the U. S. Holds Reunion," in the Aug. 15, 1983, *Times*; Kenneth W. Wachtel's article on Norman ancestry in *Genealogical Demography*, edited by B. Duke and W. T. Morrill (Academic Press, 1980); James E. Smith and Phillip K. Kunz's "The Kinship of the World," in the Jan. 1977 *Ensign*; Francisco J. Ayala's *Population and Evolutionary Genetics: A Primer* (Benjamin/Cummings, 1982); William F. Bodmer and L. L. Cavalli-Sforza's *Genetics, Evolution, and Man* (Freeman, 1976); Victor A. McKusick's "The Royal Hemophilia," in the Aug. 1965 *Scien-*

tific American; Debrett's Royal Scotland, by Jean Goodman in col-
laboration with Sir Ian Moncreiffe of That Ilk (Debrett, Webb
and Bower, 1983); Guy Murchie's Seven Mysteries of Life
(Houghton Mifflin, 1978); Richard Lewontin's Human Diversity
(Scientific American Library, 1982); "Democrats' Genealogies
Show Some, Ah, Royalty," in the Oct. 26, 1983, Times.

For "The Mountain of Names," I talked with Ansley J.
Coale, who reviewed the section on historical demography and the
history of record keeping. The following members of the Gene-
alogical Society of Utah were particularly helpful, in many cases
supplementing our discussions with in-house publications: Thomas
E. Daniels, Herbert White III, Robert C. Gunderson, Monte
McLaws, John Laing, Kenji Suzuki, Dennis Neuenschwander,
Gregory Gubler, Ted F. Powell, Henry E. Christiansen, Reynolds
C. Cahoon, Brent Barlow, Esther Smith, John C. Harman, and
Vance Standifird. I have rarely come in contact with such natu-
rally open and friendly people as the Mormons I met in Salt Lake
City. I hope they will not feel their trust has been betrayed, but
that this write-up will make them even prouder of their extraor-
dinary operation. I also talked with Pat Gregory, O. Theodore
Dinkins, Jr., and Mary Smith Fay; the section on the Utah Re-
sources for Genetic and Epidemiologic Research was reviewed by
Mark Skolnick and other members of the research team. I read
Nathan Keyfitz's "How Many People Have Lived on the Earth,"
in Demography, vol. 3, 1966; Edward S. Deevey's "The Human
Population," in the Sept. 1960 Scientific American; Fawn M.
Brodie's No Man Knows My History (Knopf, 1945); Robin Fox's
The Tory Islanders (Cambridge University Press, 1978); Mary
Smith Fay's "Genealogy of Howard Robard Hughes," in the May
1984 National Genealogical Society Quarterly; Mark Skolnick's
"The Utah Genealogical Data Base: A Resource for Genetic
Epidemiology," in Banbury Report 4; Cancer Incidence in Defined
Populations; Who Shall Live?, edited by Victor R. Fuchs (Basic
Books, 1981); and Donald G. Schueber's "Our Family Trees Have
Roots in Utah's Mountain Vaults," in the Dec. 1981 Smithsonian.

Index

About the Author

Alex Shoumatoff is a graduate of Harvard and a staff writer for *The New Yorker*. He is the author of five previous books: *Florida Ramble, Westchester: Portrait of a County, The Rivers Amazon, The Capital of Hope,* and *Russian Blood.* He lives outside New York City with his wife and their two sons.